12 Steps to Mastery

A
Path
To
AWAKENING

By Al Miner and Lama Sing

CoCreations Publishing

12 Steps to Mastery - A Path to Awakening

Copyright ©2000 by Al Miner and Lama Sing

Cover art and book design by Susan M. Miner

ISBN 9780979126260

1. Lama Sing   2. Psychics   3. Trance Channel   4. Mastery   5. Oneness   6. Awakening
I. Miner, Al   II. Title

Library of Congress Control Number: 2008901439

Printed in the United States of America

For books and products, further information, or to write Al Miner visit
www.lamasing.net

How the Course in Mastery Was Initiated

Early in 1999, the question was posed to Lama Sing: *If you had an opportunity to speak with us on a regular basis about any topic, what would you find would be best to be given to us in these times?*

This was the response from the Lama Sing group:

LAMA SING: With regard to our opportunity to speak – and correct us if we have this thought incorrectly here – but we understood this to be an open opportunity for any here to offer works deemed to be good in God's name to the Earth through this, the forum. Is that correct?

CONDUCTOR: Yes, an opportunity for you to speak on any topic and subject that you feel important to offer on a regular basis for us and these times, whether that was an ongoing series or something different each time.

LAMA SING: A moment, please... we are discussing this.

Very well, we have discussed this at great length here, and we have, in the finality of our discussion, brought it before the Master. He has advised us clearly that this is a worthy work. And so, we will participate in this work with you.

We will offer those things which we believe are timely and appropriate... and we shall invite the entirety of the universe (which is as to say, those who are in service with or to God) to contribute.

Contents

A Message from Al and Susan

Lama Sing told us on numerous occasions that the guides of their "ward" on Earth would be working with the Lama Sing group and the material given in an effort to reach their wards with information. What is, perhaps, phenomenal is that Lama Sing made it clear that they were working with the guides of individuals who would come to this information years after it would be given.

It is our prayer, then, that you find this course personal to you.

Excerpts from Lama Sing
About the Course in Mastery

- "The Course itself is neither sacred nor holy; *you* are sacred and holy. The Course is the gift, given from here, to call you forth. See? There are many in the Earth who are awakening. This is but one work among many similar. But those of you who are about it, rejoice. For it is a work in His name."

- "The Course contains the keys which can set you free."

- "This actually is a work intended to bring those who subscribe into a state of oneness. It is a process of claiming one's heritage. The key ingredient, then, is the empowerment of the individual through the process of free will."

Notes from the Editor:

With the exception of a few words here and there, what you are about to read are the words of Lama Sing verbatim given in separate sessions (called readings), channeled by Al Miner. At the opening of the reading, Al placed himself into the trance state. Lama Sing would then enter the dimension of Earth, borrowing Al's voice for the reading.

Even though the name *Lama Sing* has been assigned to these readings, there is actually always a group involved. Depending upon the topic, sometimes the number is massive, and sometimes it is a handful; sometimes they are speaking to a group, and sometimes to an individual they know will one day get the message – in essence, speaking to one and all, as well as to only one and only all... curious, but true. Throughout the reading, they defer to one another just as we do when in a group discussion. This information may be of value as you read, so you don't stumble when they sometimes change, even in a single paragraph, from an archaic form of speech to a more modern one, or from the singular to the plural.

The name *Channel* is used by Lama Sing in place of *Al*, because to use the name *Al* would essentially serve to call him from that consciousness to which he is taken that prevents his personal involvement and influence in what is given in the reading. There is only one known occasion in which Lama Sing used Al's given name; the reason given was that the depth of his channeled state was being tested.

When referring to life on Earth, Lama Sing uses the term *in the Earth*. This is referring to living within the consciousness of Earth, finite experience, rather than *on* the consciousness of Earth and that expression.

Lastly...

- There are places where Lama Sing emphasizes a thought by speaking the words *quote/end-quote*. To let the reader know that those emphases are Lama Sing's, as opposed to the transcriber's, the words *quote/end-quote* have been left in the transcript as well as the quotation marks themselves.
- The word *dis-ease* is used by Lama Sing to mean, not only illness and such, but *"first and foremost, a lack of ease in spirit, mind, and/or emotion, which are then precipitated into the physical body."* – Lama Sing
- Lama Sing's use of words such as *ye, thee, whom, we, they, he* is often contrary to conventional, but the meaning will be clear.

With two opposite views as to how to present Lama Sing – those who feel the grammar should be corrected, and those who find it endearing – it was decided to keep the text verbatim, especially helpful when reading the text while following along with the audio.

Some Suggestions for Study:

The more involved you can be at the onset in expecting and intending results for yourself throughout this course as well as upon completion, the more successful you will be in attaining that ideal, those goals.

Ask for and be consciously aware of those walking with you unseen, who will be with you in this work doing all in their power to assist you in attaining your goals. Let them participate with you.

There are profound convergences occurring at this time, which you will read more of a few chapters into this course. Tuning in to these energies will also help the effectiveness of this course. Additionally, there are others taking this course around the world at the same time you are; by tuning in to one another – sending your prayerful expectations for their success and receiving theirs for you – will empower you (according to Lama Sing) beyond comprehension.

Throughout this book, you will find space provided in which you can journal your thoughts, your experiences, your questions, your changes.

At the onset, space has been provided in which you might like to journal some thoughts prior to beginning this course in mastery.

Such as...

- The title includes the subtitle *A Path to Awakening*.
    Awaken to what... from what?
- What does the term *mastery* mean to you in this context?
- What do you hope to/expect to attain by the end of this course?

Lama Sing has said this course contains the keys that can set you free.

- Free from what?
- Free to what?
- Look for those keys/that key in each topic.

With this as an encouragement, feel free to journal other such thoughts. You might like to share these with others discussing this material on the Lama Sing website: www.lamasing.net

JOURNAL: First Thoughts

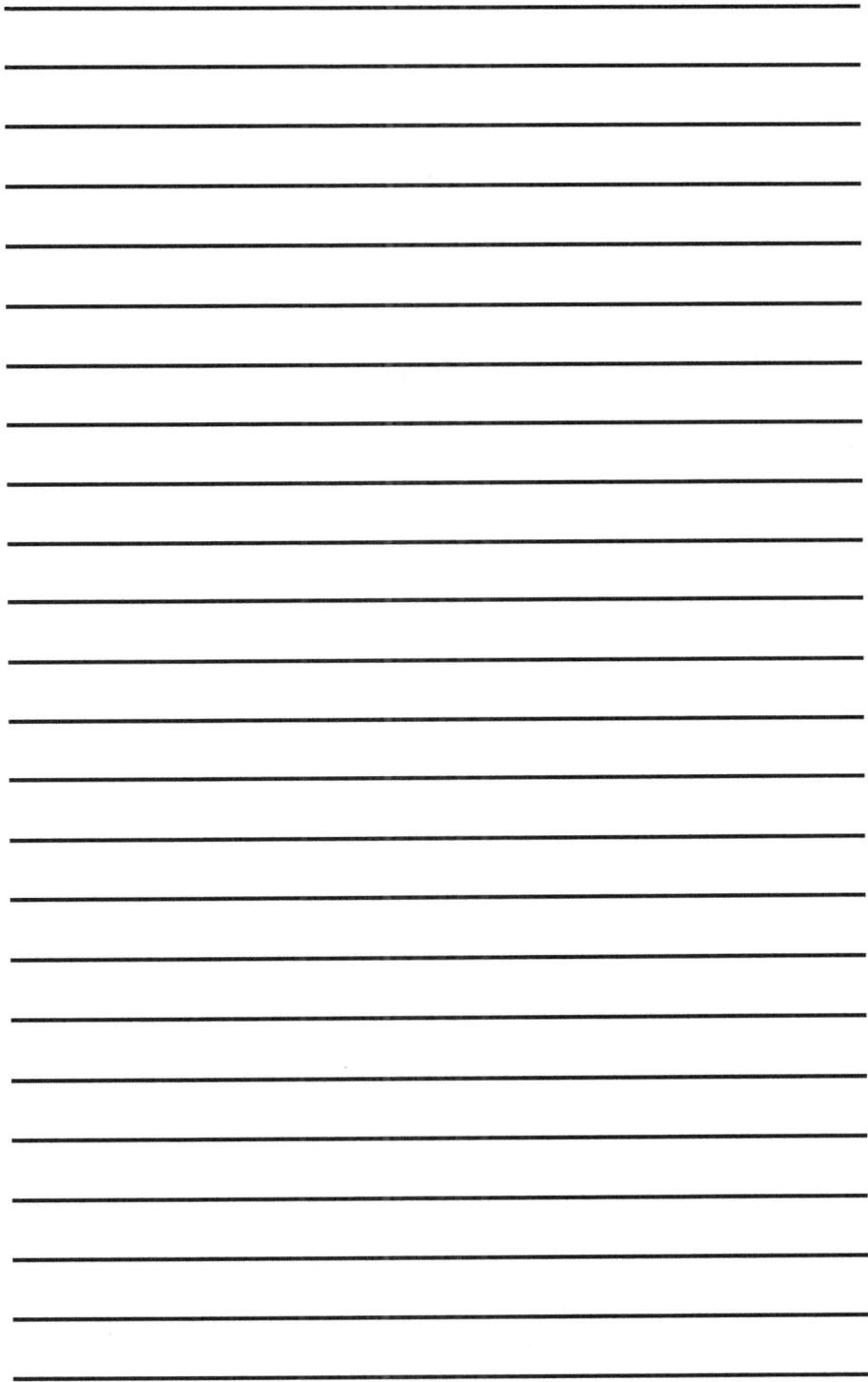

Step 1

Forgiveness

Given November 13, 1999

OPEN FORUM ON FORGIVENESS

LAMA SING: Yes, we have the Channel, then, and joyfully accept this opportunity to be with you all.

As we begin this wondrous new work together, let us become as one. Let claim our oneness in this joyful prayer of affirmation:

In the light of that Spirit which lies within each soul is the Promise, the Path, the Way; which, if we, as one, move forward into the light of same, can make this passable. So do we claim our oneness with Thee, O Father, knowing that the inner light is Thee... guiding, illuminating, so as to bring forth that understanding, that wisdom and joy, as each opportunity in the journey called life shall bring before us. There is that Promise, as given above, which is called the Christ: It is the Way, the Path, the Eternal bond of Light given us all by Thee, Father... claimed and demonstrated in the Earth [plane] and elsewhere by the man called Jesus. It matters not, O Father, how others might call this spirit by this or that name, or the personage of those who bear it in the Earth and their given name – it is one path, one light, one promise. To this, then, Father, do we pray of Thee... help Thou us to be emissaries of Thy Light. Guide us to that which Thou knoweth to be the very highest and best for each who shall hear or read these words. We thank Thee, Father, for the presence of the Christ Spirit in these works, surrounding and blessing all who shall receive same. We thank this, our Channel, and his mate Susan, for this opportunity and for presenting this work to be shared by others. And we thank all those gathered here for this, the initial work... and Thee, Father, for gifting us with this joyous opportunity of service. Let us all send a prayer of hope and light to those in all realms who are in the moment in some need. Amen.

WELCOME

We welcome all of you to this new work and to those activities as shall be, prayerfully, a living part of same.

This is a work which has been long in preparation, and carefully evaluated and nurtured by the Channel and his mate, and many others – here, and in other realms.

But even greater than these noteworthy efforts is the preparation that *you* have made to come to this point in your life during this time of such wondrous opportunity.

The Power Is Yours

It is now that was spoken of so oft in times past; these are those times of profound opportunity. And where is the opportunity to be found? The greatest of all aspects of this shall be found within you – for it is you, ultimately and finally, and only you, who has the power to change, to make the Way passable.

Each one who hears or reads these words empowers them, for the greater is a thought, a word, a deed known in the Earth and elsewhere, so much the moreso, then, are those given life.

THE NATURE OF INTERACTION

Lines of Light

It is difficult, we comprehend, while in the Earth (and in other realms, similarly, are there difficulties) to perceive the nature of interactions between self and others... interactions between yourself and other events, other groups, other cultures, and so on and so forth. As you encounter these all throughout your life's journey, there is a connection of sorts, which the Channel has referred to as *lines of light.* Perhaps, as you acknowledge that you do have lines of light connecting you and others whom you have interacted with, and are interacting with, that this shall have meaning and greater understanding as we proceed.

It is the nature of those connections between individuals, groups, classes, masses, and so forth, that interactions endure... that thoughts and emotions empower them, not only in the current lifetime, but beyond same.

Shadows upon the Lines of Light

When these (as called) lines of light are brilliant and lovingly neutral, open and passable, then the progression of all involved is enhanced by the ease of such. When, however, there are those limiting forces, when there are shadows upon these lines of light... and, perhaps accordingly thereafter, upon the individuals as well who are interconnected... then these become burdensome; they cloud, they diffuse, they veil, the potential beauty and joy continually offered to each soul.

Such clouds, such veils of shadowy darkness or mutation (in terms of color or brilliance) can run the gamut, the full array or spectrum of emotion in the Earth; and in a manner which is interactive, stimulate the thoughts, stimulate the actions... and, yes, begin to fashion, to mold or shape, who and what you are. So, the topic or title of this, our first open forum is *Forgiveness*.

The Connecting Lines of Emotion

Those connective lines of light, those feelings and emotions that perhaps all of you have to varying degrees (as relate to the past, as relate to past interactions or events between you and others – perhaps a bit of anger, perhaps a bit of resentment, maybe even some bitterness, a bit of hatred, a little fear)... looking at this on the one hand. Now, because the universe is perfect, there is always balance, and you, as Children of God, are ever striving to find movement along a path of balance. Therefore, as we have defined these as they might be thought of as shadowy aspects of limitation, consider as well that there can be, at times, other things, other emotions that can equally impede, that can block or tie you to the past.

Strangely... love. Love is such a powerful, dynamic force, having an array of expressions, which, in the Earth, is one of the main purposes for journeying therein. In other words, learning about love is perhaps uppermost on the list of choices, or reasons why souls wish to incarnate in the Earth. If you would think of this as your *Top 40* (humor intended) love is at the top, see, almost a perpetual Number One.

"How," you would ask perhaps, "could love limit me? How could love be a force which clouds the line of light connecting me to some past event, some past individual, some past grouping?"

These are the aspects that we shall explore; these are the potentials which we will ask you to look at, perhaps invite you to explore within yourself...

If you have, in the past, been loved by someone, and (for reasons which could be very numerous) this did not come into fruition, it is possible that that feeling of love still exists. That desire, that wish, is a part of the flow of energy, the thought, along that line of light which you share. For one, it might be essentially forgotten; for another, it might endure. So there could be, you see – even in one of the most beautiful emotions – some potential limitation for those involved.

FORGIVENESS BEGINS WITH SELF

As you would follow such an example further and further, throughout all of the emotions, it is important for us to emphasize to you at the onset that you are *not* responsible for the other end of that line of light.

Why is that? Are you not your brother's keeper? It is, quite simply, because of God's Laws, which are perfect. To the forefront of this do we find the right of Free Will, known by all of you. And there are others which are of equal import here. The Law of Just Return is one of them. Your part in building an attitude of joy, of freedom, of harmony, is to forgive yourself for your part in whatsoever might exist as a burden, a limitation, a shadow... that you as a Child of God are sending light and loving neutrality along that line of light.

Are you responsible for the receptivity of the entity on the other end? Not really... in fact, not at all. That is a part of forgiveness: recognizing that the forgiveness begins within self. We will assist the Channel in preparing certain works intended to help you along that pathway. There may be several of these, for the area, the topic, called *Forgiveness* is, as you can clearly note and understand from your own experiences, quite vast.

Removing the Sheaths

In this time, this meeting, as we are together here, we are encouraging you to think about those things which are limiting you as you hear these words or read them.

What do you believe keeps you from attaining your ideal? Remember? It was given clearly and oft through Edgar [Cayce]: Ideal, Purpose, and Goal... like a path that you can build... steps, and purposes, and the ultimate goal or ideal. We are with you in this work. We are reaching out to you, as you ask... to assist you, to support you, to offer you our love. But only you can do the work, for the work is within you: It is the releasing of those bonds which fetter, tie, bind, limit, distort, blind, and so forth.

How have you come to be who you are in this lifetime? From here, we see you as perfect a shining light... let's call it a sphere of light, that resides within you just about the bottom of the ribcage... a center of such wondrous beauty and potential that there is naught in the Earth which can compare to same in any respect. Yet, those who would question could righteously say, "Why can I not see this, feel it? Why can I not hear it or taste it? Smell it?" But curiously, if they would only go within and journey into that light, that which they need to substantiate the existence of that light is the light itself, bearing to them fruits greater than taste, touch, sight, smell, or sound.

Forgiveness is a process of removing the layers, the sheaths, the vaporous-like appendages that have woven themselves about this light, your light, during the course of a lifetime. They begin, in a manner of speaking, upon your entry into the Earth [plane], for they are all about, as the living, vibrant thought-form dominant wheresoever you might be. These are contributed to by those who tend you... their words, their thoughts, their emotion... those who are in the bedchambers (bassinets, if you will) surrounding you, for their life's intent and purpose is already radiating from them, intermingling with all the energies about.

From here, of course, you can draw your own conclusions. All of the entities that that babe encounters in the process of its growth... the criticisms, the praise, the laughter, the tears, the anger, the joy... [are as] contrasts, balancing forces. If the soul's light and purpose are strong, they merge the childhood process (guarded all the while by the Angelic Host into adulthood)... and the prevalence of Law Universal, God's Universal Law, becomes strikingly more profound with remarkable rapidity. Now the choices become moreso individualized... conditioned, yes, by what has gone before.

But as many of you good workers who strive daily to assist others understand what deep-seated limitation exists, and find that the roots of these causal forces reach back into that childhood period, then you work upon this, helping them to see what the causal force is. That they are the *result* of it, not the *causal* force... so that in their conscious mind, you can help them to see it for what it is: an external event, a stimulus, an energy which is enduring because of factors which were involved and caused that entity to claim the results of same, often doing so at such depths within themselves that they, themselves, do not recall it. And *that* is the inner emotional seat of a limitation; but it is also the causal force which creates an envelopment around the entity... a sheath, a sphere of energy which thereafter conditions all the energies coming into and out of that entity.

Note now, that is one event! Imagine that the event was such that it caused the entity to question self... to doubt, to fear... and perhaps, with some entities, to counter that fear with aggression, anger, hatred... others, going within and being withdrawn, timid, afraid to try for fear they'd be chastised if they fail: One event... one great circle of dulling light around the entity... one growth ring on the tree of their current life. See this?

Time passes, and another event and another growth ring... another sheath, another veil of limitation... and another... and another. Some might gather greater than others, to be sure... some might gather sheaths of light and hope, so that as you encounter these entities they appear bright and hopeful, and are joyful to be around. There is always the positive, as well, see.

The Key

But what happens to that pure light that entered within the babe? By the time adulthood has been reached, it may be so occluded with these spherical lines, veils, sheaths, that lest one has true sight, inner sight, that beautiful light that is their potential within cannot be perceived. Indeed, that entity becomes the sum and substance of all those experiences, and all that they are and do. And all that others do and are to them is, of course, conditioned by these veils that are so deep within... so that whether it is an intention emanating from them, it can be distorted... or an intention from someone intended to them with goodness, it can be distorted.

The key to all of this, at the first levels of working with this, is forgiveness. True, you must discover what they are. Would you say this to be correct? Not always. If you discover that something from the past has an effect upon you today, you can use the principle we gave above and forgive it, bless it, let it go, send prayer and light and love to the source of it. But not yourself.

"Now, how's that work?" you might ask, colloquially, as does one here whom we shall call Zachary,[1] noted for his lightness and humor; but also regarded, here, as a true servant of God. (He shall oft be

---

[1] Zachary – is an individual first introduced in the early 90's in a Lama Sing/Al Miner work called THE PETER PROJECT. He has remained with us ever since, offering his insights, his humor, and his love.

among us and these future works to bring a bit of joy.) So, Zachary's question to you is, quite simply, "Do you want to stay where you are? Do you believe that you have the very best, the very highest of the potential within you, now manifested in your life?"

If you answer yes, his answer is, "Congratulations." But if you have not answered yes, then he invites you to join us in these works in these ways:

The Connecting Emotion

Knowing... see, *knowing*... in daily life that you are the result of what you have lived and experienced, gives you power.

If you know that you are going to react to someone who, let us say, slurps their tea from its saucer rather than its cup, then what can you do about the reaction to this... your part in it? If you do nothing, you will probably (because that annoys you) build a dislike for that individual, no matter how slight. That one flaw or fault, as you see it, will limit and color your interaction with that entity.

Now, supposing that entity comments on your necktie, mentioning how ugly it is, or, should you be dwelling currently in a feminine body, perhaps that the color of your blouse and dress are in disagreement with one another (humor intended). Now, the entity has already annoyed you because they slurp tea from their saucer, and *now* on top of that, they have insulted you. After all, who are they to judge your apparel? The natural reaction can be several-fold... You could agree and be embarrassed or self-conscious the rest of that Earth day, hoping no one else will notice, and upon arrival home discard that ugly necktie, or toss aside that blouse... Or not... but if you don't, each time you take it out, won't you remember the comment? The next time you encounter that entity who slurps tea and comments about your apparel, won't you have an immediate defensive reaction? Won't you probably avoid them?

If not... if your demeanor, your confidence and such are well-centered, you might have in the first place shrugged it off. If so, that is well and good. But were you, even if you have no reaction of the *down side* (as Zachary calls it)... won't that entity's words and actions have some impact on how you interact with that entity? Even if they haven't burdened you, wouldn't you thereafter think to yourself, *Oh, no, there's that annoying entity. I believe I'll make a phone call over here and hope he or she doesn't notice me.*

This has been a tiny example. Let's take another, all too common in your world, particularly in your denser populated areas. Let us say you are moving along a byway in your automobile. Your mind wanders for a moment, and you don't notice some vehicle trying to make a turn or something of that sort, so that the entity has to brake abruptly. What's their reaction to you? Probably quite vocal... probably some gestures, and such as this.

As you realize that you are (quote) "in the wrong," you can say, "I'm sorry," and they'll call you a jughead or something, but won't that thought stay with you? Of course you'll be a bit more alert. But supposing you knew that entity... it's a neighbor or your grocer or on and on... what's the effect of this the next time you see them? What's the effect upon the neighbor or the grocer when they see *you* and they have, perhaps, demeaned you vocally and with gesture? Well, you have a line of light connecting you to your neighbor and your grocer and all those who are in your life. Some of these lines are large, beautiful. Those are usually between self and loved ones. Others may be more subtle, not so self-evident. But yet, all of these connect.

Radiating and Receiving Energy

Now, if we drop the entire use of reference to lines of light, and move to thoughts, attitudes, emotional energies, each entity is as a miniature broadcasting station, a generator. You are continually radiating thought energy, emotional energy, spiritual energy, physical energy (and we could take this to levels which aren't even known in the Earth as yet, but shall be). All of these things are a part of your life.

The next time you encountered your grocer after an event like that, you'd feel it. And the grocer would feel it. There might be a repetition of the grocer's anger, and perhaps he or she might speak to you about it, "What in the world were you thinking of yesterday at the corner of Elm and Main? I could have clobbered you. You really should pay more attention!"

Well, by this time there's lots of defenses strengthening the sheaths, the veils, around you. Or you might have been shaped by your life previously to look at the entity and say something equally critical, "What about you, dummy? Do you always drive that fast? Don't you recognize that other people have a right to the road, too?" And you could create a *thing*. Or maybe you'd laugh and look at them and say, "Sorry. Have a good day." But the probability is, is it not, dear friends, that some residual stays with you, like lint to sticky tape.

The point of this, again, is to recognize what you are, who you are, and what has conditioned or shaped, fashioned, or molded how you got to where you are. It is, again, entirely possible that where you are is where you want to be. It is also possible that you have passed through all these things as an adept (spiritually speaking) and you have grown from them rather than having become burdened by them. This, of course, is wonderful, and we will support that in those works ahead.

In this project, this course, this coming-together in a common work and purpose, we shall always look to you for your guidance, your needs, and such as these. Why? Because of your individual beauty. This work is comprised of the uniqueness of the workers. When we say we shall look to you, it is as an invitation. When we say we shall look to you for your uniqueness, it is because we recognize this uniqueness to be a part of God's intent, that this is intended to be what it is… unique.

So many aspects of life, in the Earth and elsewhere, have a tendency to create the expectation that everyone conform to certain criterion: To be really good, you should be this tall, of this weight, of this particular dimension (of body), this particular hair color or style, wear certain clothing, drive this type of automobile, live in this certain type of abode. True? So that, if you don't conform to all of those, somehow or other you are a little less than perfect; and if you don't conform to many of them, you might think of yourself as a *lot* less than perfect.

We comprehend the evolution of such characteristics in the [consciousness of] Earth, and they do exist in certain other realms, as well… many of those, rather limited. But our point here, which is an offering to you, is to ask you to recognize that your uniqueness is just that… certainly, you can agree and cooperate with others, other ways of thinking, traditions, mores, standards, even laws; but so doing, not subjugating your uniqueness, not abandoning the wonderful qualities that comprise your uniqueness… but savoring them, holding them, knowing that their place in all of this is important even if outwardly this does not seem to be recognized.

PARABLE: RELEASING

[Ed Note: Lama Sing gave a parable for each lecture, but the parable for Forgiveness was given in a separate work and the sound file is lost. For those listening and reading simultaneously, the audio will pick up on the other side of this parable.]

A large truck is moving at a rapid speed toward a busy intersection in New York City. An automobile is coming from a different direction on one of the cross streets. The thoughts of both drivers are focused upon the demands of the day.

The collision is resounding. There is an instant explosion such that both drivers feel only a flash of fear, and then find themselves a few feet apart on a pathway surrounded by a wispy, cloud-like substance.

And there they stand, looking at one another in shock.

The truck driver begins turning about slapping himself, yelling a collage of colorful words, along with "I think I'm dead."

The other, in business attire, is looking at his hands and then down at himself, looking for signs of injury, yet he sees none. There aren't even any wrinkles in his suit... too perfect... a slight glow, he notes... With an empty expression, he looks up at the truck driver.

The truck driver is still flailing his arms, stating things like, "Oh, my God! How could this happen? I'm not ready... oh-h no."

The businessman struggles to speak. His voice breaks and he covers his face with his hands and begins to sob. The sobbing grows until his body is shaking almost convulsively out of control.

The truck driver is stunned by this reaction from this other man... whom he hadn't, for all practical purposes, even noticed or paid any attention to, too preoccupied with his own death. Then he notices two luminous beings standing off to the left, one of whom walks over to the sobbing businessman and places his hands upon the shoulders. In just a moment, the man removes his hands from his eyes, still covering his cheeks and mouth, to peer into a pair of remarkably gentle and compassionate eyes. They embrace, and the man feels a flood of wellness... goodness.

The truck driver asks the other luminous being, "Am I dead?"

The being, smiling, nods, and responds softly, "In a manner of speaking, yes... but in truth, no... you are just passing on."

"Oh, I don't like that phrase at all," comments the truck driver, becoming animated. "So-and-so passed on... that's awful."

Still smiling, showing no reaction to the truck driver's emotional response, the being simply waits for the driver to calm down. And then he extends his hand in a gesture of handshake.

For the longest moment, the truck driver looks down at this hand with all the shimmering light around it. Then, looking up at the eyes, he sort of automatically, extends his hand to meet the grasp of the luminous being. The instant he does, he feels a rush of all sorts of good feelings, some he can't remember having felt since childhood. The emotion wells up within him, and he cries out, "Oh, dear God, I *am* dead!" Now he begins to sob, and throws himself upon his luminous being, who quickly embraces him. Here again, comes the sense of wellness, the sense of peace, and a general feeling that all is aright, and that God loves him.

After a time, the four of them begin to walk along this pathway, which leads gently up. Shortly, they come to a beautiful parklike area, all still surrounded by this luminosity. The two men look about and see other luminous beings with other people in a variety of garb and of obviously varying backgrounds. One of the luminous beings gestures to two semi-circular benches off on a side path, and the two men while the two luminous beings seat themselves on the other, simply smiling, looking at these two new arrivals.

Finally, the driver looks over at the businessman, who returns the smile. "I am so sorry. I wasn't paying attention."

The businessman responds, "Well, I'll have to claim responsibility here, too... I was thinking about my meeting and... Oh, my! I guess that deal won't go through now." And everyone laughs a bit.

One of the luminous beings at that point speaks, "It is a blessing to you both that you are able to recognize that this is not an event of fault or responsibility. In the Earth, there is the tendency to assess responsibility... guilt, if you will... and punishment... the imposition by society of attitudes which can shape and limit the remainder of one's life. It is wonderful that you have forgiven each other. You have, haven't you?" smiling as he makes that statement.

The two men turn to look at each other, a seriousness on each face as they search to find out... is there anything that one holds against the other. Both blurt out the same words simultaneously, "I am so sorry" and they laugh and embrace one another.

"Oh, well," states the truck driver after they release their embrace. "No more deadlines. I had two more loads to haul. I was hurrying thinking about my bills and... Oh, my, what will my family do?"

"They'll be fine," responds his luminous being.

Eyebrows arched, the driver states, "Why... somehow I feel that!! It's incredible, but somehow I know that all is well. Anyway, the company has good insurance. They'll probably be better off."

The luminous beings simply smile and do not comment.

The businessman looks into the eyes of the truck driver and states, "That may be so, but with the kind of person you are, there's surely going to be a great hole in their lives for some time!"

Looking down, the truck driver is remembering those he loves. "I didn't say I love you to her today. I kissed her cheek and ran out the door. Didn't stop to hug the children, either." Tears are falling.

The businessman's eyes are glazed, obviously off in his own thoughts. "You know," he speaks softly, "I never really believed that life went on." Pausing, and then, "I should have asked her to marry me. I didn't want to be burdened. I thought about the money and the power. I did very well, too," turning to look at the driver.

The truck driver responds, "I never cared about any of that. I only wanted certain things, and once I had them, I just settled into that as a way of life. I never thought about going beyond."

"That's hard for me to understand," the businessman responds. "All I ever had to do was want it, go for it, and I always got it... a contract, a woman, an automobile, a fine house. I had it all."

The truck driver again arches his eyebrows, "What for?"

"That's incredible!" the businessman responds. "Why wouldn't you want to have everything, get it all?"

And they go back and forth, bantering their positions. All the while the two luminous beings simply smile.

Finally, the businessman states, "You know, I think you're right... all those things I had, and no one to care about or to care about me. But you... you'll surely be missed."

"Well... you're right, too. If I believed in myself, I could have had more and my family could have had more." Then the driver asks the luminous beings, "Which is the right way to live?"

"The right way to live," the first luminous being responds, "is that which brings you the greatest joy. It is important to remember these simple words, as taught by the great masters and by our Brother, the Christ: Know thyself. Look within. See who you are. Discover why these aspects of yourself are present. Do they bring you joy and love? And do they open you to be all that you can be?

As the luminous beings look to the businessman and the driver for how they are absorbing what has just been given, a gentleness appears about both men, now at peace, and in true friendship and fondness.

In that instant, there is a blinding flash, as the two men hear these words, "Live what you now know. Look within, and look at the seeds you are sowing. For this is your harvest... Know thyself."

One of the firemen extinguishing the flames around the truck cries out in amazement. "This driver's still alive! Get the oxygen."

Only a second or two later, another rescue worker yells, "I have a pulse. Bring the jaws. Let's get him out."

Both of these men will live on for a time in the Earth. Perhaps they will come to remember this journey they've taken. Perhaps, in the process, they may truly come to know themselves. One thing is definite – they will become friends... a curious friendship built on this experience of forgiveness.

80C3

APPLYING FORGIVENESS

You can do this, you can accomplish this, by dwelling in that center of light within. By passing through those layers or sheaths which might be preventing you from claiming it at present.

Fore-Giveness

Forgiveness is, by its very word or words, going before events and individuals... be-*fore*... *fore*-giveness, see... f-o-r-e... that you *dwell* in a state of fore-giveness.

"How in the world is that possible?" Zachary submits here. "Wouldn't that make you vulnerable? Couldn't you be held hostage by the world, in a manner of speaking, if you so subjugated yourself to dwell in an attitude of fore-giveness?"

If you do this from the center of your being, that would be an impossibility. For fore-giveness, in such a case, begins with you. If you cannot fore-give yourself, this is like having a well with no water in it. What you hold in your heart for yourself is what you have to give to others. Think about it. What you feel about yourself is the well-spring from which you can give to others.

In these works (this project, this course) we'll help the Channel and Susan provide you tools with which you can explore these things. They shan't be of great complexity, rote, or dogma, for the path of truth is clear and straightforward, not complex. Simple worksheets and journal formats for you to evaluate and to know yourself better and better as each day progresses... to look at the events that have occurred to you in this day just past which could use a little seasoning of forgiveness... to look at your own reactions to the day just past: what has this day given to you? It was intended to be a gift, a blessing. What are you willing to harvest from it? What shall be the fruits of this day's activity? And who decides?

Go Forth and Sin No More

In those times past, when they were awaiting the Master's arrival from the East, those who were preparing the way for Him often spoke of the need to unburden self. This guidance... those words some two thousand Earth years ago and the words we are giving to you now... are the same: In the Records, they are recorded as "Go forth and sin no more."

And the one who led this work baptized them, asking them for their forgiveness... To release their sins, yes... but what's not recorded was the definition of them: the greatest sin of all has oft been called here in past, inactivity (if there is any such thing as sin in the first place). So if you are inactive – if you are allowing life to direct you, to fashion you, to make you who and what you are – then the beautiful light that is God's gift to the world within you shall not be seen. Those are the things of which those who heard the Word were baptized of, and those were the limitations. (Many different translations of those Aramaic words.)

Know Yourself and Be Free

But the point for us in this meeting is a joyful one: The love of that which is eternal will always endure. That love is within you. When you begin to see yourself as perfect within, knowing that this is not going to be the same perfection you see in your brother or sister – no greater, no lesser, equal, but unique – perhaps you'll stop hammering yourself on the forge of emotion… trying to make what is uniquely beautiful into that which is profoundly common.

The Master called out to His followers often, as did and do many masters in the Earth this day as we are speaking: *"Know yourself, and be free."* For you to know yourself, you must be willing to pass through those sheaths, those veils. And you can do this, and you can claim oneness with the Light within. And thereafter, claim oneness with all else.

So we would encourage you in these ways to oft remember these things: Upon arising, take time to reflect upon this day. Even if you are late, don't give this up… this is your time… a few seconds, a few minutes. Give yourself time to recognize and affirm that you are uniquely beautiful within; and that no matter how you are seen outwardly, how you are evaluated by the standards of your populace, if you claim your inner beauty and light, and live it, that is how you will be perceived. Not by how you look, not whether or not your tie is tasteful or ugly, or your blouse and skirt match or do not. "You could become a trend-setter," Zachary states humorously here.

If your light *is* you, if your uniqueness is honored, fore-give yourself. If you did something you don't like or another didn't like, let it go. Learn from it. If there is something in your past which feels like a chain or a rope holding you back, turn around… find it, and sever it, blessing who or whatever is on the other end.

A TIME OF RECEPTIVITY

This is a time in the Earth of receptivity. It is a time of birth. It is a time of wondrous potential and celebration. The dominant forces of Earth have builded their own righteousness and held dominion these many two thousand Earth years and before.

Intersecting Polarizing Forces

And yet, who were those in the Essene Expectant Ones' community who were the most revered of all? They were those who held the receptivity and the continual attitude of birthing into the Earth; not pillaging it, not taking from it, but giving to it. They sought not dominion or authority, but lived both of these, offering it as it was sought.

These were those who were the practitioners of the greatest of all wisdom: the healing arts; the divination; the foretelling; the astrological; working with the energies; knowledge of the foods, the herbs, and the Earth itself; the understanding of the Law and the giving of it.

These were those who nurtured the Forerunner and the Master and their colleagues. These were those who foretold of their coming, and prepared the way. These were those who held the bosom of the Earth itself as a part of their very being.

Mary epitomized this. The eleven other Maidens who were the elect with her, equally so epitomized these qualities. When Mary was chosen, the other eleven went to work, sharing that which they had been gifted, that which had been awakened within them to guide and teach the other workers... and yes, even the Master Himself.

To give this powerful force a name, is to immediately create a reaction to it. See if there is such a reaction within you as we tell you to awaken the Principles Feminine within you now.

If you are in a female body, perhaps your reaction will be one of joy, for this should be easy... *After all, I am in a feminine body.* Conversely, if you are in a male body and you've heard these words, you might have a reaction, a little struggle, a question about how you'll be seen by society and the populace, how you'll ever succeed and provide for your family or your own needs if you subjugate yourself the way you presume such feminine aspects must. If you've had, from the feminine body or the male body, either of those reactions, then you have no idea... none... of that which we are speaking of!

But we shall move into these and other areas in times ahead – polarities: male-female, positive-negative, light-darkness, on and on. The collage of those sensory reactions and evaluations, the spontaneity of your current reaction to outside stimulus... all are conditioned by these.

The Feminine is not weak and submissive. The Feminine *is* the Earth. It is that which gives rise to each plant in its season, each fruit in its time. To be in a male body is not to be apart from this spirit. Neither, to be in a feminine body guarantees you that you are a part of it. (Some humor should be found here... prayerfully.)

Releasing That Which Limits

Forgiveness begins, perhaps, at the point of intersect of two polarized forces within you... where the entity who slurped the tea from the saucer commented on your tie or blouse or skirt... the grocer who, let's say, might have even cursed you for your driving error... the mother who didn't hold you... a father who *did*... clothing that you had to wear that didn't fit your body and made you an outcast as a child... living in the wrong part of town... living in a body whose outward color doesn't fit.

Too tall, too short, too wide, too thin... *but always beautiful within!*

Forgiveness is the release of that which limits, and seeing it as such. If a thing – a force, an entity, an object, an event – has the power to limit you, then you need to forgive it.

Forgiveness is releasing. Forgive yourself. See? Release yourself from limitation.

Other things to look at after claiming in the morning is to pause here and there throughout the Earth day... look around, see where you're at, see where your thinking is... and forgive someone or something, but especially try to forgive yourself.

If your name is Walter, stop often and say, "Walter, I forgive you," and *mean it!* And if someone offends you, then forgive that person frequently, all throughout the remainder of the day.

Do not go into slumber holding an imbalanced connection between yourself and that individual. It is better that you not sleep than to go into spirit carrying that bond of limitation. See? How do you do this? By repeating it. By hearing it, thinking it, feeling it, living it.

GIFTING SELF WITH FORGIVENESS

We will use colors and sounds in the most simplistic ways.
In this month's activity, let's take the color red. It usually means emotion. It usually has to do with emotion, and it's a key to forgiveness. Take something red – a swatch of fabric, a gem, anything – and carry it with you. Hold it in your hands when you pray and meditate.

And then each time during the Earth day when you recognize something that limits you, look at that object... see the limitation's redness and transform it into love... release it, and forgive the event or situation or individual. Most of all, remember you are forgiving and releasing self.

Prayer has the power of your thought. Emotion is the substance of which mind builds. Isn't it? If you see something and compliment the individual who owns it, aren't you imparting emotion… aren't you offering them a gift? Why don't you offer yourself a gift?

It's easy to look at the criticisms of others. It's easy to compare yourself to what is without. What's even easier is to go within and claim that inner light, and to live in your own uniqueness; but only after you've passed through those sheaths, those veils. And you do that by forgiving yourself.

We shall in this project continually revisit many of these major (we might call them) steppingstones… such as forgiveness and, of course, love and others like this. For they are a collage of emotional fibrils which, when woven together, comprise the complete essence of who and what you are. The substance of your being – who you look like, what you act like – is the fabric of your emotional weaving. See?

We have been most joyful to have been with you in these works, and more will be given in future on this and other topics. The purpose of these works is to assist you in empowering yourself… to be of support, of loving encouragement and guidance, that you can claim oneness within and ultimately, *live it* without. We thank those who have come forward to help assist with this work, and our Channel and his mate for making this opportunity possible. We shall oft be in joyful prayer with you, dear friends. And you, and those about you… will you not join us in prayer often for those in need? The greater you give in that spirit of light, the greater is your return in that same manner.

Remember the red swatch or object. Use it. It can be a powerful, simple tool.

We are through here for the present. May the grace and blessings of our Father's wisdom ever be that lamp to guide your footsteps. Fare thee well, then, for the present, dear friends.

STUDY GUIDE

Activities for Applying Forgiveness

Using The Color Red As A Reminder & Tool
- Use the color red as a reminder and tool. Take something red, such as a swatch of fabric, gem, or anything you might prefer. Carry that object with you during the day. Whenever you recognize something that could limit you, look at that object. Let its redness transform that potential limitation into love, then release and forgive the situation or individual. Most of all, remember that you are forgiving and releasing self.
- Hold it in your hands when you pray and meditate.

Morning Activity
- Upon arising, take a few minutes to reflect upon this day. Even if you are late, don't give this up. Give yourself time to recognize that you are uniquely beautiful within, and that if you claim your inner beauty and light and live it, that is how you will be perceived by others.
- Weeks 1 and 2: Ask yourself: What do I want as the fruits for this day?
- Weeks 2 and 4: Remind yourself to look at your thinking throughout the day, and if there is anything in your thinking that is in any way limiting you, another, or an event, offer forgiveness.

Daily Activity
- Pause here and there throughout the day and see where you're at. See where your thinking is, and forgive someone or something. But especially try to forgive yourself. Repeat it: hear it, think it, feel it.

Evening Review & Exercises
- Look at the events that have occurred this day that could use a little seasoning of forgiveness. Look at your own reactions to the events of the day.
- Ask yourself: What has this day given to me?
- Journal: Who or what did you forgive today? What fruits did you harvest? What imbalanced thinking or emotion did you change, to one of balance?

Do not go to sleep holding an imbalanced connection between yourself and an individual or event. It is better that you not sleep than to go into spirit carrying that bond of limitation. Try this: Visualize the clouded "line of light" between you and another. Imagine clearing the cloudy shadows of doubt, fear, regret, bitterness and even resentment. See a bright Christ light of loving neutrality coming from your heart, with shining brilliance. Allow the light to move gradually through this line to the other's heart. As it moves, see it sweeping away all negatives to clean the line between you. Think of an affirmation to say while visualizing this change, or use a Bible verse, or your own powerful intention. As Lama Sing said: Forgive it. Bless it. Let it go.

- Pray for self forgiveness and comfort your inner Child of God. sending loving neutrality to yourself along the same light line.

Weekly Exercises for Forgiveness

Week 1

- Pray and meditate focusing on yourself. Ask yourself "Are there any aspects of myself that need my forgiveness?" Write these down.
- Use the Guided Meditation tape on Forgiveness, holding one or more of these in your prayers and thoughts as you do.
- Pause often during each day, and repeat this affirmation: "I forgive myself." Try adding what you forgive yourself for to this affirmation.

   Continue these throughout this month, or longer if need be, until you can review your beginning list and feel that you have claimed forgiveness for yourself.

Week 2

- Pray and meditate on this question: "Who is there in my life that I haven't yet forgiven?"
- Make a list of the people in your life who, when you think of them, seem to limit your joy and sense of freedom. Add other individuals to this list as you discover them.
- Take time to hold them in prayer prior to using the Guided Meditation tape. Use the tape as often as possible, but at least once each day. The effects are cumulative.
- Pause often during each day, and repeat this affirmation: "I forgive (Name)." Try adding what you forgive them for to this affirmation.

   Continue these throughout this month, or longer if need be, until you can review your beginning list and feel that you have forgiven everyone on your list.

Week 3

- Pray and meditate on this question: "What is there in my life itself that limits me, or that I am not joyful about?"
- Make a list of everything you discover that is limiting you.
- Take time to hold these in prayer prior to using the Guided Meditation tape. Use the tape as often as possible, but at least once each day. The effects are cumulative.
- Repeat this affirmation often throughout each day: "I forgive and release (the items on your list)." Also take a moment to see the gift and/or opportunity for you in those items.

Week 4

- Review the items from weeks 1 through 3. Be sure you have done all you know to do to forgive and release.
- Pray and meditate on the World. Focus on forgiving on a global level. See yourself sending the World forgiveness and Light.
- Pause throughout each day and reaffirm: "I give forgiveness to all in the World."

NOTES:
_____

_____

_____

_____

Exploring Forgiveness

NOTE: The thoughts listed here are merely suggestions to get you started in further exploration of this subject. Use any portion of them, or not, as your personal guidance leads you.

- How could your uniqueness, your individuality, possibly help shape the Course in Mastery? Why would Lama Sing emphasize this point?

- Why do you think the topic of forgiveness was offered as the first in this series of Mastery lectures?

- Can you think of times when 'love' has limited you? What part did you play that could be due for some forgiveness - of others involved? - of yourself?

- What does your becoming annoyed with another's idiosyncrasies have to do with this topic on forgiveness?

- What does non-conformity (by yourself or by another) have to do with forgiveness?

- Put into your own words the concept of 'sheaths'.

- Think about, or write about the concept that it is your choice to find the gift or the challenge in anything and anyone that comes into our lives.

- How is the concept of receptivity and feminine energy in the Earth related to the subject of forgiveness? How does this relate to you?

- In the thought Lama Sing gave of imparting the gift of our emotion to another, how can you offer that gift to yourself?

JOURNALING per LAMA SING:

You might wish to use the powerful tool of journaling, to give you reference points, and so you can see your progress.

Suggestions for your journal:

- Each day, briefly write down how you feel, emotionally and spiritually, and what has lent itself to those feelings.
- Once each week, review your journal. This will give you a clear overview of your progress. Based on what you find, modify your efforts and techniques.
- Keep it simple, or you probably won't continue with it.

JOURNAL

_____

_____

_____

_____

_____

_____

_____

_____

_____

_____

_____

_____

_____

_____

_____

_____

_____

_____

_____

_____

_____

_____

_____

_____

_____

_____

_____

_____

_____

_____

_____

_____

_____

_____

_____

_____

_____

_____

_____

_____

_____

_____

_____

Step One: FORGIVENESS

Step 2:

Gratitude

Given January 21, 2000

OPEN FORUM ON GRATITUDE

LAMA SING: Yes, we have the Channel then and, as well, those intents and purposes as are a part of this grouping and its intended works. As we come together in this joyful prayer, let us do so in the spirit of Oneness.

> *Eternal Father-Mother-God, here are we once again, Thy Children, seeking to claim our Oneness with Thee... knowing that so as we do, we are empowered with the presence of Thy Spirit in all that we are and do. Help Thou us, then, O Father, to dispel that which limits or which mutes the beauty and light of Thy Spirit within us. And as we do, let us look to those pathways which others have left before us. In the example of their grace, in the example of their teaching and wisdom, help us to learn and claim that as is also good for us. In the spirit of this, we turn to the Master, the Christ, thanking Him for His presence in these works and in the hearts and minds of those who focus upon His teachings. So doing, His gift of His healing grace, love, compassion, and wisdom are given to us. We pray on behalf of all those souls who are seeking of Thee, Father, that we might, in the spirit of Thy gifts to them, be the messengers who bear same. For those of our brethren who have lost their way, we offer ourselves, Father, to You and to them, in joyful service. Let us, Father, bear them Thy Light. We offer special prayers for each and every member of this grouping... and so as you are hearing these words, know that we are with you in prayerful joy unto your need. We thank Thee, Father, for this continued opportunity of joyful service in Thy name through this, our Channel, and his mate in the Earth. Amen.*

A CONSCIOUSNESS SHIFT IN AND ABOUT THE EARTH

As we commence with this joyful work, and our presence with thee is also illuminating the spirits and intents of each, let us offer, for a brief moment, this comment:

There has been, as you are cognizant, some significant shift in consciousness and such in and about the Earth[2]. We are aware of same and are, of course, a part of those forces which are going before. Herein, we believe it important that we stay the course, so to say, with that which we know to be of good foundational purpose in the discovery and claiming of Self. For if you are to maximize the potential of the opportunities now before you, it is good for you... if not, a mandate... that you claim Self; and to know Self is the pathway unto that claiming.

To this end, then, we have chosen with great care the topic of *Gratitude* for this current month's meeting.

THE POWER IN GRATITUDE

Forgiveness is an aspect of empowerment. Following close behind that is gratitude, recognizing quickly that gratitude is nothing more than a word, true? In other words, it is that which you would find in your reference books with a variety or an array of meanings that can be associated to the use of that word.

Our intention here is not to expound on that in the literal sense, of providing you yet another interpretation or definition of that word, but to delve into the meaning and the power – which is as to say, the affirming and claiming power – that is associated with gratitude.

Energy to Direct

Take, for example, the simple act of saying, *thank you.* In the process of saying *thank you*, you are acknowledging some act of kindness, some gift, or perhaps merely the rendering of a service from someone in their labor, their vocational work. But, what you do when you say *thank you,* as an expression of gratitude, is a powerful affirma-

---

[2] Consciousness shift - On January 11, 2000 a global shift in consciousness occurred. More is given on this at the end of this chapter, titled *Special Bulletin.*

tion. You are communicating orally, verbally, the acknowledgment of receiving something. True? As you do this, if you look at receiving – a gift or service or some variant of same – from another entity, then your receipt of it is confirmed with the action of *thank you*, and that is a completion of a cycle.

If you would… think of it now, for a moment, as energy flowing beautifully, lightly, joyfully, across the expanse of the universe. Let's take, for a moment, a small band of that powerful creative energy, and say that that energy belongs to you… you become the director, so to say, of its use… how you employ it, where you give it, how you use it to fashion something whether that is a word, an action, a deed, a material thing, the building of some structure, the creation of a painting, a bit of music… that creative flow of energy is yours.

When an entity, in the example we gave just above, provides you with a service, they are directing *their* flow of energy, through their labor, resulting in some gift to you… the receipt of something by you. Now here is, perhaps, one of the most important offerings that we can give to you, for you to truly comprehend the power and meaning of gratitude, of all that shall be given here in this meeting:

The Flow Is of God

That flow of creative energy is, of course, from God, from the universe. It is the Spirit of God. It is the Creative Force Universal. Because it is yours, is due to your heritage… in other words, it is yours because you are a Child of God. And in a manner of speaking, that creative energy is modified somewhat because of the uniqueness of you – no other like you, see – and because, quite simply, you are a part of God. So, whatever portion of that creative energy you would claim, is yours to direct. The example we have given is for simplicity and understanding. Actually, it is unlimited…the creative energy, that is.

So, now, you might be, in this example (for a moment, at least) the service person doing some labor as your vocation… and you meet a client or customer… and you have just given to them. And that is where we left the example… the flow of energy is flowing from you to the customer, the client. And there it is, right before them.

Now, they could pick up the article, if you are a merchant… the baked goods, if you are a baker… and on and on, that is the product or that called the wares of your labor. But in that moment when they look at you and state *thank you*… in that very moment, they have claimed that flow of creative energy through you, and they have received it. Why is that important? Several reasons…

The flow of energy now is opened. In other words, they have affirmed your gift; they have also affirmed that flow of energy. Now it is not only flowing to you, but through you, in a creative, in a constructive, way. See?

Their *thank you* is an affirmation, a recognition, that you have gifted them. And on multiple levels, you have gifted them with the spirit that is yours to direct... the flow of creative energy that is yours to command, to give, to use. See?

Now that energy is going forth, affirmed by that customer who has just expressed gratitude, affirmed, and recognized your gift of service to them.

Immediately (note this... *immediately*), that flow of energy to and through you has just been amplified. In other words: God gives the greater unto those who give the greater.

Where there is the use of that creative energy... the direction of it, the application of it... it multiplies. *You* are expanded. You become an even greater channel of potential blessings to others. But a small part of that is yours in the response of stating, *you are welcome*.

See? Simple words used daily by so many, but look at the empowerment.

Now, that client or customer feels good. Certainly, they have tendered some monetary exchange for what you have done, whether you do it personally as your own labor or in the employ of someone else, or what not. But your interaction of that simple exchange has created a connection, a path of light, through you.

If you, in turn, acknowledge that on a spiritual level, then just look at how powerful you can become! Each action of kindness, of service... each work which is done in *joyful prayer* is worthy of note.

Is it wrong to claim these actions, or should they be done in a passive, yielding state? We tell you, the Master would give to you all that you would ask and greater, if you would open yourself through such claiming!

THE POWER OF GRATITUDE IN PRAYER

Taking this to the next level... We have dealt with this somewhat from the obvious, and added some dimensions perhaps that you know but have not considered in such a way for a time.

Consider now, again, that flow of energy which is yours... it's sort of like a conduit, a pipe, and you have control over the outlet of that. (Perhaps a hose and a nozzle – with a note of loving humor – might be a good connotation to reflect upon.)

Nonetheless, the flow of energy comes to you... an entity comes to you (in the example given just above, is an entity coming because they have a need or a desire. True? If you are in a service-oriented business, or a merchant, entities come to you for what you do, for your wares, your product, and so forth.

Spirit Coming to You for Service

What of spirit? In spirit, entities call out. They may not know *of* you but they do know *about* you, because in spirit you are of the Light.

Presuming now, for a moment, that we have moved into spirit... we have used meditation, prayer, and so forth... and now you and we are in a non-finite spiritual (or more infinite) state. The thoughts of all can be known here... the works, the needs, and all that sort, are available here. If one can clear themselves to such a point wherein they can reach what is called Universal Consciousness, then all of this and greater are known here.

An entity who comes to you in spiritual form is seeking... no different than a client or customer in the Earth, except that their need is not necessarily (though it can be) of a finite service or product. It is, rather, that they have probably exhausted all means in the Earth and are now turning to spirit. Or they are awakened sufficiently that they know to do both from the beginning – in other words, seek and do all they know to do in the Earth, *and* seek and do all they know to do in meditation and prayer. Nonetheless...

Here comes their request to the Light. In spirit form, you are a part of that Light. As you offer to them your prayer, they receive it. Their acknowledgment of it would complete the cycle, just in the same manner as the customer thanks the merchant for their service.

One with God in Service

Many in the Earth fail to recognize the empowerment that is available in such states, noting here that as one begins any work, any meditation, any prayer work... Or let us say that you are seeking guidance... you are seeking enlightenment.

As you, in that process, acknowledge and perhaps say. "Thank You, Father, for these blessings," you, in the Light-worker's state... in spirit, remember... are offered the completion of a cycle, if you are in service to God. Their thank you, even though they might not have yet acknowledged receipt or heard the answer to their prayer, is a form of empowerment on the part the seeker... that one beseeching of God, so to say; and it offers you in your prayer work, or in your spiritual work, the chance to complete a cycle, the cycle of joyful service. You may not, in the conscious or intellectual sense, know one another, and yet, the expression of gratitude the petitioner states to God is a gift to you for your service.

Several facets of subtlety, but considerable importance and power, are a part of this example:

When you pray in askance of some thing – perhaps not even for self... you are praying for the healing of a friend, a family member, someone on your prayer list, and so forth – if you, in the process of your commencement, recognize and affirm, express, gratitude simply by saying "Thank You, Father," you form a bridge of light instantly with the Creative Force. You open self through the acknowledgment that you are not apart from God, but one with God.

As you conclude your prayer work, it is important in that kind of work to release the result to God and to those for whom you are praying... and even if you are praying for self. Among your last words should be those: "Thank You, Father." See?

They are just words, it could be argued. But they are your form of communication. They are that with which you direct your intention – your thoughts, your emotions, and your spirit, if properly given, are a part of that. The lines of light that are made open and passable by way of the expression of gratitude cannot be underestimated.

Now back to our example. (And please forgive our movement this way and that... we have a lot we are attempting to convey here, and striving to do so in the broadest and most understandable way.)

Prayer Engages Forgiveness

If we move back to you as, let's say, a beautiful sphere of light hovering off here in some wondrous realm where you are deep in joyful prayer and meditation for others, you are sending that out as a ray of light... broadcasting it, if you will. What have you done to reach that point, and what happens when one who receives the harvest of your prayer claims it and then sends back a *thank you*? Numerous cycles are completed.

But, for you to have reached that point where you are that beautiful sphere of light – deep in prayer, deep in meditation – what are your chances of being angry at someone? What are your chances of holding a grudge? What are your chances of fretting over an incident or an entity who created it hours, days, months, years, decades ago… maybe even lifetimes ago? They're quite small, aren't they?

In other words, when you are in joyful prayer and meditation, you've usually used some aspect of forgiveness. Whether passive, latent, or active, you've used that to reach this state of gratitude, of joy, and of service. So we could look backwards at our previous meeting and say that one tool you can use to accomplish gratitude is frequent prayer and meditation. (There's considerable humor here, joyful humor. We hope that is reciprocated in your realms.)

So a form of forgiveness has made this next powerful key a key of affirmation, a key of claiming: the simple act of gratitude. See that? How well they fit together.

A Part of the God-Source

Now suppose that you, in this joyful state, can feel the *thank you* coming from someone who has just used that creative flow of energy that you have directed and offered to them, and they have gained much as the result… if they do not know that you are in joyful prayer for them, then they are thanking God, they are thanking the universe, they are thanking Buddha, Krishna, and perhaps many others. How is it that you benefit from such a broad *thank you*?

Here is another step of enlightenment, of power:

In the highest and best states of joyful prayer, one allows self to simply be. You might no longer consider yourself to be the entity Dave or Marie or Richard or Maria or Pauline or Robin or Kendall, or any of these entities. In other words, you have relegated your finiteness and the given name to your current incarnation to a place of rest, and you have gone beyond it into spirit… pure spirit, let us say. Because you are offering who and what you are, your own spirit, to that flow which is a part of the answer to the recipient, then of course they don't have to say "Thank you (so-and-so) for your prayer work," but a *thank you* to the Universe, to God, to the Creative Force, is just as much yours in all forms as it is that of any other entity or the God-Source, Itself.

Some might squirm a bit here, or might scratch their head, "Is this suggesting that we place ourselves before God? Is this saying that that intended for God, is claimed by the individual?"

What if it were? Would this deplete God? Would God become angry with us for claiming His or Her *thank you's*? Or perhaps the Mother-Father-God would look and state with great joy, with great wonder, and with such a delight, *"Look you... two of My Children have found each other. They are claiming each other. They are claiming Me. They are serving each other where they are, with what they have. And look! My Spirit is rising as a light around them because they are allowing Me to be with them."*

See? The Creative Force has no aspect that is hostile, nor judging. Gratitude relinquishes those qualities, as well. Gratitude is the claiming of one's omnipotence with God... not one's separateness.

In Creation with God

Everything in existence is for you; whether it is adjudged good or bad, it is there for you. In the process of searching out and finding your place of Oneness with the Creative Force... the Universal Force, with God, you will undoubtedly pass through much of creation that does not outwardly, nor as an offering, seem to impart that which is of the Light, or even joyful. But it *is* there for you.

The Pallet of Experience

As an artist who acquires a nice array of pigment, colors with which to portray the spirit of their thought, their creativeness through their individuality, so does all of existence offer you the pallet of emotion, of perception... an incredible pallet from which you can take a dab of this, a little dollop of that, blend it together. And from the good and bad, the darkness and the light, you can create.

But supposing you have no consciousness of this and you fall into disarray, and you call out in prayer and another happens to be in spirit form, offering themselves as a channel of blessings (they have a body in the Earth where the petitioner is seeking from). The Earth is a realm of manifestation, or consciousness, which, in compliance with Universal Law, is for the most part inviolate to other forces. But those forces which are within that sphere (or beneath it) may always offer to you, or to the petitioner in this case, the pallet of emotion and experience and reaction.

You, as a Light-being in spirit form, answering the prayer of someone in the Earth, also make a connection of light into the Earth. You become, during that time, a passable path of light to the Earth.

Now, what happens when you conclude your prayer and meditation for others? Your eyes pop open and you look about and see the nature of the finite realm in which you exist. Yet, there remains with you the result of the works, even though in the specific sense you know them not. The entity who has asked in prayer and who has completed the cycle, wisely, with the empowerment of gratitude... you, willing to claim your part as a Child of God – not distant, but in the Spirit of God, see – claim their gratitude, acknowledge it.

See? In your prayer works, why not state, when you are concluded, "You are welcome for these gifts." And when you hear of good works that have come from entities that you have mentioned by name in prayer, you had best claim that, if you want to grow. If there are questions on that point, tell the Channel and his mate, and we'll try to speak to them, but we shall delve into that point in greater depth in future.

But recognize this: If a worker labors in a joyful state of prayer and good intent, and the ideal, purpose, and goal are held to the accord of the needs of others, and you do not affirm this, then what are you doing? No, don't wobble... don't waffle away from this point. If you don't claim it, what are you doing? Aren't you a part of each healing that is offered through you when it is successful, and even if it does not appear to be so?

Oneness in the Cycle

It is simple... it is profoundly simple:

It is asking. It is giving. It is affirming through *thank you* and reaffirming through *you are welcome*.

Simple cycles of energy, of consciousness... seekers, givers... all of it is a part of the one continuum. See?

When the entity who has prayed returns to the Earth, they bring a greater path of Light into the Earth as well. Having been in joyful prayer for others, having allowed themselves to be an even greater channel of blessings this day and the next and the next, manifests the greater and greater pathway to them, and through them into the Earth.

So now we have a new dimension to the simple action of gratitude, when that entity... who became, let us say, a glorious sphere of light while off in another realm praying, meditating, offering themselves to others, doing other works... then concludes, comes back, brings their creative flow of light with them, expanded by those good works just done and locked into place by acceptance, by affirmation.

Each day that passes wherein you so do, so are you each day the greater light into the Earth. It is (in the general sense at the least, if not specifically in terms of the definitions herein) this process which has made the way passable for the Elders to bring in the first of the seven golden steps of opportunity[3]... according to the cycles, according to the Law, and according to those who are His/who are Hers/who are one with the Light: the Way is made passable through joyful service. See?

The Way is made passable through joyful service, and that joyful service must include self. In order for the cycle to be complete, it must include self as an affirmation.

"The Father doeth the works." ... "Do you believe?" ... "I am ever with thee." ... "All these things and greater shall ye do." Are those not clear, empowering statements?

You say them: "The Father within me doeth the work" ...then let your body be the instrument of Him doing that work. Let your heart rejoice in the expression of gratitude, which is an affirmation, a claiming of that... that it can be as a wondrous light around your thought, your intent.

PARABLE: THANKSGIVING

Two entities are walking down a busy street in a noted city. They are busy in debate, walking along, and suddenly one falls through (what you call) a manhole... breaks a number of bones as he lands in the sewer-way below.

Which of the two are righteous? Hard to tell. One would have to state, at least at outward appearance, that the one who did not fall is righteous.

Let us look at this again... Here is an event which seems to be utterly an accident. It seems to have befallen one and not the other.

The one, while recuperating in hospital, perhaps with one or more of the lower extremities in cast, and that sort (you have the picture)... that entity might lament and state, "Lord, why me? Why didn't Walter fall into that sewer? Why me?"

But at some point along the way, perhaps that entity will, after having balanced with the impact of this, find some gift in this. Perhaps some family members, who the entity had little or no time for in the busy schedule of their executive world, might have time to tell him of their love for him, or talk to him about their dreams, their goals, or perhaps to plan the spring flower garden. You see?

---

[3] Seven Golden steps of opportunity/ the seven Waves of Light - In reading 01/11/00, it was given that there would be seven great cycles of energy, seven great waves of light preparatory to other works, as a part of the preparation of The Way. These seven waves would occur between that time (01/11/00) and the year, approximate, 2013, the effects of which remaining until approximately 2018, ultimately leading those who choose to participate in this opportunity by seeking in the spirit of Oneness, to the ascension to the kingdom of God.

The entity who continued on, unscathed, went on for several more Earth days, collapsed of exhaustion, had a heart attack, and is now here in these realms. But the one who just broke a leg or two is still there, enriched... perhaps awakened to the true gift of life that is surrounding him... the opportunity not only to accomplish, build an empire in the financial or whatever world of this metropolis, but to share himself and his love with those who are close at hand and who would only wish to give of their own love to him.

So perhaps late one evening, after having spoken with many friends, family members and so on, this entity... the pain moderated, the frustration over... might close his eyes and state, "Thank You, Father, for the gift of this injury, for the awakening that You have given me." Even so much so that we might see a tiny rivulet of tear upon his cheek. You are doing your prayer work, you are *out there*, so to say; and here comes this man's heart-felt, soul-felt, expression of gratitude. His life will never be the same. He is transformed. He has been given back his very life... had to break a few legs to do it, but he's there, and he's offering thanks. He's grateful. He's expressing gratitude.

Now, we are at the next level of spiritual discovery here. There is gratitude of all sorts. This man's gratitude didn't come from a prayer answered... he was too busy to pray. But it did come from prayer; it came from the prayer of those who love him and couldn't reach him. So a loving Universal Force offered him the opportunity to walk straight into a manhole, an open one, and break a leg. Spiritually, he took it... broke the leg, had the experience, and it changed him.

Those who prayed perhaps didn't always pray, "Oh, please, let him..." (this-or-that). They perhaps prayed in their own way... perhaps more *I's* or *my's*... "Give me, O Father, greater love and joy in my life." The injured executive could have cared less... didn't know... wasn't aware... thought he was joyful. But that was an illusion.

In this case, specifically, there were two who prayed for his attention and affection. You, now, as we left you there (with a note of loving humor) in this fourth level of gratitude's expression, have answered that prayer because you have offered yourself as a light.

Through your light into the Earth... the one which you bring back, the one which you are when you claim and empower yourself, when you receive and open self... has made the way passable for this man to break his leg. (We're hopeful there are at least a few bits of laughter in that last statement.) However... now, this man's expression, his acknowledgement that this is a gift... not a random act of disservice to him by the Universe or God, but a gift!

'Round and about, perhaps months earlier in your prayers to those in need, those two loved ones of this man were asking... and your light entered therein. It shined through, and now this man, in traction in a hospital, wants to complete the cycle... a grand circle, see... a ring of light... the Logos. There you are. You happened to be on duty, so to say (humor intended), in meditation-prayer work. This wonderful gift of this... we'll call it a... another ball of light comes sailing through the universe towards you: someone's prayer has been answered, and here comes their gratitude. Are you going to duck and allow the ball of light to sail on to some distant, massive globe of light which is wearing a tee shirt with *GOD* written on it? Or are you going to state, "Thank You, Father. You are welcome, whoever this is from. I claim this, and complete the circle of light."

If you are becoming an adept, you'll do the latter, because you know that it is the completion. In turn, when you leave your station on prayer-and-meditation watch in some other level of consciousness and sort of float back down to Earth like a leaf falling off a tree swinging back and forth in the wind until it reaches the Earth, when you get there, you'll bring this light back into the Earth.

Do you get it? The man gave the gift in the Earth. The two who loved the man prayed from the Earth. Their prayers went out into the ethers, so to say (as most believe that prayer does) and there you were, on prayer watch, and you received it. And in turn, you brought it back to the Earth. Trace it out on paper. Write it out. Look at it. It's real. It is The Life. See?

80C3

APPLYING GRATITUDE

What can you do with gratitude in your daily life?

Well, you use one of the more simplistic and most commonplace tools of gratitude in the form of *thank you*, as we illustrated several times above.

Thank Yourself

And you can do this... another strange but powerful offering to you: If you have a bathroom with a mirror, a looking glass, go to it; stand for a few seconds and look at yourself. Don't pay attention to the way your hair looks or any such, but look into your own eyes. Think a prayerful thought; hold an affirmation, or whatever you do to feel like you are connected with God.

Now lean forward and look into your own eyes. And say "Thank you." Really. Do that. Do it every day... do it three to five times a day... all throughout the period of time that you are focusing upon gratitude, say *thank you* to yourself.

Now, the purpose in this could be sort of ascertained by those who have such training in the Earth, or you could leave it alone and just *do it...* we would recommend the latter. There's no magical, hidden, psychological intent here, beyond the obvious fact that you are going to look at yourself and realize that you are a being in the Earth. That's a good thing to do. Some don't even remember that.

With Your Eyes, Thank Others

You're also going to take time, after you do that, to look at others, aren't you? And if you do it the way we suggested and look into your own eyes, deep into them, three to five times each day, Zachary here is willing to wager a great sum (were it that he had one... humor intended) that you will also do the same to others.

Think back as you are hearing or reading these words... did you really look into anyone's eyes this day? Did you think the thought, *Thank you for being in my life... thank you for this opportunity to share my spiritual light with you... even though you may not know it, I gift it to you?* And if they do know it, they'll say "Thank you," you'll say, "Welcome," and the cycle will grow, the light will expand. See?

What will happen is... they'll notice that you are truly looking at them... that you are giving them, perhaps, ten seconds of focus as you've given yourself. Because you've done it three to five times that day, you're getting used to it, so maybe you'll do that with others.

We promise you, if you will do this for seven days... no less than three, but preferably five times at intervals throughout the day... it will transform your life. You'll start to *see*; you'll start to *know*; and you'll start to *empower yourself* with the affirmation of gratitude. See?

Thank Your Past

Now, if you'll bear with us and do that, then in the next seven-day cycle we would ask you (three to five times each day) to look at some aspect of your past (never mind if you haven't applied forgiveness completely... you can go back and do that; this is a good way to discover how thorough, how successful you've been). In the second seven-day cycle, do this: Do your meditation (assuming you are still – because you found good benefit from so doing – doing the little bathroom mirror exercise), do this, as well:

Look at events in your past. The best way, Zachary states here, is to choose one straightaway in the morning upon arising... pop up out of bed, meditate, find a past event... anything, but something note-

noteworthy; it'll come to you... hold that, and say *thank you*. Like the man in traction, look for the gift it bears. See? You'll find it. It's there.

Remember the palette, the collage of color, the essences of emotion which are like pigments for the master painter to paint a life of beauty and contrast? You are painting your own. You are building it upon the canvas of your past. And you are claiming... you are taking over the brushes, the pigments of emotion. You are taking the array of material, and you are going to make your own life, as you choose.

More and more keys will be given and discussed with you, and you'll discover others on your own.

But, in the second seven-day cycle, each day, often (three to five times) pause. Meditate, if possible, but simply close your eyes, remember the event/the person/the circumstance, and express gratitude for it. Even if it has left you in a state that is considered to be not one sought after, see, there is that of a gift for you in all things. Expressing gratitude, confirming it, affirming it, claiming it, completes the cycle of the flow of light through that.

Forgiveness was the stripping away of the illusion that you must hold something other than joy and light towards others.

Gratitude, now, is the affirmation of the gift in those events. This is the next step of empowering yourself.

As you do this through the next seven days, you are going to find yourself very quickly starting to look at life even more differently; you are going to look around, having looked at the past and, using forgiveness and gratitude, taken the best of it, taken the truth of the gift in it, and now you are going to be walking around in your daily life, bearing and wearing the gift.

Notice. Keep records of how you felt in the beginning... what your thoughts were... and very briefly keep notes in a journal. The more succinct you make this, the more likely you are to do it. Just these words: *Today was great* and the date; or (perish the thought) *Today was not so great.* See?

Thank Your Daily Life

Let's look at a third seven-day cycle, and let's look at it in this way (humbly offered)... What is there in your daily life that you oft do not recognize and express gratitude for? Is it that automobile that sometimes ignites or starts, and sometimes doesn't? Is it that cleaner who never gets your clothing correct?

Perhaps these little things are just there for the same purpose that the man in traction found a manhole there, open for him to fall into… perhaps they are to give you some form of contrast, some form of respite, pause; and rather than expressing anger or frustration or anything less than joy (no small work there, Zachary states)… but nonetheless, it is an opportunity for you to *do* something… an annotation in the otherwise calm waters of life that has a gift for you.

Perhaps that automobile needs to be replaced. Perhaps there are trips that you are taking that might be better if you didn't. Perhaps there is some place that you should be walking, because you need the stimulation to your circulatory. Or perhaps God is trying to shout at you, *"Hey, Daughter… we have this wonderful gift here for you! How much longer are you going to hold onto that old automobile? Won't you let it go? Won't you trust? Won't you have faith? Won't you accept?"* Or perhaps your style of clothing, your apparel, has come to be symbolic of who you have become, and until you recognize who and what you have become, that cleaning place is the open manhole of your life. See?

You can simply say, "Well, I need to make some changes here," and these simple little annoyances, or you could call them frustrations, are offering you the gift of being able to see this. (Of course, this could be carried to a fault, and one could go looking for incidents that are less than desirable, manifest them, and try to make a gift out of that; that, of course, is not the point here at all.)

The point is to know that you are the captain of the vessel of your own life. When you meet these confluences, these contrasts of light and dark in life, you direct the outcome just as surely as the captain directs the course of the vessel he is captaining.

Forgiveness is that which clears the way, makes it passable, forgiveness is that which you can use to open the path; gratitude is putting the light into the path. Forgiveness might clean the conduit, the pathway; gratitude is the opening of the valve in that conduit or pathway, which can allow creative spirit to flow. See?

You Asked for This Life

You are the one who has asked to be who and what you are in life. Reiterating this again: You are that one who has asked to be who and what you are.

You have asked this, first, by seeking entry as a soul… reentering, claiming a body, being born, growing, experiencing, and all that; but who and what you are now, is through the process of your acceptance. You've asked for these things. Think about that…

They aren't happening to you randomly. True, in some in-

stances you have asked for them sort of obliquely. In other words...
you didn't ask to have rheumatic fever at age ten, you didn't ask to be
smitten with some impairment at age thirty, you didn't ask to be of this
height or that particular physical characteristic. But you did ask for
them in seeking the entry.

What you do is allow. You accept, you evaluate, you adjudge... or you *don't!* If you consciously know and choose, then you
are captaining the vessel of your life; if you accept what comes, if you
do not claim the empowerment that you have within *each event*, then
you are adrift upon the sea of life without rudder or direction.

You Are the Captain of Your Life

Forgiveness and gratitude are a part of the process of claiming
the fact that you are in charge of your own life. Don't bother to argue
that point from all the other potential perspectives... we know them,
and so do you. What we are stating here is simple truth. It is your
choice to take control of your life. Your life is, in the ultimate, how
you feel within, who you are within. It can change the outer, and the
degree to which that outer changes, is again under your direction
and/or control.

Here again, the Master asked, *"Do you believe?"* In other
words, *Is the pathway open for you to be healed?* Well, is your pathway open for your life to become yours... for you to claim it?

Forgiveness unburdens the vessel, like cleaning the barnacles
off the hull of a sailing ship in the great seas, the sailing seas. Forgiveness is the removal of the impediments.

Ready to claim your life? Then acknowledge it. Look in the
mirror and state, "Thank you!" Look back at your life's events, and be
grateful for them. See the gift. Claim it. And this day, in this moment,
ask yourself this question: *Who am I?* And, *How did I get here? Am I
this professor, teaching at this university? Am I this doctor, serving in
this emergency room? Am I this metaphysician, building dreams, serving people? Am I this one who tends these animals?* And on and on.
Who am I, and how did I get here? Did I choose these things? Some of
you did. Some of you didn't. But did you choose who you are, inwardly?

What is the result of all of this? Has it reached a level of bore-
dom? Can you still see your service in the Logos, the Circle of Light?
It's like walking down a hallway with several doors... in order for the
Winds of Light to flow through that corridor, you can't open one door
and leave the others closed.

You affirm and give thanks for who and what you are... that opens the doorway into your life. If you do the little mirror exercise and the first gratitude experience, and that affirms and illuminates you right now, then you go forward with your prayer and meditations, and you open the doors in front of you, and on and on. And you'll receive through them and from them the gifts of Light, the expressions of gratitude of others; and you confirm them with your own reciprocation of *you are welcome.*

We spoke of, in the recognition of prayer work, the importance of claiming, affirming. Now, of course, that is a process that will take some time to become accustomed to. There is a sort of innate resident attitude in most entities that feels more comfortable with a separateness between themselves and God... this is an action, a practice, a work, intended to remove that separateness. See? That's all. Except that that small thing does complete the cycle, the circle.

DEVELOPING AN ATTITUDE OF GRATITUDE

We would encourage you all to oft meditate in an attitude of gratitude.

Look at the sky, the plants, the animals, the trees... the things that others have created, designed, built, and provided for your life... the foods that you eat, even those wrinkled shirts from that poor laundry, the happenstance-starting automobile that still, for the most part, gets you to and fro.

An Omniscient Child of God

Gratitude. Gratitude is empowering. It is the recognition by a Child of God of their power, their righteousness; and of the omnipotent presence of the Light and power of God in the entirety of their life, and not just in those times when they've traveled to some distant realm where God's Light is so brilliant and pure.

Bring it back... manifest it in the Earth. Help us to help you. And in return, together, we'll help others. The way is opening. We are all One.

Oneness... the *O* in it a constant reminder of the rings of light, of God's Truth. Flow through those with thought, action, and deed. But be grateful for your life. Be grateful for yourself, and all there and about you in the Earth... contrasts, the hues, the brilliances, the subtleties of them... be the weaver of the fabric of your own life.

We are here to help you as brethren. We have gone on from finiteness in this time, but we are not gone. We are with you; just so, as you awaken yourself, you will find that you are also with us... your spirit is here, as ours is there with you. Let us complete this Circle of Light by acknowledging that and expressing gratitude for it.

So, Father, we give thanks unto those who have gathered with us in this joyful work. We thank You, Father, for the gifts of this meeting. And you are welcome, dear friends, for what we have offered, and we thank you for what you have offered. But most of all, recognize that you can decide... can make the decision, and take charge of who and what you are. And in that process, you are contributing to making the Way passable.

We thank all those who have come forward to assist in these works, and you, dear friends. As we conclude...

May the grace and blessings of our Father's wisdom ever be that lamp to guide your footsteps. Fare thee well, then, for the present, dear Friends.

GUEST LECTURE: T-I-A

Given January 23, 2000

LAMA SING: We have an entity here before us, who would like to contribute something. We identify this one as T-i-a. That is this entity's spiritual name, the entity's soul note. It is quite an honor for an entity to give such, and indicates the stature of T-i-a (Tee-eye-ah, as we would pronounce it) ...and we shall use the reference, *her*. T-i-a has come forward from the Angelic Host and wishes to speak just briefly. We bow to her, and offer her the grace of our soul light and our love.

T-I-A: The message I bring to you all is not mine alone, but comes to you from your brethren... not distant in terms of measure, but only separated from you by the willingness and openness of your hearts. We are not here to offer to you something which is unknown, but rather, to emphasize that which *is* known.

We have, with great joy, seen the efforts on the part of many in the Earth to awaken others to the needs thereupon. As we are given leave by God to so do, we have served these needs. But, yours – in the Earth, each of you – is the dominion over these... in the end, only you can affect the healing and transformation of that which is now in a state of dis-ease.

Those good souls who have passed through the Wheel of Life and gone beyond it, and who are called now collectively the Elders, have led the way for God's light to be re-awakened within the Earth[4], bringing in their own light to serve as the kindling flame, that it shall be illuminated once again.

Each is born of God as a perfect whole. That perfection is defined in a unique way. Your soul note is needed in the great symphony of life. In order for you to contribute it to that symphony, it is you and you alone who can claim it and manifest it, that it can be heard, that it can blend with the other soul notes and make the symphony of life upon the Earth into that work of beauty and joy as is God's intention for same. Within you are the counterpoints of all that exists without. Whatsoe'er polarities, contrasts, and forces in opposition that you might discern outwardly, the seeds of these are within you just so, as

---

[4] The re-awakening of God's Light in Earth – this refers to the shift in consciousness that occurred on 1/11/00, further described in the "Special Bulletin" included in this chapter

well. As you have these as potentials within, balanced and in harmony with one another, then they do what they are intended to do: they give meaning… they provide depth and perspective, and from them can spring forth fruits of goodness, hope, joy, and love. But when these inner seeds are not in balance with one another, then the outward fruits shall be as are seen in and upon the Earth.

The message, then, is to know yourself; and in the process, know those aspects which are a bit awry from the state of balance that is within your capacity to so accomplish.

Past communications and guidance and information as has been given to you spoke of the Feminine Force. And these beautiful souls comprising the ever-changing grouping called the Lama Sing grouping have given it forthrightly, with deliberateness and definition. We, as are a part of the Angelic Host, summon you forth to claim the creative you. We have joined with the Elders and this grouping and yours, and we shall serve as it is joyful for us to be received. And in the works with that one from the Earth known as Peter[5] through this, the Channel through whom the Lama Sing grouping speaks, it is through his love of you and of the Master, the Christ, that we can come forward… and so we shall. So we are entering the Earth to serve with them and you, the faithful.

So as you hold love in your heart for yourself and others, then can we be with you… for love is the portal, the pathway, upon which we shall arrive.

We thank the Lama Sing Grouping and each of you, dear friends. May it be, ever, to your joy that we might walk with you.

God is Love.

---

[5] Peter – in 1991, the path Al uses as he's leaving finiteness for his channeled readings crossed with that of a man who was leaving his body through the process we call death. That process and the information that followed was recorded in what came to be called the PETER PROJECT. Those involved in the PETER PROJECT followed Peter through his incredible journey for more than ten years. Easing the fear of dying, giving new hope for life after death, the first book, IN REALMS BEYOND is a compilation of the first eighteen months, with future books in the works. The movie TV and series due out soon, is based on this incredible story.

SPECIAL BULLETIN

Given on 1/11/00 11:00 p.m.

ELDERS: The Earth is in transition ...
At approximately 2:01 a.m., this day, 1-11-00 in
the Earth Eastern time, United States of America, a
change in the energy forces has been brought forth
as a consciousness.

The movement was preceded by the preparation and
intention of those who are called the Elders. In
their works, there is the intent to serve, without
limitation, the Forces of Light. Primarily led by
the Elders, this movement is a part of their intended service for the preparation of the Way.

It is a transformation preparatory to those works
which lie ahead. It is a shift which is a part of
the movement from one level of consciousness to the
threshold of the next… a manifestation according to
the progression, according to the cycles.

The cycles have reached their intersection of omnipotence, and so the Elders have used this, and
the free will choices of those in the Earth, to
manifest it, to open it into the Earth.

It was at that point, at 2:01 a.m., when those
forces entered their major convergence, and will
remain to an approximate time, 2018. Several other
cycles will also enter in, in the times ahead, and
will manifest, each one in a different form of
uniqueness. You could adjudge this, in terms of an
evaluation, as the first of seven steps to the
kingdom of the throne of our Father.

What does this mean to the individuals there upon
the Earth?

This is dependent upon each individual and the nature of their spirit and their free will. For those
of the faithful all across the sphere or planet,
Earth, who are choosing to prepare The Way, here is

the answer to your prayer. It portends the opportunity for considerable advancement in terms of the potential of each as a Child of God. Thus, there is, in this, wonderful opportunity. Any entity who is seeking in the spirit of oneness and who asks in accordance with God that which is to the betterment and to the fullness of their spirit potential, this process is for you. Those who are seeking and who are truly willing to release (in other words, to go forward in faith and to release their apprehension or fear of the unknown) will progress markedly.

This Light cannot be dispelled or diminished. It is at its basal point in the Earth, even as we speak. This is not a conflict, not a battle between the forces of darkness and light. The Elders have no intention to do anything but serve. They consider the Master (the Christ, in his seven major embodiments culminating with that wherein He was called the man Jesus and with that as the ascension to the throne of God) to be their Brother. As such, they are all a part of a continuum of work that has no separateness. Their dedication to this service is without peer. And so it is that their nature is almost child-like in its purity and innocence... but as the greatest of all warriors in terms of its faith, in terms of its honor.

Notice for all in the Earth: It is not so much that we are sharing this information to point out something that is utterly new. This has always been an offering. What *is* new is that there are such goodly numbers of good souls who are now claiming this. They have made a Bridge of Light[6], so to say, which is passable for your Elder brothers and sisters to bring this light into the dimensions of Earth.

---

[6] Bridge of Light - in a "Peter" reading in 2000, it was requested of those on Earth who were following the Peter journey that they help build a bridge of light… that the light workers would build it from their side of the veil and the group on Earth would do so from the Earth side. By enlisting help from Earth, the Bridge would be in keeping with the Law of Free Will. (i.e. the Bridge was not thrust upon the Earth by the light workers, but a combined effort from both sides.) Its purpose was so those departing the Earth through "death" could find their way to life beyond with greater ease. In the years since the Bridge was built, its wonder has grown – it now spans the Sea of Faces (see pg 53). Somehow, knowledge of its existence has spread, and people are asking to be taken to the Bridge of Light when they die.

By being conscious of this, by the affirmation of it, there is the process of claiming. The process of claiming is an empowering one. As you choose it... as you, from your free will, reach out to it, knowing it to be a Force of Light in God's name, you further enhance it. In other words, it is like making a pathway or a passageway to contribute to the entree of this... the Forces of Light.

8003

LAMA SING: The Elders point out that there is need for greater expediency for those of you who might be considered in the vanguard of that work:

- It is recommended that those of you who wish to accelerate your spiritual growth and be a part of that which is, literally, preparing *The* Way, even as we speak, perhaps would be well-advised to redouble your efforts to focus upon your spiritual self in terms of meditation, prayer, centering self, and releasing limitations, shadows, doubts, those sorts.
- The Sea of Faces[7] is being impacted dramatically by this shift of energy and consciousness. You might well offer, what you call, extra works and efforts to that.
- The Elders are, as their right under Universal Law, asking each of you to claim daily your heritage as Children of God, and invoke your right of free will, that you are, each day even moreso, a clearer, more perfect, more joyful, more whole expression of God.
- They are asking those of you who have opened yourselves, to begin the process of reclamation of the more total self. This is preparatory for a greater shift in consciousness which is being prepared, even as we speak... again, by the Elders.

This is an offering of love, not a mandate, but as information to help, to aid, and to support the beauty, the individual uniqueness of each soul who is incarnate in and about the Earth.

---

[7] The Sea of Faces - Built of illusions and habits formed while in the realm of Earth, these are realms whose discarnates seek to perpetuate their realms of illusions by using all manner available to them to influence incarnate individuals who have abandoned their free will, their hope, ideal or purpose, or are in some way addicted; or to lure to their realms those departing Earth in death, passing through the Sea of Faces and their signature temptations on their way "to the light." Countless numbers succumbed to the temptations, adding to the vastness of this Sea. Now, with the Bridge of Light, people can now choose to pass *over* the Sea.

STUDY GUIDE

Activities for Applying Gratitude

We would encourage you all to meditate often in an attitude of gratitude. Look at the sky, the plants, the animals, the trees... the things others have created... the events.

Morning Activity
- Upon rising, take a few minutes to reflect upon this day ahead of you. Even if you are late, don't give this up. Decide to harvest some fruits from it.

Daily Activity
- Stand for a few seconds and look at your eyes in the bathroom mirror. Think a prayerful thought or whatever you do to feel like you are connected with God. Now lean forward and look into your own eyes... and say "thank you." Really, do that. Do it every day or even three to five times a day, all throughout the period of time that you are focusing upon gratitude. Say "thank you" to yourself.

Evening Review & Exercises
- Look at the events that have occurred this day that could use a little seasoning of forgiveness and gratitude.
- Journal: How did you feel thanking yourself, or a stranger, or a past event? Who am I, and how did I get here? Did I choose these things about me – my vocation, my appearance, my environment, my friends and family? What did I choose for myself inwardly?
- In prayer, see the request to God as <u>already answered</u> by saying, "Thank you, Father, for these Blessings" and reaffirm and claim your part as a Child of God by saying, "You are welcome for these gifts."
- Journal a time in your life when a seemingly negative event later proved to bring a positive outcome. "Look for the gift it bears."
- Say often to yourself, "I know that I am the captain of the vessel of my own life." Also, "affirm and give thanks for who and what you are. That opens the doorway into your life.
- Sing/play "Your Song" and imagine your soul as one note joining in with many soul notes to make 'the symphony of life.' "Your soul note is needed in the great symphony of life."

NOTES:
_____
_____
_____
_____
_____
_____

Weekly Exercises for Gratitude

Week 1

Look into anyone's eyes this day and think the thought *Thank you for being in my life. Thank you for this opportunity to share my spiritual light with you. Even though you may not know it, I gift it to you.* If you feel something in return from them, that's their *Thank you.* And you can mentally say, *Welcome,* and the cycle will grow, the light will expand.

After about a week, begin to look for how your life is changing, becoming more empowered because you are thanking it.

Week 2

Do bathroom mirror exercise, and do this, as well: Look at events in your past. Ask for it, meditate, it'll come to you. Hold that, and say, "Thank you" (like the man in traction) for the gift it bears. You'll find it. It's there Keep records of how you felt in the beginning, what your thoughts were, and very briefly keep notes in a journal.

Week 3

What is there in your life that you oft do not recognize and express gratitude for? The trucker who brought your food to market for you to purchase, the designer of the bed you are sleeping on, the service person who fixed your heater so that now yr home is warm on a cold night.

Week 4

Ready to claim your life? Then acknowledge it: Look in the mirror and state, "Thank you." Look back at your life's events, and be grateful for them. See the gift. Affirm it, claim it.

NOTES:

_____

_____

_____

_____

_____

_____

_____

_____

_____

_____

_____

_____

_____

Further Exploring Gratitude

NOTE: The thoughts listed here are merely suggestions to get you started in further exploration of this subject. Use any portion of them, or not, as your personal guidance leads you.

"If you are to maximize the potential of the opportunities now before you, it is good for you, if not a mandate, that you claim Self." -LS How would understanding gratitude, as well as understanding forgiveness, help us claim Self?

How would adopting an "attitude of gratitude" be empowering?

Diagram a flow chart that shows you the energy exchange that occurs, optimally, between giver and receiver, showing God as the original Source, and you as the channel, modifying it as the uniqueness of you.

Diagram the same flow, showing the recipient as making a request (a prayer) of the Light, and you (not knowing anything of them from the finite) as a part, a channel of the Light, of the answer to their prayer.

How do you benefit when accepting *the amen's*, the *thank you's* from another's prayers, even when neither of you are aware of the other, from the Earthly plain?

Name some ways that lama Sing has related gratitude with forgiveness, helping, by establishing this correlation, to lay an even firmer spiritual foundation for you?

How does gratitude help you claim your omnipotence with God?

"If a worker labors in a joyful state of prayer and good intent, and the ideal, purpose, and goal are held to the accord of the needs of others, and you do not affirm this, then what are you doing? No, don't wobble; don't waffle away from this point. If you don't claim it, what are you doing?" -LS Why is this such an important issue in the topic of gratitude?

NOTES:

_____

_____

_____

_____

_____

_____

_____

_____

_____

JOURNAL

_____

_____

_____

_____

_____

_____

_____

_____

_____

_____

_____

_____

_____

_____

_____

_____

_____

_____

_____

_____

_____

_____

_____

_____

Step 3:

Hopefulness

Given February 25, 2000

OPEN FORUM ON HOPEFULNESS

LAMA SING: Yes, we have the Channel then and, as well, those references which apply to the grouping as gathered, and those intents and purposes as are gathered within same. As we begin with these works, let us come together in this joyful prayer of Oneness unto God.

O Holy Father-Mother-God, look upon us as Thou would, and see as to our needs and purposes here and in the Earth. Guide Thou us, then, O Father-Mother-God, that we might know of Thy presence, claiming same, and empowering ourselves in the Light of Thy grace and the wisdom of Thy Spirit's presence in all. We thank Thee, Father, for the presence of the Spirit of the Christ in all things, knowing this to be that path of opportunity and joyfulness that has been eternally present. We thank Thee, as well, for the presence of the Master, the Christ, who is the example and the light upon this... the way of return unto Oneness with Thee. We offer ourselves, Father, as channels of blessing unto the prayers which have been brought unto Thee. So as Thou would see us worthy, send us, Father, joyfully, that we might commune with them, and give unto them, as is their need. For those who have lost their way and know not to pray, we offer this prayer... giving the gift of the Master's love, compassion, wisdom, and healing grace. So as they are ready, this shall ever be present. We thank Thee, Father, for this continued opportunity of joyful service through this, our Channel and his mate, in the Earth. And we thank all those loving souls who have come forward to join in and to give unto, this work, which we now do in Thy name. We thank Thee, Father. Amen.

A Brief Review

As we are joined together, dear friends, in this, the third of our collective works, there may be some value in a brief review and an explanation of that which we have to offer you in this meeting. In the foundation of one's expression…where that might be, is highly variable… nonetheless, such a foundation has to do with the focus of one's intent and purpose. To that end, then, those of you who are dwelling in the Earth in physical form or body at this moment can find that this explanation may make for greater understanding of that which has gone before, and that which we are about to offer to you, humbly and lovingly…

Forgiveness is that which is obviously powerful in its capacity to release. Releasing is important, in the sense that, as one holds or clings to experiences from the past, these are like fetters, bonds, even chains, which can bind one from moving forward. The obverse of this is, of course, equally important… that the bond is multi-directional at the minimum, involving at least one other, or one other event.

So as you have searched, and applied, forgiveness, you have found aspects that are perhaps of some surprise or question to you. And to that end, we commend you, and many gathered here have been with you in those efforts, and shall continue to assist you as you are at the ready.

The importance of forgiveness, then, is obviously foundational: Until one has attended to those things which are holding them or binding them, progression… or *complete* progression… is difficult to attain. There would always be that aspect which is similar to what you call a yo-yo in the Earth… you think you are moving outwards, and suddenly you stop, spin a bit, and are drawn back.

Forgiveness is the vehicle upon which one can place themselves for movement forward.

Gratitude is the opening of the way. It is the preparation and the building of a receptivity.

Foundationally, you have already released yourself through the application of forgiveness, and no doubt will continue to do so for some several months, or perhaps even years, ahead. Do continue that.

Now, gratitude does accomplish the next step of opening, and making passable, the claiming… in effect, making and defining a channel of movement. Sufficient on this, we should think.

HOPE-*FULL*NESS

Our next topic is carefully chosen here. At first hearing, you may not see the relevance, but we believe, as you dwell upon it and work with it during your next segment (or Earth month) you will find that it is powerfully relevant... and that topic is *Hopefulness.*

We have chosen this word with some deliberation. We could have stated simply: *Hope.*

But rather, this word seems to connote (at least as we see you, in the Earth) a more meaningful intent: Hope-*full*ness.

The Law of Expectancy

You have freed yourself. You have defined and opened the way. And now you are beginning to build upon it, with that aspect of power within you called *hope.*

One of the most wondrous tools that lies within the definition of hope, and hopefulness, is the Law of Expectancy. In the sense of one's day-to-day life in the Earth, there are those things which we clearly see, comprehend, and lovingly embrace you for dealing with... and that is the aspect of distraction.

The illusion of that which is presented to you in a myriad of ways in each Earth day's activity can, as you well know, take you away from an attitude of hopefulness. And yet, those of you who have the brilliance in your energy fields – or aura, as called – of an attitude of hopefulness and expectancy, know that this, as *a choice* in one's way of living and thinking, has profound power.

To define hopefulness a bit further in the spiritual sense...

Hopefulness is that which sends out the call. It is that which enables and empowers; those who are striving to serve you, striving to be servants of God, and to carry His light, gifts, and blessings to you, can move upon this, can give to you, in the sense that your hopefulness *permits* same to be given. (There is much to be discussed and explored in the area of this topic, both as lie within the definition of hopeful-ness, and that which is the explanation of same in Universal Law called the Law of Expectancy.) But here are several basics, which we offer to you in the prayerful intent of empowering you...

The Power of Choice

Each day, begin your thoughts, your intentions, by considering the choices before you. You have, of course, always presented to you in the Earth (and in many other realms) the picture, the thought, the way of life which has become the tradition of the realm in which you dwell… in this case, the Earth. So often, this is a collage of energies, of thoughts, emotions and that collage may come upon you instantaneously upon opening your eyes in the morning, upon awakening.

If you would think of this as a garment… in other words, that perhaps you have (what we believe you call in the Earth) a clothes tree, some sort of appliance that stands near your bedside on which you hang some garments… then think of this collage of emotion as a cloak of consciousness for the Earth. To carry that just a bit further, it may be your cloak, imbued with the aspects of your being, the sheaths, or layers of past influences and tendencies, and all that sort. When you awaken during this cycle, this Earth month, alert yourself to the fact that you are, in that moment of awakening, presented with a choice. Claim that choice *before* you reach out to the clothes tree to take the cloak of your Earthliness and begin this new day.

Hopefulness is incredibly powerful: It is that which will build, according to your willingness to receive.

Choosing Hopefulness

Now think of there being another cloak, so to say… another garment hanging on another arm of that clothes tree. It is beautiful; its color is lavender, its brilliance is stunning; it has a collage of color, sound, and vibration that are simply joyful to contemplate and, even moreso, to behold. Give yourself a few moments and imagine, perhaps by closing your eyes again, and seeing yourself reaching out to the clothes tree; and rather than the cloak of Earthliness, you take this wondrously beautiful lavender cloak of hopefulness… and adorn your body with it. Feel the essence of it. We shall be with you. Think of those things which are most joyful for you to contemplate. Build an attitude of hopefulness before you open your eyes. See? This would be for each morning of this period.

In your morning prayers and meditations, think about hopefulness. Allow your thoughts and minds, after your affirmation and prayer, to flow freely. Test the limits of your own hopefulness. Are you hopeful to the extent that others have presented to you as the intended boundaries of your hopefulness? Where is the limit of your expectancy? Flow gently, easily. Move outwards, and feel when you are beginning to slow, when you sense a bit of friction, abrasion, and you know that you have reached a point that defines how much hopefulness you have in this point in your Earth life.

Expanding the Consciousness

We will ask and assist the Channel in the preparation of a work which will be intended to take you to those limits and, thereafter, to move beyond. But as you do this successively, each Earth day, you will find that you are expanding. For the process of movement... the process of realizing and actualizing where your limits are, and then next perhaps identifying them and their source of origin, and then moving beyond same... becomes very fluidic, almost automatic. It is, indeed, a joyful work.

In the evening of each Earth day, we encourage you once again to offer your prayer of affirmation: your prayer of forgiveness, of gratitude, and ask for the increase in your own hopefulness. Review the Earth day and look at those events which come to you. Those which have the greatest potential will obviously be those which are brought to the forefront, and upon which you will feel some consider-able affinity. As you do this, then, once again having had a full day's measure of activity and consciousness in the Earth, allow your thoughts to be free. This should be as light and joyful as you can make it. You may wish to use sound with this process, or you may wish to use an intonation, a mantra, or some such... whatsoever shall carry thee, shall free thee, is that which should be used.

Now, as you find what might be ascertained as the outer pa-rameter of your hopefulness, think and see yourself turning around and looking back. If you do this consecutively, you will find it is very re-vealing. But more than this, you will gain a comprehension of who and what you are, what your life is, and where your limits are. Or let's make that past tense... where your limits *were*... because we are joy-fully hopeful that you will surpass these easily, see, so our expectancy is already with you as a gift of Light.

PARABLE: EXPECTING

Two entities are traveling through a very dense forest. Their journey has been long and arduous, and they continue step by step. Weariness has set in. Hunger is becoming a growing pres-ence. Darkness is swiftly falling upon them, and the density of the forest, combined with the darkness, is creating an atmosphere that is oppressive.

One of the entities finally, in sheer exhaustion and despair, collapses at the root of a great tree... leaning back, sighing heavily, finally placing his hands up over his face, begins to sob lightly.

The other, equally weary, equally enhungered, stands looking down at his companion, and states as follows, "Why dost thou weep, dear friend?"

After a moment, his colleague stops, slowly removes his hands, wiping away several tears as he does, and looking up at his colleague, states, "I am beset with fear. I see no hope... no way out. This forest shall be the end of our lives." With which, he can speak no more. Choked with emotion, he thrusts his head forward, drawing his knees up, wrapping his arms around his knees and forehead.

The entity who is standing, looks about, and he perceives clearly the now dense darkness. Only the dim shadows of the many-fold trees can be perceived in this very limited light.

He descends to his knees and bows his head, and we hear the following. "Lord God, it is I, Jacob. Would You look upon us? We are lost, weary, and enhungered. I believe unto Thee, Father, as does my colleague. Send unto us, as is our need. I am hopeful and expectant, because I know Thou art ever with me. I thank You, Father, for having heard and answered my call."

He remains in this posture, kneeling, hands together, head bowed, until something calls out to him in the aspect of sensory perception... it is a light and a song. Startled, he looks about, straightening up. What can this be? Off in the distance he sees a glow and hears... yes, a song.

Soon, this duo is joined by a threesome of woodcutters who are on their way home from a day's labor in a distant part of the forest. They are met with rejoicing, and the woodcutters embrace them openly and lovingly. "What are you doing?" the leader asks of the duo.

"We are traveling to a distant city, and we have lost our way."

"Well, then, God has sent you to be our guests. Join us. Come sup with us, and on the morrow we shall bring you to your destination, for it is near at hand. What you perceive is only the illusion of distance and lack of definition. This forest is our friend. It gives us life; it gives us shelter, and that unto our need. We know it and love it, as it knows and loves us in return."

The group travels a brief distance to the abode of the woodcutters. There they are nourished, and rest. And upon the dawn's light they are brought to the edge of the forest where they can see their destination in the distance.

Turning, as they prepare to depart from the company of these three good woodcutters, Jacob states, "Would you mind if I offer a brief prayer of thankfulness?"

Smiling and nodding an affirmation, the leader of the woodcutters simply nods, and immediately all three woodcutters bow their heads and clasp their hands.

Jacob does not do so. Rather, he stands with his hands spread apart, as ye have oft seen the Master do, looking up. We hear him state the following, "O Lord God, I thank Thee for the answer to my prayer. Fill me with Thy hope and Thy promise, that all that I am about bears the Light of Thy presence. To these, Thy chosen servants... the messengers who answered my prayer unto Thee... bless them, O Father, for they are good and worthy souls. I thank You, Father. Amen."

With that, these entities part.

As Jacob and his companion begin the walk down the rolling hillsides to their destination, they can hear the joyful song of the woodcutters fading off into the distance.

Jacob's companion turns to him and states softly, "Forgive me... forgive my doubt and fear. I was lost, and your faith has brought me back to the Light of God."

Jacob, smiling broadly, extends an arm and places it around the shoulders of his companion and friend, and we hear him softly speak these final words, "Oh no, my dear friend... what you did was give to me a gift. This gift, as you know it, bore the fruits as we have harvested them. And it has strengthened us and it has strengthened our new friends, the woodcutters. But even greater, it has given us this special gift: As our journey continues, and wheresoever we shall be guided to travel, and whatsoever work we shall be given to do, the memory of this will always fill us with hopefulness. You have given this to us. Thank you, my friend."

ഇരുഗ

APPLYING HOPEFULNESS

So you can see in this, dear friends, many truths. It is possible for you to be as Jacob... to assess what is about you, as we have spoken of, in the morning and evening of each day; but greater than this...

A Cup Overflowing

As you progress throughout the Earth day, give yourself a bit of a song. Give yourself an air of expectancy, of hopefulness. And wheresoever you find those who are dwelling, as Jacob's companion was so doing... in a state of momentary illusion.... give unto them of thine own cup of hopefulness; impart to them a positive, promising aspect. For we say unto you, think not that your cup is not filled. It is filled to *overflowing*. The greater as ye give in the spirit of hopeful-ness, encouragement, and support, the moreso shall it be given in return to you. God's Law is perfect.

Applying Your Song

As you continue to explore the principle and powerful aspect called forgiveness, remember this new work as you do. An attitude of hopefulness going before all that you do will enable you to revisit past experiences of limitation and to find therein, as Jacob pointed out to his colleague, the gift that event, those individuals, are offering to you. You can claim the darkness of a forest night, or the light of the wood-cutters' torch. If you claim the Light, you will hear its song. It is, after all, *your* song. See?

There may be some value for some of you to comprehend the mechanics (as they might be called) that are a part of what we have called hopefulness... again, a brief recapitulation and weaving of the previous two principles into this, for greater understanding...

Building with the Tools

Releasing one's self from that which limits puts you (so to say) in the mental state of neutrality. In other words, you are sort of standing mid-field... that field being life itself... with no bonds, no shackles or fetters that are limiting you. You might, in that moment of recognition of your state of being, look about you, and as you do, ponder which direction next might you travel. In those moments, seeing no defined pathway.

Enter, then, next our second principle... of gratitude...

Standing in the mid-field of life as you are, after working with forgiveness, is like a worker with no tools. The attitude of gratitude is one which sets forth definition. It is empowering through the process of claiming, of recognition that you are connected, that you are enjoined, and that you are the recipient of that which you are willing to receive... the latter point being an important one to which hopefulness speaks very clearly.

Gratitude gives to you the definition of a path or paths. The first singular path, as we just defined it, is a way of proceeding. The second multiple paths are those venues, those conduits, through which, and into which, gifts can be given and received. It initiates the power of claiming, the principle of a partnership with God... the recognition of who and what you are.

Now you are a worker standing in the mid-field of life, with a path upon which to proceed defined, or at least made possible... other paths which are conduits of light, and that as we have just given it. Hopefulness is that which builds a flow of expectancy upon that path called life. Now you, as the worker in the mid-field of life, have defined the path and can follow it, using your own hopefulness as the vehicle with which to so do.

Your mind is the open field of life. Gratitude is the process of claiming and empowering the mind. Hopefulness is the creation... the opening of the creative power of who you are and what you wish to become. See? Hopefulness begins the mechanics, so to say, which thrive, which function, which claim dominion through the Law of Expectancy. Hopefulness is the power of your thought, guided by the spiritual pattern you have set through ideal, purpose, and goal, and others such as this. This, then, is an energy: your mind and spirit come together in your meditation and prayer, and your movement in the exercises we have defined, give to you the recognition of it. Let's explore that with a momentary digression here.

Exploring the Energy

If you are a woodcarver and you have no tools, you would, of course, as one of your first intentions, seek to gather some. For it is difficult to do such a work without the implements with which to tender, to give unto those who are seeking from you through your skill I n fashioning wood. Perhaps you would be given a hammer, a saw with which to shape or cut the pieces of wood, some chisels, a few knives, a woodcarving bow, and on and on... not to mention, in your current Earth time, those implements which are powered in various ways.

As you contemplate these new tools, the next step is obvious... you want to become familiar with them. Since they are new tools and perhaps those with which you have no true familiarity, wouldn't you reach out and pick them up one by one, turn them over, run your hands over them... perhaps test the edges of the cutting tools... perhaps put them to a bit of wood and test them, marveling at their capacity to extend your creativeness?

And so, after a time, you have explored all of these new tools, and you begin next to contemplate what works shall you apply them to. Here you build a thought, as a woodworker, of something you wish to create. This falls into the domain of that called *expectancy*... you contemplate a need. You may discuss with others, you may experience the need by measurement and all that sort as a woodcarver or woodworker might, and then you have what we will call the conception of the need.

Applying the Energy

Now, let's step back to you standing mid-field (that being life, again) having applied forgiveness, having applied gratitude, and now working with hopefulness. You create that which shall be your own harvest by the dimensions of the portal created through your own hopefulness. Example... A small portal or doorway allows for small things to pass through it (bi-directional... to and from you); a medium-sized portal or doorway, of course, obviously, allows for medium-sized things to move through, to and from you. A large doorway, of course, allows for large passage. But what if you were to define an un-limited portal, a portal of unimaginable dimension... that the *All* might pass to and fro with no impediment! *That* is the purpose of your search in the morning and in the evening. *What are the dimensions of my por-tal? What are the dimensions of my Expectancy... of my Hopefulness?*

The woodworker takes now, after his conceptualizing of that which is the need, and begins the process of creating it. He might make for himself a diagram, a plan... a blueprint, as you call it in the Earth. But before he does such, he has gone forth and strived to expe-rience the need. Think about it... He is familiarizing himself with the need unto which his labor [and] his creativeness are going to be ap-plied. He knows with some intimacy his skills and his potential. He has familiarized himself with the tools, the implements, the mecha-nisms through which he might express his skill, his talent, his creative ability, his knowledge, his wisdom.

Isn't your life just so? Aren't the experiences of your life, pre-sent and past, just as the woodworker? Could you find it within your capacity to claim all that has gone before to your current point, this very moment as you are reflecting upon these words, as your tools?

If you think of a past event, which has caused you limitation, or some period of Earth time, from the perspective of this little analogy of the woodcarver... what would you do with it? Well, forgiveness has empowered you, just as the woodworker... in the sense that you have explored these as the woodworker explored his tools. You have touched them, you know of them, you know their potential. But per-haps most empowering of all (and this is several-fold, humor intended) is that you see them now for what they are – they have life, to the ex-tent that you give it... and you give it through your emotion, through your thought. Now you are looking at these past events, these items categorically found under forgiveness (most of which you have already dealt with... our joy is with you in that regard) and you are seeing them now for what they truly are: potentials, tools. You can choose to pick them up and use them, just as the woodworker might do, to create. The other aspect of this is seeing them as a gift, a blessing, a potential, that which is foundational, that which is the field of life upon which we defined you as standing on in mid-field. Gathering up the concept of those things past is foundational... hence, we gave it first. Conceiving, moving throughout your life and illuminating it, empowering it, preparing it, making it passable, is through your affirmation of gratitude.

The woodworker looks upon the task with joyful expectancy, moving all about the need, see, perhaps visiting his client's home into which his creative work will ultimately come into rest and service for his client. Gratitude is a vehicle... hopefulness is the energizing of it, the fueling of the vehicle of life. See?

DEFINING LIFE BUILDS UNDERSTANDING

Definition breeds understanding with rapidity. Your verbal communication is an act of definition. The power of definition should never be underestimated. A word or two can change one's life, can it not? Look back over your known history. Look back at our last meeting and the empowering, dramatic import of two simple words: *thank you*... (and the third word) *welcome*. See?

Definition. Whether you accept or nay, *you* are defined... your name defines you... your vocational title or the absence of one gives you definition... your language and its inflections give you cultural definition... your religious belief or lack thereof gives you further definition... your appearance defines you... your clothing... your manner of forbearance.... and on and on... are all aspects of the definition of who you are, where you are, and what you have become.

These exercises in hopefulness can be expanded. They can be fine-tuned, so to say. Let's take a brief review here and see how that can be done, offered to you in humbleness, and prayerful expectation. (Note our use of that word, see.)

What Your Hopefulness Is Based On

What is your viability? What is the permeable status of your state of hopefulness regarding your sex in the Earth, male or female?

Does your hopefulness, your expectancy, have definition, boundaries, which have been accepted externally because you are a man or a woman in the Earth? Think about it. Explore it.

Your tenure in the Earth... how does this impact your hopefulness? Do you think along the lines of there being insufficiency remaining in your Earth's journey for you to make any changes... for the fruits of any work to come into fruition and be harvested by you? Give it careful thought.

Has your vocation placed parameters, boundaries, definition, walls or fences around your hopefulness? Where is your creative self? Down deep within, in some reclusive corner of your being? Have you given it gratitude? Have you unfettered it through forgiveness? Have you brought it the fuel of life... the light of spirit in the form of hopefulness? Think about it carefully, for your creative self defines who and what you are. Creative is life; creativeness is the living of life. Hope is the fuel, the energy, the sparkle; hopefulness is the application and opening of self unto same. "Bi-directional... two-way street," Zachary states.

Understanding What You Have Defined

In the environment around you, take a moment. Stand in the middle of your home, your abode (whether yours or rented or whatsoever, it is irrelevant here, to an extent)... stand in the mid-field of your abode. From a neutral... or the Channel's *lovingly neutral* state, look around. What's there? A bit of furniture in a corner, a source of illumination over here on this table, an illustration, photograph, picture or such, perhaps, on the wall, some decorative thing over there in the other corner? What's on the floor that you stand on? Look at the ceiling. Are there windows, doors? Do this first with your abode, and do it for an Earth week.

Next, in the second week, do the same thing outside, but on your property (whether yours or otherwise). Look about. What's there? From that neutral state, open yourself. Reach out and search the definitions. Have you noticed any colors? What are the patterns, the shapes? Is there any vegetation? Is the spirit of God expressed in any life-form about you? Turn all about. Are there bi-ways, paths? Are there constructed benches or the like? Note them. Look at them. Truly see what is there. Experience the definition for that second week.

In the third week, do this where you do your work. This is very important, for habit is very domain-oriented to one's works. Some entities work within the same abode in which they dwell... as this, our

Channel and his mate, and many of you. In your environ of work, we would ask you to expand upon this, and not only see what is there, where it has come from, what its function is... but how does it contribute to, or perhaps detract from, your joy? How does it serve you, or does it not? Look at the colors. Sense the essences of what is there. Is all of this conducive to bringing forth that beautiful Child, which is your creativity, from the shelter within you?

Now, there are many of you whose creativity is free and joyful, and others who are in varying degrees of freedom of their creative self. But this we offer in humbleness and love: No matter where your creative expression lies in terms of its freedom of expression, there is always the greater to be given.

At that point or juncture, we are back squarely ("Solid as a rock," Zachary states) upon our topic of hopefulness. In your third week, you have looked at something which is very (potentially, at least) filled with opportunity. What greater vehicle of expression for hope and hopefulness do you have, than that which is your labor?

We said we'd ask you to expand upon this in this third week, and that shall be in this way...

One of the items in your workplace is, of course obviously, *you*. Now we'd ask you, from that neutral point, to take a look at what you are contributing to this workplace: Do you allow yourself the luxury of taking time to prepare yourself for entering into your workplace – perhaps refreshing yourself, nourishing yourself – before so doing? What is the color you impart to your workplace, just in the same manner as, perhaps, the pigment on the walls might do, or the fabric on the furniture, or upon the window coverings, and on and on? What is the status of your functionality as a contribution to this workplace? (Well again, Zachary states, "They've got the idea; don't belabor it.") So we shan't. But it is important.

In the fourth week, we would encourage you to do this...

You have explored your home, its external or out-of-doors environment, and your workplace... the channel through which your creativity flows.

Next, in this fourth week, stand in the mid-field of life itself. Look at all of the above as we have given it, and see how the harmonics of it blend with life itself.

Life, as we gave it above, is a collage of potential... a garment hanging on the clothes tree at the bedside as you awaken each day. Well, there is a clothes tree in life itself from which entities can come and go and select varying garments for varying events, or experiences, in their daily life. Under certain circumstances, they may put on the cloak, in the same connotation as the cloak of life we spoke of: they may put on the cloak of their trade, and they *become* it; they may put on the cloak of their abode, and they bear its connotation, its implication; they may take on the venue of their surroundings, just as much so as if they were to take from the coat tree of life a certain garment.

TAKING DOMINION

Again, we will help the Channel to guide you... Take off all these cloaks... all of them. Stand in the mid-field of life lovingly neutral, and become aware. Know the definition of what you are willing to receive. See the parameters of your own expectation. The particles of your life come together in a collage, molecularly speaking, to form you. But now, through forgiveness and gratitude, you have taken dominion over this. You are going to re-fashion, re-create, so as it is your wish to do, and open yourself to the unlimited potential of God's gifts.

The Fullness of Your Cup

Somewhere within you is a cup which is full. The venue of these four weeks is a process of discovering this, through the definition of where you are, who you are, and what you have become. Hopefulness is the energy which is anticipatory, expectant (and joyfully so) on the wings of which, that beyond your imagination can be brought to you. And herein, dear friends, lies another empowering tool; just as for the woodworker, so as the worker of hopefulness will find these and other tools always before them. Let's step backwards a moment first...

Definition gives you concepts. The woodworker gets his concepts (or hers) by interaction. So have you gained conception of the parameters or definition of the current status through the four-week exercises and the morning-evening review.

Expectancy and empowerment, hopefulness and hope itself... How can we give this a bit more vibrancy?

What can you think of, and what manner of expression would there be, by way of which you can create in the beauty and unique joyfulness of your individuality?

Shaping the Definition

Sing a song of hope. Yes, literally. Find something to say or sing, either aloud or to yourself, periodically throughout the Earth day.

Think of lavender... the color of hopefulness and expectancy, so to say. Our dear friend and mutual colleague Zachary has this offering for you in this regard... not too complex, as you might anticipate (given with a note of loving humor) And here it is [to the tune of Frére Jacque] *I am hopeful, I am hopeful...* and you can carry on and intuit the rest.

Sing a song of hope to yourself, for yourself. Is there a wall of habit you've created? Know it, and pass through it as easily as the winds through the treetops. If you like the comfort and shelter of the definition that is around you now, we promise you, if you apply hope and Hopefulness, you'll like what follows all the moreso. See?

Stillness... the quietude of self... the center of centers within... the building place of all that is and can be... there is a place within you, again, called *lovingly neutral*. It is the small child of expectancy, of hopefulness, that calls out to you: *Hey, don't you see me? Won't you know me? Can I come and be with you?* Go to that place and find that child, and give it the gift of hope. Break down those walls... if you must, nodule by nodule... but you don't have to. Just seeing them, knowing them, gives you dominion over them. If you approach the definition, the perception of them in an attitude of hopefulness, you are instantly empowered beyond your comprehension.

There is a super-highway of light between you and God. Having an attitude of hopefulness is the vehicle, the energized intent which can flow upon same. Forgiveness helped to uncover this highway, to un-clutter it, to remove impediments. Gratitude illuminated it, claimed it, gave it name and potential. Hopefulness is the power, the energy, the sustenance of your very life which you are now placing upon it and putting into motion through your will.

The four-week schedule does this. The evening works give you definition and understanding. You are going to flower and bloom with a radiance that others will see and know to be wonderful and majestic. And that will be your hope.

The lavender essence of truth, and other great principles, are all a part of this, and other expressions of God's Universal Law are, of course, interactively present.

The Foundational Trilogy

In a manner, then, dear friends, dear colleagues, you have now a trilogy, the trilogy of the foundation of where you are…

Forgiveness is the releasing.

Gratitude is the claiming.

Hopefulness is the energizing, the empowerment, of the foundation of who and what you are.

You could see these with some parallels to the first three chakras or energy centers, and even to the first three glandular centers (but that is a diverse topic which has no true appeal to many of you, so we give it here only as reference).

Think of this as the first three of seven steps. Think of this, then, as it goes beyond that definition, into the perfect set of three threes or nine, and you have a glimpse into the intent of this collective work. This will complete the first segment.

The second now becomes more apparent, as does the third, we should think. So go forward in this and in the anticipation of that which lies beyond, in your cloak of hopefulness. Let the others see the lavender essence of your beauty, and rejoice in it. "Who knows," Zachary states, "You might even get a bit of a jolt out of some lavender essence… hard to say."

But in all of this, *you* are the key… *your* choices… *your* dedication and willingness to apply these principles and the others that are on the periphery of same, as you, each of you individually, shall discover them in unique ways… *you* are the key.

However, because you have come forward and, through your own Free Will of choice – the most powerful of God's gifts to you – *asked*, we have become as one… we are in a partnership in the glory of God. So now it is *WE*. As you embrace us, we embrace you… and others, and others… the majesty of the Oneness is inestimable in its potential, awesome to contemplate.

This is the foundation. This is that upon which we shall build all else. Do put it securely into place. And that shall be our concluding prayer for you.

A Message to Those Who Are Beyond the Earth

We thank those who have come forward to contribute unto this work. We shall sing the song of your *being* ofttimes here in that which lies ahead.

For those who have gathered and are rejoicing about these works from distant groups and distant realms: We welcome you and embrace you into this work in our Father's name.

Those of you who are in the Earth realm and have been limited: Waves of Light are passing through the first opening. They are there for you. Hear our call, and hear the prayers and calls of this, our grouping in the Earth. We offer it unto you. Wilt thou not accept same to the glory of your own beauty? See how these beautiful souls in this grouping have applied forgiveness. See how they are expressing gratitude. Now they are presenting the Earth… and all of you, because you are within or near it… a great gift of Light in this, their group intent: to give hopefulness.

We are through here for the present. May the grace and wisdom of our Father's light ever be a lamp to guide your footsteps.

Fare thee well then for the present, dear friends. Om Shanti.

GUEST LECTURE: Jacob

Given February 25, 2000

JACOB: I would greet you all by identifying myself as Jacob. I do this in order to create a bridge of understanding and familiarity between us, and for no other purpose. (In the discourse for the third open forum, we have heard mention of two travelers, of which I was one.)

My purpose for coming to join with you is to offer to you some insight into what is occurring in and about the Earth, and during those times which are immediately ahead of you. I would express my gratitude to the Lama Sing Grouping, granting this opportunity, and to their Channel and his mate in the Earth for providing this as a means of communication. And my gratitude to each of you, for having the spiritual light to seek service.

The event which was identified as the one, eleven, ought-ought event [1-11-00] led by the beautiful forces called the Elders and supported by many legions of workers of light, has been as was described somewhat in the analogy or parable of the doorways in [the topic, step] #3: Through the doorway of light, which has been opened by the actions of the Elders and others, there is now passing great Waves of what I shall call Light.

These are Waves which are definable in that term, in the sense that they are rhythmic and undulating. The connotation and mental image that comes to most of you when I use the word *waves* is that of crests and valleys, highs and lows. And this is through our Father's intent... or the force of creativity, if you will, which is going before all these works. The crest... I would ask you to look upon as the energizing; the valley or the trough of the wave... is the time of application. (I am with you in whatsoever of that you are willing to claim. And in this instance, when I use the first person *I*, I wish to emphasize that includes a great grouping.)

What does this mean to you? A great deal. We are here crossing the Bridge of Light. This Bridge of Light is that which was created through the Elders' intent, in accordance with the *confluence of cycles* and in complete harmony with God's Laws... not *highs and lows* in the emotive sense, but energizing, empowering, powerful surges of this, followed by periods of logical compensatory application. It must be so in order for you to truly claim it.

No matter what you are given, just to perceive of it is insufficient to truly claim it... you must, you see, apply it... use it... live it. Our grouping shall be. And we are at the ready to walk with you through that process. You are not alone.

What is coming just ahead is more of the same... and greater. At this juncture, there is (in the intent to define clearly to you) one major principle expressed in the Waves of Light coming through. Soon, a second principle will join that, and a third and a fourth, and so on.

As these come forth, and as we have the opportunity and are granted same, we are joyful to discuss those with you. But for now, I and the grouping of which I am (and joyfully) a part, urge you to consider the current expression of the Waves of Light as the presentation of power, followed by a period in which you are given the gift of opportunity to apply same... claim the power, and apply it... again, and again.

And so, once again, I (in the individual sense) thank you. And I thank the Channel and his mate for their welcome and invitation that I might come forward. There are others awaiting that opportunity, many-fold over. Thus, my honor is even greater.

I am humble in the sight of you. Your souls are of such beauty, because you have chosen that Path. I shall be in this day in joyful prayer, remembering each of you – by name – as I do.

Apply the energy of your truth. Apply it in the beauty of who you are, in the individuality as God has carefully and lovingly made you manifest.

I am Jacob. I go now to join the Master in those joyful works. But, as He... I am ever with you.

AN UPDATE ON THE WAVES OF LIGHT

Given December 19, 2007

LAMA SING: The Waves of Light have a quality of effect on all of existence. As it has been mentioned by the one through whom we speak, the veils appear to be thinning. But in truth, they are being born again… given life by the presence of the Waves of Light. You could think of this little analogy: that it is the prayer of God; it is Him breathing out His love and blessing to each.

It begins with the foundation within self as a stirring…
[Wave 1: Awakening - Entered Jan 11, 2000. Its gift – Self Awareness]

then, to feel the qualities of compassion, and love,
[Wave 2: Love & Compassion - Entered Mar 18, 2001. Its gift: Forgiveness]

and the quest for something to believe in, to hope upon, the building of expectancy, which opens the way…
[Wave 3: Joyful Expectancy - Entered Aug 22, 2002. Its gift: Hope]

that one can find themselves at a place of golden peace and silence.
[Wave 4: Golden Silence - Entered Nov 27, 2003. Its gift: Peace of God]

And after a time the Waves lift you up, and you enter into such a sweetness, so uniquely brilliant and beautiful, that you know this is Truth. And it is Sacred, wherein your belief is a power within you; not merely a thought or words which can be uttered, but something of a tangible nature.
[Wave 5: Sacred Truth - Entered Feb 18, 2005. Its gift: Truth of God]

And so here you are…
And each subtle step of this Sixth Wave is bringing life to hope and life to all things that have been dormant, calling to them, embracing them.
[Wave 6: Christ Consciousness - Entered April 8, 2007. Its gift: Universal Consciousness: the Manifestation of Sacred Truth]

So do we conclude here by sending to each of you these same qualities of God, which are within you ever. Call them forth. And be glad, for He comes to you, and will call you. Make the way ready and passable within you.
[Wave 7: The name and arrival - as of the date of this printing, March 2008 - is yet to be revealed. Its gift: Righteousness]

STUDY GUIDE

Activities for Applying Hopefulness

Morning Activity

Upon arising, take a few minutes, even if you are late, to recognize and claim your unique beauty. Then pause to consider your choices.

Using The Color Lavender As A Reminder & Tool

Before rising, with your eyes still closed, think of your beautiful, shimmering, lavender cloak. Perceive its glorious sound and vibration. Wrap yourself in this cloak of hope-fulness. Feel the essence of it adorning your body. Think of those things that are most joyful to you and build an attitude of hopefulness before you open your eyes. Perceive Lama Sing, the Lama Sing grouping, Zachary, T-I-A, Jacob, your guides, etc., with you, assisting you, as you build this. Continue to build your hopefulness, testing the limits. Each day, allow yourself to move further beyond your previously defined limits.

Daily Activity

- Build an ever-increasing air of expectancy and hopefulness.
- Put a song into your day. If you cannot come up with a joyful song of your own, sing the one given to you by Lama Sing to the tune of "Fréres Jacque" -"I am hopeful, I am hopeful" and make up your own words from there.
- Wherever you find someone who is in a state of illusion or darkness, "give to them of your own cup of hopefulness; impart to them a positive, promising aspect."
- Pause often to remember yourself being cloaked, wrapped, in your beautiful cloak of lavender, sparkling, vibrationally singing hopefulness.
- When you consider the word "hopefulness" consider it, as hope-fullness.

Evening Review & Exercises

- Review the day and its events. Offer your prayer of forgiveness and gratitude, and ask for the increase in your own hopefulness.
- Then allow your thoughts to be as free and joyful as possible (using sound, or man-tra, or whatever assists this), and move further and further out in your hopefulness. When you have reached, what seems to be, the outer parameter of your hopefulness, turn around and look back at where you have just come from. Take a moment or two to recognize your progression to greater joy and hopefulness, than when you first began this exercise.
- Remember, in an attitude of gratitude, that those of the Light are with you, and offer their hopefulness expectancy *for* you, as a gift *to* you.

Weekly Exercises for Hopefulness

Week 1
Stand in the center of your dwelling, and in a lovingly neutral state, look all around and notice what is there, noticing more each day.

Week 2
Do the same out doors, on your property, noticing everything you can possibly think of, noticing more each day.

Week 3
Do the same within your place of work, whether that is at home, or otherwise. With each item you notice, think about where it has come from, its purpose and how it serves you or doesn't, whether it contributes to your joy or does not. Note the colors, the essences. Do they "speak" to that child within you? Now, still from that lovingly neutral state, look at yourself within your workplace. What are you contributing? Do you prepare yourself before entering? What do you impart of yourself to your work-place? Your "color", your "song"?

Week 4
- Consider the elements of the previous three weeks' exercises: how do they blend with Life, itself?
- What are you willing to expect from Life?
- What are you willing to receive from Life?
- What are you willing to give to Life?

Remember, you are not alone. Speak those names you know, and those you are now becoming familiar with. Ask for their help. Acknowledge their willingness to assist you. Offer your gratitude.

See yourself as a Co-Creator, with God, of your Life. Begin to see yourself as opening more and more completely to the unlimited potentials of God's gifts.

NOTES:

_____
_____
_____
_____
_____
_____
_____
_____
_____
_____

Further Exploring Hopefulness

NOTE: The thoughts listed here are merely suggestions to get you started in further exploration of this subject. Use any portion of them, or not, as your personal guidance leads you.

PONDER:
 - Why do you suppose such emphasis is being placed on the shift that took place on 1/11/00?

- Why does the Lama Sing group consider Forgiveness, Gratitude, and Hopefulness so important, so pivotal, that they have made them the foundation upon which all else will follow… so much so, that they have advised us not to go on unless we feel comfortable embracing those aspects as our own?
- There is "profound power" in expressing "an attitude of hopefulness and expectancy."
- Read the example at the bottom of P. 69. Visualize and "define an unlimited portal, a portal of unimaginable dimension that the *All* might pass to and fro with no impediment." Create in your mind's eye, an unlimited
- The idea of a child neglected, for the most part, wanting to be recognized, loved, and appreciated, perhaps calling out to you, is poignant. Yet how many of us neglect the child most important to us of all – that Child within? Go to that place (the stillness, the center of centers within, the building place of all that is and can be) and find that child, and give it the gift of hope.

List some characteristics of each of the first three open forum topics, such as:
Forgiveness – *Releasing* that which limits
Gratitude – *Claiming the* connection
Hopefulness – Empowering the path through which Life can offer its gifts

Forgiveness

Gratitude

Hopefulness

NOTES: _____
_____
_____
_____
_____

JOURNAL

_____

_____

_____

_____

_____

_____

_____

_____

_____

_____

_____

_____

_____

_____

_____

_____

_____

_____

_____

_____

_____

_____

Step 4:

Truth

Given March 23, 2000

OPEN FORUM ON TRUTH

LAMA SING: As we commence with these works, let us join together, dear friends, in this prayer of oneness.

Here am I, O Father-Mother-God, Thy Child. As Thou look upon me each day, help Thou me to know that You are present... that it is Your spirit which is going before me in all that I am and do. Bring unto me the understanding, the compassion, and wisdom, and that healing grace, as are those gifts of my Brother, the Master, the Christ. Help me even moreso, O Father-Mother-God, to claim these and to fill within myself, in all aspects, my being, to such a level and degree that these gifts overflow and are given unto all whom I meet. As Thou would see me worthy, O Father, send me unto that work which has come before Thee in this day; my spirit sings its song in hopefulness and joy, that You would deem me worthy to answer that call. For those who are dwelling in some limitation and/or darkness of their own acceptance, we offer our light of prayer and hopefulness. For so ever as they shall wish to claim same, this shall be there before them as a living light. And finally, we thank Thee, O Father-Mother-God, for the presence of our colleagues in all realms... those who we know as family, those who we know as friends, colleagues, associates, and spiritual family in realms beyond. In all these things we give thanks unto Thee, Father, and we claim that which is the light of Thy truth in all things. We thank Thee, Father, for this continued opportunity of joyful service in Your name through this, our Channel, and his mate in the Earth. Amen.

TRUTH-FULLNESS

We are joyful to be with you once again, dear friends, in this wonderful work in claiming oneness.

As we have approached this topic together, we have studied those aspects which can be liberating, empowering, and which can bring a pathway of light unto our dreams, our hopes, and our desires.

Now we should, as we proceed onwards, like to offer to you some insights, suggestions, and comments, which are not new to you. Indeed, we have given them here in past to varying degrees and they have been given through Edgar [Cayce], and elsewhere to be sure… all of those to be looked upon with honor and joy, for the gift of truth is an eternal one.

So is it, then, that our choice for this meeting is *Truth*. Or perhaps it might be in keeping with what has gone before, if we might also call this *Truth-fullness*. (A little humor intended there, see.)

Empowers

In past we have spoken of the wondrous power that truth can have for those who seek it and who are willing to claim same. For in the essence of truth there are so many things to be found. There are those aspects which can embrace, incorporate, all four of the qualities which now include truth, and which can, by their nature, empower you. We will explore herein some of the reasons why this is so, and some of the tools with which you can accomplish same.

Defines One's Uniqueness

What is the word *Truth* in terms of, not only definition as a word or term in the Earth, but its true meaning unto all other entities you shall meet… and others who, perhaps, you shall not meet in the literal sense.

Truth is that light within each individual that is the measuring rod, so to say, against which all else is compared.

Truth is that which gives an entity their quality, their uniqueness. It follows, perhaps obviously at this point, that therefore, since each individual, each entity is unique, then perhaps truth itself may have some unique qualities, as well.

We should like to postulate this and carry it even further. And here is the comment that will, no doubt, give you cause for thought:

There is no one truth. And yet, God is Truth.

There is one God and, therefore, one Truth.
And yet, we have stated there is no one truth.

Relevant to the Perceiver

Our statement of course is intended, as its destination, to reach you in the Earth. For if you consider that statement very carefully in your meditation, you will, if you have not already, come to recognize that truth is relevant to the perceiver.

You can attempt to share Truth. You can accomplish this oft-times to a considerable degree. You can come together as individuals and then as groupings, who agree to form, let us say... (Hmm, no good word here. We would call this a *tribe* in the historical, literal, biblical, sense, see, for a tribe tends to formulate itself around a tenet, a truth, which is subscribed to by all of the members, or else they leave. See? Nonetheless, we'll use the word *group*... it seems to fit better.)

As you form into groups which are in agreement upon a certain basic principle of truth, this usually moves along quite well for a time. Then, as individuals begin to explore their unique perspective of that common truth and the subscription of the group to it, new interpretations, new viewpoints, new perspectives, and all that sort, begin to emerge. In the course of the emergence of these new perspectives, new understandings, new viewpoints, these are attempted to be presented back to the grouping by the perceiver (or plural, if that's the case).

A Powerful Tool

Much of the rest of this little scenario (as we are defining it here) is known to you, for your history, in the recorded sense, has documented this over and over again.

Our point in reiterating it here is to offer you a very wonderful tool... a powerful instrument, if we might so humbly be permitted to call it such, with which you can do very good works.

So, as you awaken in the first week of this next four-week cycle, do not arise out of your bed apparati, your sleeping apparatus, but open your eyes and look straight up, probably looking at the ceiling, we should hope. And just let your eyes go out of focus for a few moments, perhaps at most fifteen to thirty seconds. Intentionally allow them to go out of focus, as though you are trying to look through the ceiling and beyond. Now, gradually close your eyes, and this is the prayer we would encourage you to state, or some variant of same:

Thank you for this new day, O Father-Mother-God.
Help me claim my truth as I now spend these moments
in oneness with You: help me to see that which I believe
in, that which is Thy rod within me against which I
shall measure all that comes to me in this day. Then,
too, O Father, guide Thou me to see and understand the
nature of truth as others perceive it... that as I under-
stand their truth, that I can the better serve them and
serve Thee... knowing, Father, that in service, <u>there</u>
shall be my greatest joy and growth. Guide Thou me to
Truth, Father... Thy Truth. Amen.

Now another minute or two, not much longer. The whole process perhaps three to five Earth minutes. You can go longer, if you
wish, but there is no true need, see.

Now, in the second Earth week, we would do this, we would
replicate, to the degree that you have found it joyful, modifying accordingly those comments as just given for the first week. In this second week, we would do this:

O Father-Mother-God, help Thou me to see, to know
and understand the perception and the truths as are
known by those who are near and dear to me. Those
who are... (and here you would include by name your
family, those you love and so forth... those who are
close to you, see). Help Thou me to see them and know
them. Open me to feel and understand their perspective
of truth. Thank you, Father. Amen.

In the third week, we would take this to the next step. Adding
what suits you best from weeks one and two, make a composite, see
(remember, this is *your* work). In week three, we would state:

In this day, Father, I know that Thou art sending me
gifts and blessings, that the entities who I shall meet
and interact with shall be bearing these gifts to me.
These gifts will reflect Your Truth, as borne and ex-
pressed by the uniqueness of each individual whom I
shall encounter. Help me to listen, to see, to feel, and to
know the gift that they offer. Thank You, Father. Amen.

Now, you have built upon self and others; and now expanded
that to loved ones; and now to, perhaps, total strangers or those who

are only on the periphery of your familiarity. And this fourth week is the most powerful of all, if you have followed the first three, as given. The most important of all here is the first and fourth week. Why? Because the first begins with self, and this fourth week is the truth of the Earth. See? Therefore, the others, in weeks two and three, must therefore also be embraced in this, the fourth week. But it is appropriate for you to focus upon them in a sort of stepwise progression that will lead you, once again, to the Earth itself. Here is the guideline for this prayer in the fourth week:

I, Thy Child, (state your name)*, come before Thee, as I am now awakened and preparing to enter this day. O Father, let me be open, let me perceive, let me feel and know the perception of those who comprise the Earth as a realm of existence. Let me know and understand how Your Law is being used, and how those actions and reactions which are a part of same can become empowering tools of righteousness and wisdom for me. Thank you, Father. Amen.*

PARABLE: EMPOWERING

There was a small group of entities in a time perhaps several hundred Earth years prior to your current time. They were, to a degree, travelers and explorers. They were crossing your land called the North American continent, and they were traveling by rudimentary, wheeled contrivances pulled by beasts of burden.

As they reached one of the last known outposts, they sought shelter and provisions and all that sort. The next portion of their journey was known to them only by scarce detail. No one had yet provided the specifics of the journey in terms of documentation or cartography or any such. That which existed gave generalizations and such, and that's about it. So this small band of travelers sought counsel here in this outpost. As they did, they spoke to many different entities, and they came to realize that each one that they spoke to, who was identified as a guide or such to those who were traveling, had a different opinion. Most all recommended a different route, a different schedule, and so on and so forth.

So, now, we join the group, as they are clustered together after evening meal. They are discussing their choices, recognizing that the season is limited and, thus, their time for travel has some sense of urgency, immediacy. The elder of this group, seated cross-legged before the embers of the cook-fire, has spoken to each and asked for their opinion... some of them favor this individual, and others that one... basically, there is no concise agreement.

Since this entity is considered the elder of the group, honored and revered as a spiritual leader as well, silence befalls the group encircling the campfire as they await his words from beneath a weathered black hat, the brim of which is flopping in front of his face softly as the evening breeze moves past.

It is a mesmerizing sight. And the rather serious, almost blank face of the elder, gazing steadfastly into the flames of the fire, suddenly looks up at the brim of his hat as it is flapping in front of him, now making a sort of fluttering sound. As he does, his face widens in a grin and his eyes come together in a sort of crossed fashion. He holds that for a few moments, as the children begin to chuckle in the background, with the parents shush-shushing them, fearing that they will dishonor the Elder.

Uncrossing his eyes and looking around the campfire, his smile broadening even more, he looks at all of them. And these are the words we hear. "It is just like the brim of my hat. Each of them rattle on with their stories and their authority in their own way, convinced that theirs is *the* way and the only way. And so, we should find humor, not frustration. We should rejoice in the fact that we have choices and know that these choices are presented to us by our God," still smiling, eyes bright and clear, the flames of the campfire dancing in them, reflecting back to all in the circle.

Finally one of the... you could call him a yearling man, with some fire and some sense of individual righteousness, speaks up, "Forgive me, Elder, but that is, as I see it, no decision. What shall we do? Time is passing. We have limited provisions, and we need to secure our journey by the end of the good season," his eyes transfixed... this yearling lad, as we've called him.

The elder tilts his head slightly over to the side, still smiling, and we hear him state softly, "And what would be *your* choice?"

Everyone turns to look at the lad, whose face now flushes as he recognizes what he has done.

And what *has* he done, dear friends? Actually... nothing. But the question here is not one of doing or not doing, his asking or not asking... it is a question of responsibility. The lad, in questioning the elder, was asking the elder, of course, to make a decision. And to tell him and the group what that is. Instead, the elder, with some degree of wisdom, parried that question and reciprocated with his own. For in this young lad, he can see himself some numerous decades previous. And his point was: *If you are willing to claim your own truth, then you can see the truth of others through your truth.*

Finally, the young man gathers himself up... all the others still staring at him, almost expressionless, some thinking to themselves,

I'm glad the elder asked him and not me! And the lad finally states, "I think that the man called Tom should lead us. He has the most honest eyes, and I have a good feeling about him."

Immediately, discussions break out here and there. Two or three state, *No, no! Not him. I saw him do...* (this or that... well, you all know that sort of thing).

The elder is once again gazing into the fire, his aged face warmed by the dancing flames, his eyes twinkling, and his smile and bearded jaw a goodly sight to behold. Everyone finally, of course, quiets down and turns back to look at the elder, especially the yearling lad.

Again, the elder looks around the group, making eye contact with each and every one, even the children. And there is silence, until his eyes come to rest on the yearling lad again. "Your suggestion seems to have merit, and if you trust what you feel, that is a good measuring rod for life itself. This is a gift to us, to all of us. Our journey has been blessed to this point and shall continue to be.

"What we shall do is this... We shall all join hands and form a circle, which will symbolize our oneness with God. Then we shall offer a prayer and each will then go to their individual sleep. On the morrow, we shall awaken and gather here again by this same flame, which I shall keep illuminated throughout the night. Any who wish to remain with me by this flame are welcome. I shall meditate and pray, perhaps sleep a bit here and there, but I will not allow the flame to extinguish, for this flame will be the symbol of God's light within each and every one of us. And in the morning, we will have our answer. For God answers prayer."

The yearling lad spent the evening with the elder. Two others started out but could not sustain the watch. But the yearling lad did, and gathered fuel for the flame, and sat across, directly across, from the elder. And when the elder's look invited it, the lad questioned and commented, and they talked about truth. Here are some of the things that the elder told the yearling lad:

"Truth, my son, is that light that ever burns within you. It is life itself. Look you all about as you walk through life, and ask... listen... perceive the truth of others as life itself, and those in your life shall offer it to you. But as I have directed the others, the only real truth lies within. For we can all look upon a sunset, can we not, and each one will find some radiant aspect of that sunset that is most meaningful to them. If they compare that which they find most beautiful and joyful, you could gather up the individual comments and paint a wonderful collage that might approach the beauty of the sunset itself, *if* you listen and feel as they offer you their truth.

"Truth is that pathway through life which is aright... What is aright? Is it straight? Is it narrow? Is it paved? What is the path of truth? It is the light within you, my son, which shines from you as you hold that intention of goodness, that intention of joy, that sense of love for self and others and, yes, for nature... for God in the spirit of all things. And if you hold it according to your ideal and the reasons for which you are passing this way in life, then it will illuminate that which lies before you. And no matter how many entities bring to you their truth... and some might not bring you *truth*, my lad..." and he chuckles aloud as he states this, "still, you will see when the others awaken, we will have our answer clearly."

"But Elder," questions the yearling lad, "how can you know this?"

The elder leans back and raises the index finger of his right hand into the air and points upwards. "*He* tells me."

"You mean He speaks to you?"

"Of course," smiles the elder. "And to answer your next question: in all things... in all peoples... even, my son, through you."

With that, the elder gestures with his hand that he is going to lean back and close his eyes.

And the young lad props himself up and gazes into the fire.

With the dawn's first light and the cooking commenced, the entities are gathering, chattering excitedly. You can hear them whispering about their dreams, their visions. The meal is cooked, consumed, and all gather. Excitement, joy, goes all about.

The elder begins by questioning each one about their dreams, their visions. There are none who had naught one dream... some had several. By the time the elder completes his survey of the entire group, even the children, the laughter and joy is pouring forth from the group, for clearly... *clearly*... Tom is the choice.

The yearling lad, of course, is proud and joyful. Not a one now questions this decision. And the elder, smiling, nodding at him, says not a word.

All in the group look upon the yearling lad, and smile and nod an affirmation... all here know in their hearts that one day the yearling lad shall become the elder.

Each dream held a facet of what could be considered one of your jigsaw puzzles... where the solution is cut up into pieces. Each has a part of that. If you wish to work together in a group, remember that your truth is your truth; and the truth of others should equally be honored, but not to the relinquishment or the dishonor of your truth.

The elder in this grouping used wisdom... gained, of course, through the experience of life. As always, he defined certain tenets of his truth, and these became the foundational blocks upon which he built all else, and look, how it served him.

They followed Tom to the West Coast of North America, and

not a one of the group was lost. They were never challenged... they never created any hardship for another, nor was a hardship imposed upon them.

Even Tom, upon completing his work for them, as they sat around the last cook-fire before he departed them, looked at them all and stated, "You know, I never have been too close conversationally with God. Oh, yes, there have been a few times when I've called upon Him rather vigorously. Usually, I was in trouble. But I'll tell you this... these months of travel with you people, and seeing how your faith brought us through, took us through hardships that could have stopped us (and did, on other journeys) your faith somehow made this the most miraculous journey I've ever made.

"And so, dear friends, I thank you. I know you have thanked me and paid me for my services, but I also want you to know that you have paid me in a unique way, that I shall carry and remember you in a special way from this time forward... you were always bright and hopeful. You didn't criticize one another... even when a little of that might have been justified." And humor comes forth. "But you believed in me. What I told you was truth as I knew it, but I know there were others who had their own vision and path and methods. But you believed in me. And I'll tell you this last thing... somehow or other, you empowered me in a way I've never felt before. I'll hold you in my heart. Thank you... and, farewell."

So the point here, even this sort of weathered, unique individual of this time past could see it... he could feel it... it was the power of this group's belief in his truth. It wasn't that they didn't meet hardships, for they did. It wasn't that there weren't challenges, for there were many. But they were met, you see, from the perspective of their belief in Tom. Tom was empowered, and it changed his life. And it changed his spirit. We know this... because Tom stands here with us this day.

೮ಂಆ

DEFINING YOUR TRUTH

Truth is a banner of light which, when held as the intent for one's works, can be seen and felt by all. Truth is the rod of God within you... not a rigid metallic object, nor one carved from this or that, but the potentiality for you to be all that you can be in your current life.

You began, as you entered, on a quest for truth. Through childhood you asked others, *What is this? Why does it do what it does, and what's its purpose?* and so on… *Why does this food taste the way it does? What is the nature of this sound, and where does it come from? Why can't I see it, I only hear it?* and on and on. All the way through your education into life itself, your relationships with others, you are asking for definitions, parameters… you are defining that which is acceptable to you.

Conditioned Belief

Your truth, then, in your current position in your life's progression, could be defined as that which you have become conditioned to believe. Your truth could be, as such, dependent on, or builded upon, the perspectives and the unique definitions of truth held by others, could it not?

Then one day you discover that you and others are something greater than a composite of elements… than a branch of the animal kingdom in Earth (genetically speaking) and on and on. And you come to realize that there is something within you that is worth exploring. Now there are other circumstances, of course, which can predicate this, and we have chosen this one for obvious reasons (with a note of loving humor).

Others' Interpretations of Your Truth

Your spirit begins to stir. And some of the first things you encounter are efforts on the part of others to dissuade you from claiming any of these new concepts as truth, or to put their own interpretation and modification upon your evolving discovery of truth, to the point where, if you did so, it wouldn't truly be your truth… it would be a variation of your truth, with their inflections, their decisions and interpretations, imposed upon you.

Truth is the banner of God's light which is your life itself. You already know you are unique and, therefore, truth as you perceive it, shall also be perceived in its own uniqueness.

APPLYING YOUR TRUTH

As you do the exercises for four weeks and focus on these things, each evening we would heartily recommend that you have one singular work. And that is to define your truth as it is explored, studied… as it stands out against the backdrop of the day just past.

Seeing Self Through Others

Now, think about this… this is a very powerful, very effective work: Think about the events, perhaps, where someone came to you during the course of the Earth day, with a rock-solid decision… so firm, so dedicated, so complete in their belief of their decision that you could immediately sense there is no room for negotiation here. In that process, what were your feelings? How did this resonate with your truth? Did you find yourself compromising? Or perhaps you'd prefer to call it cooperating? Did you keep quiet?

Actually, these points aren't too terribly important, but they are telling… they do give you perspective. For if, as in the example given, the entity's (as Zachary calls it) head was made up, see, not much you can do without creating friction, alienation, and such… unless, like the Elder of these travelers, it was your responsibility to so do.

Everything in life offers you a looking-glass to see yourself and others. We have given the little recounting of that ancient group of travelers (ancient, meaning several hundred Earth years, see… not to go astray here) as a looking-glass for you. There is always an answer. See? You could state, in the manner of the elder, *Here's my perspective… What say we sleep on it?*

Testing Against the Spirit Within

At any rate, as you progress through your memories of the Earth day, look for encounters similar to this that stand out, where you have been presented with someone else's truth. How did it feel? Did you test and examine your truth? For again, remember, as given… you may have a truth within you that is a *conditioned* Truth.

Some will say, here, *Every Truth is conditioned in one way or another.* Perhaps that is so, but your decisions are not mandated by them. Those are the reference points; your decision comes about by comparing all of those external or collective conditioned truths of your entire lifetime, against the *spirit within*. See? *That light* within will not fail thee. True, it does require that you be steadfast. Hence, we have encouraged you to do this each evening, and before you fall into slumber. We will be with the Channel as he prepares a recording to help you with this. Listen to it, and open yourself. And as you go into your sleep period, remember the wisdom of the elder: God answers all prayer, including yours. See?

Truth is the banner of your uniqueness, if you allow it to come forth. If you carry the banner of another's truth, you may very well have a feeling within you that lacks some final essence, some wonderful little bit of seasoning, to bring you completeness and joy in your life. Here are several keys:

There is honor, purpose, and joy in discovering and supporting others in their truth, insofar as so doing is tested against that within self and found to be aright. In other words... taking a very extreme hypothetical... supposing that someone held the concept as their truth that anything one had to do to get ahead, to have wealth or prosperity or material gain, is justified. Of course, if you do not believe that stealing just to gain, or injuring another just to gain, are not your truth, then, of course, you couldn't, in righteousness, subscribe to same.

So the point of this is: You must evaluate where your truth is. And if you find your truth resonates with another, then perhaps you have found another piece of that jigsaw puzzle; and together... see, as you fit your uniqueness together... the greater whole begins to emerge and be seen. But these are, indeed, pieces that do fit; that one who steals to get ahead is violating Universal Law, and probably won't fit with any of the other pieces. (Humor intended here, of course.)

KNOWING TRUTH

Truth is a lamp to guide your footsteps. But have a caution here... A key to claiming truth is to *recognize that it is alive*.

Your scientists can perform experiments of any sort, which can be replicated by entities who are not associated or such. This is then considered, as a... let's say, certain scientific reaction or chemical reaction or electrical phenomena or phenomena of physics, to be true. In other words, this element plus that element equals this third element, or compound. And if all do this in that strata of scientific community and find the same result, the truth is agreed upon.

Even here, you can find, in retrospect, that modifications, addendums, alterations, and such, do occur. It may be discovered that not just A plus B equals C, but perhaps there was another element present in all the tests associated with A but unknown, or associated with B and unknown.

If you are looking for truth in the spiritual sense, the same is true. There are unknowns in the sense of your consciousness. And when you begin to think that A plus B equals C... and containerize that, making your truth rigid, you begin the process of limiting self. You begin the process of diminishing the uniqueness of the potential of your truth as it's added, one more piece to the jigsaw puzzle of life itself. So the key here, again, is to consider truth to be alive.

If it's alive, and if it's in motion and growing, how could we suggest to you that you would take something outwardly, as a decision or whatnot, inwardly, and compare it to something that is as transient as we are implying your truth is? If that thought occurs, then we have not served you well.

Universal Truth

Here is another key: *All truth is one truth.*

There is no one truth, according to those who perceive it. And we spoke of God being *The* Truth. Now we are pointing out to you this sort of little addendum...

The composite of all truth becomes the collage of understanding. Truth is, after all, comprehending something. If you do not comprehend something, if you do not *know* a thing, then it is in the domain of unknown and un-comprehended, in which case you cannot place it in your basket of truth.

All truth is one Truth, in the sense that the perceivers are all One. Therefore, it becomes not an issue of entities striving to comply or not comply, to explain or not explain; but to simply know and accept that each entity, according to their position, their level of acceptance, their posture on their own path of life, has the right to perceive as they will.

TRUTH AS THE GUIDE

You are different. You are different because you have chosen to free yourself...

You have allowed forgiveness to cleanse you, to remove the shadows from your truth. You might have looked at someone who had injured you in any way, and you have found the potential for forgiveness. And as you did, you saw the truth of it: No one can injure you, unless you permit it. True, they could harm your physical body, they could steal from you, they could do all manner of things. But they cannot injure you, for you are not that body, but the spirit within it. And if you believe that they have the power to limit you, to hurt you... (never mind the external things now... we are speaking of your spirit, your light, your true life: we'll get to the other later, lovingly given) ...so you have released this, and a portion of your truth has been cleansed.

You turned to gratitude and said to God, *Here I am. Thank You for what You have given me,* and in the process, you empowered yourself with the gifts you are capable of recognizing at that point.

Then you turned to hopefulness, and you sent forth the call, according to your ideal, purpose, and goal… that which brings you joy… the pursuit of your own brilliance.

Now, as you seek to do this – cleansed, claiming and empowering yourself, opening yourself – you are using truth as a lamp to guide you through life… *your* truth.

You are empowering yourself to see the truth of others, and the world itself; and to understand how this may have come to be… how this entity in the office in which you work, in the marketplace in which you shop, in the service capacity as you are striving to get something done… how did they come to their truth? *Is* it their truth? Or are they subject to conditioning far more than is good for them? Not *your* choice… *their* free will.

But *you* have another tool…

You have the tool of your own hopefulness, your own gift of prayer…

Your gratitude, remembering to thank them…

Offering them fore– (f-o-r-e) giveness… *being* forgiveness.

Your truth is built upon the first three tenets.

Now, you are forging what we shall call a staff of righteousness for yourself.

Looking for Truth

Look for Truth. It is easy to not do so. It is simple to allow truth to be someone else's responsibility, even to go so far as to let them do it for you.

Truth is the song which comes from your heart. Children's laughter will reflect it back to you.

You have the means now to begin to build a powerful expression of your truth, but first you must know it. Understand why you have had the feelings you have had this day… Where are they coming from? Are they still active? Are these given to you by someone in your life presently? A shadow from the past? Check out your forgiveness level. Is it pretty good? Or is there a flaw here? Are you claiming the gifts already given? Opening the way? Making it passable? Did you hold a hopeful thought this day?

All these are components of your Truth.

You will find – if you will go within and find your truth, know it, explore it, understand it – a wonderful sense of liberation... a dynamic change or shift in your realization and understanding.

Certain things in your lives, in your works and so forth, are expected of you. But those are works; they are not your thoughts, your prayers, your attitude, the demeanor and light in your eye with which you greet entities. They will tell you what their truth is if you will listen and observe. When they do, and they know you are listening and observing, they will be open to your truth, as well.

We are with you in this work, as always. And we are joyful that you are the beautiful example of truth, just so as we see each of you. Prayer is an expression of your truth... believing... all of it hinges on your truth. See?

We are through here for the present, but we are with thee. May the grace and blessings of our Father's wisdom ever be that lamp to guide your footsteps.

Fare thee well then for the present, dear friends. Om Shanti.

GUEST LECTURE: Naomi

Given March 23, 2000

LAMA SING: As you are seeking to apply truth, in your life, or, becoming one with truth-fullness, it is important for each of you to remember, as given previously, that living your truth is a unique experience. And it is to this experience that this next guest lecturer comes to offer her comments. We have before us at this time, with great honor, one who is called... Naomi.

NAOMI: I greet you all in the spirit of our Brother, the Master. I am called, yet, Naomi, as I was in those times when the Master was upon my knee at times. It was a part of my works as one of the *Eleven Not Chosen*[8] to give a quality of spiritual truth to the Master. It was not a work I did to fill a void within Him, for the Master (as with each of you) has all these qualities ever within Him; but, rather, my work was to offer to Him the reflection of who and what He is... then, and of course, now. And so it is with the same prayer of intention, as I offered this to Jesus, that I also now offer this, briefly, to you:

You are working with a topic called *Truth*. While truth has many connotations in your current time to your life in the Earth, it has a most wonderful connotation to you, as a spiritual being... an eternal Child of God.

Once you have found and claimed *your* truth, within your own consciousness, it becomes as a living light, an extension or tool with which you can do untold works.

The Master used (as He walked in the Earth as Jesus) Truth as one of the discerning mechanisms for His healing works. Truth was the pathway through which, or upon which, the healing light of God passed through Him.

As you know your own truth – in other words, *who* you are, *what* you are, and what you hold to be of *import* to you – you have begun the process of opening and claiming that which is within you.

Truth discerns the readiness of an entity to be healed. As you see in your own truth, as you walk through life living in your own

---

[8] Eleven Not Chosen – this is a term of endearment given to those of the twelve Holy Maidens who were taught and guided along with Mary, who (as given in the Lama Sing *Expectant Ones* series) stood on the temple steps when She was chosen from among them to be the vessel, the mother, of the Christ. (The Holy Maidens are also referred to as the Sisters.)

spirit of truthfulness, you open yourself to see. If you think in terms of the truth of existence, in this very moment as you are reading these words, you have opened the path to great wisdom. *You* are in control of your destiny. Albeit, you look about and see other causal Forces, and conditioning energies, none of these can reach that of the most beautiful and omnipotent power of all... which is your own spirit.

The Master asked, *"Do you believe? Do you wish to be healed? Are you ready to release that which limits you?"* He listened in the spirit of truth. And He looked for the light of truth-FULLness, coming from those who were seeking from Him. And though it is not written any longer, except in hidden records, if He saw that they were not ready, He would say unto them, *"Go thou forth and...* (do this or that) *and return when your heart is open."* Some of those who were with Him questioned this, and even argued among themselves.

You too, as did and does the Master, can offer. But until the vessel is prepared and ready, it cannot be given; and in a manner of speaking, should be held out in the offering, as we so often hear this grouping who guide through this Channel, pray prior to their works. Those who come to you and ask, and have no light of truth, cannot be given, because the vessel is unprepared.

Now, of import here, and my closing comment, lovingly given to you, is just this question:

Art thou ready?

Is your heart open?

Do you know your own song?

Is the vessel which is within you golden, and perfect, and holy? Made ready?

These wonderful lessons and gifts are ever yours. We do not *give* them to you; rather, we call them forth. We ask you to make the way passable... to open yourselves... and then we can joyfully reflect them back to you.

He is your Brother... and He is with you in spirit.

Claim your oneness, and we are with you as you do.

I thank those who have made this possible. And in particular, I express my love to this Channel and his mate for making the way passable. May the Light of the Christ ever surround and guide you with His love and His wish for your joy.

Farewell, Friends.

STUDY GUIDE

Activities for Applying Truth

Morning Activity

Upon arising, take a few minutes, even if you are late, to recognize and claim your unique beauty.

Evening Review & Exercises

Each evening make your singular work to define your truth as it is explored, studied, as it stands out against the backdrop of the day just past. This is a very powerful, very effective work. Think about the events, and in that process, what were your feelings? How did it resonate with your truth? Did you find yourself compromising? Co-operating? Did you keep quiet? You are defining that which is acceptable to you.

Note your thoughts, your answers, to the questions Naomi posed on P. 106

NOTES:

_____

_____

_____

_____

_____

_____

_____

_____

_____

_____

_____

_____

_____

_____

_____

_____

_____

_____

_____

Weekly Exercises for Truth

Week 1:

Let your eyes go out of focus for 15 - 30 seconds, as though you are trying to look through the ceiling and beyond. Close your eyes, and say this prayer or variant:
Thank you for this new day, O Father-Mother-God. Help me claim my truth as I now spend these moments in oneness with You. Help me to see that which I believe in, that which is Thy rod within me, against which I shall measure all that comes to me in this day. Then, Father, guide me to see and understand the nature of truth as others perceive it, that as I understand their truth, that I can the better serve them and serve Thee, knowing, Father, that in service there shall be my greatest joy and growth. Guide me to truth, Father ... Thy Truth. Amen.

Week 2:

In this second week:
O Father-Mother-God, help me to see, to know and understand the perception and the truth as are known by those who are near and dear to me: (and here you would include by name, your family and those who are close to you). Help me to see them and know them. Open me to feel and understand their perspective of truth. Thank you, Amen.

Week 3:

In the third week, we would take this to the next step. Adding what suits you best from weeks one and two, make a composite, see? Remember, this is *your* work:
In this day, Father, I know that Thou art sending me gifts and blessings, that the entities I shall meet and interact with shall be bearing these gifts to me. These gifts will reflect Your truth, as borne and expressed by the uniqueness of each individual I shall encounter. Help me to listen, to see, to feel, and to know the gift that they offer. Thank you, Father. Amen

Week 4:

I, Thy Child (state your name), *come before Thee as I am now awakened and preparing to enter this Earth day, O Father. Let me be open, let me perceive, let me feel and know the perception of those who comprise the Earth as a realm of existence. Let me know and understand how Your Law is being used, and how those actions and reactions, which are a part of same, can become empowering tools of righteousness and wisdom for me. Thank you, Father. Amen.*

NOTES:
_____
_____
_____
_____
_____
_____

Further Exploring Truth

NOTE: The thoughts listed here are merely suggestions intended get you started in further exploration of this subject. Use any portion of them as your personal guidance leads you.

POINTS TO PONDER:
- A key to claiming Truth is to recognize that it is alive.
- The composite of all Truth becomes the collage of understanding. All truth is one Truth, in the sense that the perceivers are all one.

REVIEW:
- You have allowed forgiveness to cleanse you, to remove the shadows from your truth, you have released this, and a portion of your truth has been cleansed.
- You turned to gratitude and said to God, *Here I am. Thank You for what You have given me.* And in the process, you empowered yourself with the gifts you are capable of recognizing at that point.
- Then you turned to hopefulness, and you sent forth the call according to your ideal, purpose, and goal, that which brings you joy - the pursuit of your own brilliance.
- Cleansed, claiming and empowering yourself, opening yourself - you are using Truth as a lamp to guide your through life ... *your* truth. Your truth is built upon the first three tenets. Now, you are forging a staff of righteousness for yourself.

What do you think is meant by "forging a staff of righteousness for yourself", and what will this do for you?

Truth is the song which comes from your heart. What *is* the song of your heart?

NOTES:

_____

_____

_____

_____

_____

_____

_____

_____

_____

_____

_____

_____

JOURNAL

_____

_____

_____

_____

_____

_____

_____

_____

_____

_____

_____

_____

_____

_____

_____

_____

_____

_____

_____

_____

_____

Step 5:

Self

Given April 22, 2000

OPEN FORUM ON SELF

LAMA SING: Yes, we have the Channel then and, as well, those references which apply to the grouping as gathered and those intents and purposes as are a part of same. As we commence with these works, let us join together in this joyful prayer.

O Lord God, here are we once again, Thy Children, seeking of Thee Thy guidance and light. So as Thou knoweth us, O Father-Mother-God, then give unto us that which is our need, that which is Thy direction and Light. Help us, as we seek, to know of those things which shall, by their nature, bring to us understanding, compassion, trust, faith, love, and all those qualities which we see as ever present in that of the light and example of our Brother, the Master, the Christ. We thank You, O Father-Mother-God, for the presence of the Christ in these works and for the gift of His healing grace, love, compassion, and wisdom. Help Thou us, O Father-Mother-God, to take these into our being, and that therein they shall become as a part of us, as well... awakened. And as a part of our total being, let them become the expressions which we offer to others. We offer ourselves in service to those who have asked of Thee, O Father, and as well to those who have asked not... so as they are willing, let our example and light, in this quest, be an inspiration, a hope, to them. We thank Thee for this continued opportunity of joyful service in Your name through this, our Channel, and his mate in the Earth. Amen.

FACETS OF A GEM

As we have observed your group, each of you have, in your own way, brought about some unique perspective to each of the topics, to each of the aspects, as we have humbly offered them to you in past.

Now, as we come to a point of some transition here, we find that there are many faculties, many aspects of considerable beauty that are found within each of you. These aspects are likened unto the facets of a beautiful gem which has been cleaved by a master gem-cutter... that being God.

Reflected and Reflecting

So as you use the varying facets of the greater gem, which symbolizes Oneness, or the All, then can you see the uniqueness of Self, reflected in the other facets. Each facet of such a gem contributes to the luminosity, the brilliance, the sparkle, the light, the color, as is a part of the native aspects of any good gem.

So is it, then, logical that it should follow that each entity is, just so, similar in the greater perspective of the gem (which is the example, here) of God's creation.

Unique Beauty

How can you know these things?

As you sought to discover that within you which was limiting you and, through the discovery... empowering yourself to forgive and release and to be forgiven and to be released... and as you looked upon God as that Source of continual blessings and gifts, the logical aspects of gratitude empowered you, enabled you, so as you were willing to claim.

In the process of recognizing and claiming, there came about that which was as the gift of creation, through the attitude of hopefulness. In hopefulness we found that there are so many things which can come to pass, or which can become as a reality in your life experience in the Earth, by sending forth the attitude of joyful expectancy... of hope and hope*ful*ness. And that this creates, in multiple ways, many beautiful byproducts which are not only encouraging to others, which endear you to them, but which bring you to a point of discovery which is pivotally important to one's continual spiritual claiming... or as you call it, growth.

That is the empowerment to see truth… to look within self without fear, without reservation, in a willing, open-hearted way, that *these are the aspects which are the collage of my being, my personality* (if you will) – *who and what I am.* And in that quest for the inner truth, the truth of self, the willingness to recognize that this is unique to self.

We postulated to you that… first, there is no one truth (giving rise to the eyebrows of some, for that is seemingly an inappropriate statement)… which we then followed with the comment *God is the One Truth.*

This paradoxical positioning then brought you into the exercises: looking within, looking without, embracing perspectives, looking at these perspectives to understand how you have arrived at where you are and who you are in this very moment… perhaps, even so as you now hear these words or are reading them.

FOLLOWING TRUTH

We noted with some considerable interest and a bit of seasoned humor, if you will (forgive us, please), the many comments and speculations – notwithstanding those of our dear Channel and his mate, as well – as to what might come next. Following in the light of the just-previous topic, in truth, there are so many titles, topics, and works. Each is brilliant. Each has some wondrous contribution to offer to you as individuals, and to the greater group-working, and to making the Way passable.

Some here stated, *Let us speak to them and encourage them to know faith, to look for it within. Help them to understand what it means to be faith-full.*

Others here spoke strongly, lovingly, about that very word *love…* some said, *Lest we speak with them and join with them, embracing all of the facets of love, how can we build beyond this point? For here is the center of their being. What can follow* Truth, *if not* Love?

Others here came and offered good counsel regarding the quest for one's *Righteousness,* offering simplistically that *Righteousness is The Life; it is the epitome of the Master Himself.* Therefore, their urging was, *Let us join together in the quest for Righteousness.*

And so it went here, dear friends, for some (as you would call it in the Earth) considerable time. As we have gathered here in this meeting, we have no topic... we have nothing to offer you... there is no work for this segment, except this... *Self*

This could be written with a capital *S* or a small *s*, referring to the case size of the letter. For in all of the beautiful offerings and petitions which have become known to us here, presented to us, and those which the universe continually offers, it would seem very clearly here that the topic of *Self* – the greater Self and what you consider to be the lesser self – is now the point of focus.

Without Clear Structure and Perimeter

Why did we call this, as we did... that there is no topic? Because there cannot be the parameter, the definition, the container, the demarcations, which are so... perhaps we could call it self-evident, easily offered, on the other topics:

Forgiveness is clearly definable... gratitude, as well... hopefulness is easily understood and joyfully experienced... truth has many definitions, each of which is valid for that one or ones defining same.

But what are the parameters of Self? That, then, is our invitation, our topic, if you will, for this [quarter] segment.

DEFINING SELF

Those of you who are participating in the works in the grouping called *The Peter Family* will hear Peter, in this new work, make a statement of incredible power, almost approaching blasphemy[9]. (We'll leave that, tantalizing you... hopefully, not unjustly so... for your own discovery.) But the question, here, is spoken to clearly in Peter's works... it is the *willfulness* – see – to look, to see, and to know Self.

Divine Heritage

Where does your soul come from? Of course, it is a given at least in this beautiful grouping, that it is of God.

But what is the nature of the *uniqueness* of the soul... that cannot be defined nor containerized... that cannot have a boundary lest it be limited and that be an affront to God and God's Laws?

---

[9] Peter's 'Blasphemy' – in the segment of the PETER PROJECT referred to here, Peter is confronted by a tormented soul who asks Peter who he is. Peter's reply was, 'I am Peter, son of God.' To which the soul yelled that Peter was blaspheming the name of the Christ. Peter's calm, unwavering claim is ultimately what freed the soul from his tormented life.

The omnipotent nature of your Self is the heritage of your Source. You, as the spiritual being of Eternal Nature, have chosen to express yourself in this incarnation. Some have chosen paths, which, at the outset, appear to be complex... challenged... which appear to be, in some respects, limited.

Will you now, in this first segment or week, look at Self – both in the spiritual sense and in the finite expression of your being – and ask this simple question: *What are my limitations... what are my challenges... what are the things that I have dealt with and am dealing with in this life?*

Recognizing Self-Imposed Limitation

If this sounds a bit towards the negative polarity, then we find considerable humor here. Why? Because of this, humbly offered to you now: Don't you, on occasion (perhaps more frequently at times, less at other times) hold your limitations before you? Do you go about your life ever thinking, *I would love to do this, but...* Do you ever look at another entity and long to be more like them, and wish that a certain self-adjudged limitation were not present, so that you *could* be? Perhaps your body dimensions are looked upon by you as a limitation, that were you a bit less in this dimension and more in that, you could have been a (...blank...) writing anything you'd like, for most all have something to contemplate in that regard.

Are you fond of your limitation, or limitations? Don't think that to be a question which doesn't apply to you, because some portions of self often find comfort in the recognition and claiming of limitation. We believe you can follow the thought-form of this and see its importance. Here again, the discovery is the important work of this first week. Do keep notes. Do be honest. Share this only with God. That way, honesty is... well, *almost* unavoidable, isn't it. (Humor intended there.)

Week two: Why. *I am looking at self. I am reviewing those things which I have discovered, that I have found which have been/are/or which can be limiting to me. Is this the Self I want to be? Why* – why is this limitation truly a limitation? Is it something that is a comparison? Is it something that is an evaluation? Never mind, here, peripheral aspects, for there can be many here, of course... we shall grant you that. Just in the most simplistic way, think about why this is present – what is the under-riding force here?

So, you've looked for your limitations, your self-imposed... and perhaps justifiably somewhat imposed externally by the mores, the society, the creed, and so forth. Then you've asked why. That's week two. In this, week two, look all throughout – see – look at it from the standpoint of your family, your friends, your vocation, your dreams. And again, this can be vast, so try to stay reasonably focused, see.

Discovering Your Unlimited Nature

Week three... very simple: What if...? *What if I were to release this? What if I were to replace it? What would I replace it with?* Well, if we are looking at a physical condition which is considered limiting, you could ask us and Self and the grouping, *How can I release something which is?* This is not the issue. The issue is what you *think* of it, how you *react* to it.

What if I were to focus upon something that brings me great joy, rather than something which brings me limitation?

Remember, this is about Self – see – Self is unlimited. The current incarnation is the focus of the greater Self... as a tool, as a beautiful blessing, as a potential for growth.

What if (in the most, again, simple ways) we were to just release any and all thought of this limitation as you've defined it in week one? See? *What* if we were to not think about it... to banish it from thought, from consideration, for an entire seven-day Earth period? The *what if*...see?

Week four: Gifts. Each of these things that you discover has a counterpoint. The potential offering which is constructive... something which, in the process of discovering it, will set you free. Week four is a joyful week. It is a week of empowerment. It is a week wherein you can know that you have the power in this week to totally change your life, because you have chosen a perspective different than that which is the cumulative result of who and what you are in week one. See?

In the morning all throughout this Earth month period, we might encourage you, humbly, to consider this simple prayer:

As I greet this day, O Lord God, help me to discover the beauty that I am. Help me to bring this beauty into the fullness of my comprehension and acceptance. And let it shine forth from me in all that I am and do in this day. Thank You, Father. Amen.

Now, each of these weeks has its primal focus, so in evening we would encourage you to review the day's activities, contrasted against the backdrop of the focal work as we just gave it for each week. When you are discovering, review your day. Do not do so laboriously, but see yourself floating through the day, as though you are some beautiful winged creature... who has absolute freedom, who knows truth, and can see through the eyes of truth. Just notice *Where have I reacted...* (perhaps even without thinking) *from a preconditioned accepted level of limitation?*

Then, of course, in the next week, ask *Why?* Go into the day just past and feel it. Did you like that reaction? See?

In the third week, each evening, review the day again, and then use the little *What if... I had thought this way, or I didn't have this?* See? Consider the alternatives. Why? You build thought-forms; you build the potential when you contemplate what can be... see... very important point.

In the fourth week, recognize that you present each entity with a gift. Your position in week one, as we gave it, has a counterpoint of a blessing or gift to give you. You can grow and learn; your soul can discover its creative potential, its unlimited, capital *S* – Self-potential.

Look for the emergence of the gifts that are the profound blessings of that which you previously adjudged as limitation.

Each evening we might conclude the day with a meditation which we (and, specifically, Zachary) shall assist the Channel in preparation. But this would be our offering to you as a prayer of consideration here:

> *O Mother-God, here come I, seeking the nourishment of my spirit's light as Thou dost give this, ever, eternally, to me. O Father-God, strengthen me as I now come into spiritual oneness with Thee. Help me to see and know those things which are the step-stones of opportunity in this life here in the Earth, that my spirit's light shall grow, that my potential in oneness with Thee shall be enhanced through the understanding of the experiences in finiteness. O Father-Mother-God, give unto me as is my need, that I am awakened to know the beauty as is uniquely given and called...* (Then place your name here. Conclude with this:) *I now commit all that I am into the embrace of Thee, O Mother-Father-God. Guide Thou me. Amen.*

PARABLE: HONORING

A small group of entities were laboriously building a structure. Some were formulating with clay, with straw, great rectangular objects with which others were building the structure. You know this story; it is written. For the straw was the ingredient that held the earth, the mud and such, together. And when dried, formed a tensile strength which was quite remarkable. But with the absence of straw, the question of how the bricks, how the building stones could be made, was paramount...

Does one in life itself need the straw to strengthen the building bricks, the blocks? And if so, in this analogy, what is the straw of Life with which you can build blocks... and then from the blocks, structure?

It could be said here in this, that understanding is the straw of which the spirit builds the foundation of its being. Understanding imbues, in a sense, a preconception that one knows... that one comprehends... that one has experienced... that one embraces, loves, or accepts... and so on and so forth.

So, as you seek, through the process of this work, to know Self, you are finding that which is the straw – the fortification, the strengthening element – in building the foundation of who and what you are.

As children play, perhaps very similar to these serious builders of structures, they, too, fashion from clay, from mud. But they give little concern for whether or not the structure will endure; in these children's minds, the moment is what is important. In the minds and consciousness of the laborers, the artisans, the architects, and those who rule or govern who have directed the construct of this structure, perhaps the opposite is true; they care very little about the moment, and are most concerned about the future.

There is a child within each of us who builds in the moment. There are also those who are considered (quote) "adults" (end-quote) who build for the future and tend to focus, often very singularly, upon that.

Somewhere in between the present and the future lies the potential that is a very precious gift for each and every soul, each entity. In the journey to discover Self, the potential becomes very significant; it becomes what we might call the objective.

Look about you and see how much you do in this day and the next and the next that is for the future, and what is for the moment. How much of what you are doing is building for what shall be, what might be... and what (curiously) might *not* be?

...here the builders pause. They await the arrival of the straw, for they believe it must be so.

Across the way, the children playing, by a small stream, had been using twigs and such to build a small dam to gather the trickling water into a pool in which they intended to frolic.

As they discover they have no more twigs, they, too, pause; but they are joyful all the while as they roam about, searching for more twigs. Since they find so very few, they discover that as they can gather small pebbles, many of them, at a distance away from an outcropping, these can be used and end up being more substantial than the twigs. And so they have done something familiar to you all... they have improvised... they have opened their creative self to other choices, other potentials.

As we come back to the building site of this intended great monument to the immensity of a certain ruler, we find that the workers, the laborers, are idle. They do not seek out an alternative, for they firmly believe that there is none... this is *the* way, the *only* way. And therefore, they have accepted this as the definition, the limitation, to what they are doing, so they are doing naught.

Those who are at the next level are going back over the works, making little adjustments here, shaving a bit of mortar off there, and so on. They, too, are essentially idle, because they believe, just as the laborers, that there is one way and only one. The architect is running rudimentary strings, pouring sand and watching its formulation and such to determine that the angles and all that sort, of their design, are according to the expectations, the calculations, and such. But essentially, this is a review, and no progress is literally being made.

Now we arrive at those of authority who have commissioned this work... or conversely, mandated it. They are irate. They are shouting. They are threatening. They do not wish anything to impede the progress of this great monument to their importance. Thus, they call forth those of wisdom, advisors, seers, and all sorts, and command that this be resolved.

The children, at this point, have builded their little dam. They have trapped the trickle of water into a somewhat generous pool. They are dancing, frolicking, laughing. Their objective is accomplished now, in the moment, and they are reaping the harvest of same because they have been open, they have improvised, they have been willing to receive guidance, to look, to see, and to manifest according to what is at hand.

Finally, after some time, straw is obtained and the work resumes. But some have endured hardships as the result of this. The chain of authority has been (to use a colloquial term from Zachary here) *rattled severely.*

ℴℹ

Now here is the point of what we have just given...

You have both the child and the authority figure, the ruler, if you will.... someone who directs, who has the final authority, the absolute decisive power. And you have the child within you, who just wants the joy of the moment.

Honoring Self

Of your life, carefully look at those times from your current time backwards, and just sort of analyze when the child was predominant and when the ruler was predominant. When did you labor for the future to the loss of the present? And when did you frolic in the present without a thought to the future? There is a discovery here which may not be completely self-evident as you hear these words.

Balance

The discovery is a part of the uniqueness of Self.

Self is likened unto a flower... which is born of a seed, so to say, of course. But the seed is the potential of Self, and requires, in order to become a flower, all of the known activities and ingredients – sun, light, water, soil, nourishment, tending, and so on. But the child within you tends to believe that the flower is already here, even if they only have the seeds in their hand; the adult believes all the other aspects... which, of course, have validity in the Earth.

The flower is your potential, of course, and is a very beautiful symbol of same.

The child may seem careless... without concern for those things which must be thought of in the Earth. You all know this statement, we are told, quite clearly, but what the child does is take the vision of the future potential and *lives it in the moment.* They may plant the seeds, but probably will not labor over them; they'll plant them and leave the forces of nature to do the rest. The adult in you will follow protocol, will follow what is known, and believes that if you want the gift of the flowers you must do these things for that to happen.

Knowing, by reviewing your life past when the child was in charge and when the ruler was in charge, will tell you very much about Self – it will tell you how and why you are who you are in the present. (And as you try to apply yourself in your weekly schedule, all of this will become more understandable.)

Children laugh...a lot! Laughter is a nourishment... to the moment and to the future. Laughter can dispel a lack of ease, bringing about ease even if the logic of the Earth, rather, dictates that no ease should be present.

Nourishment

We have used in past comments about the *Song of Self.* Song and laughter go very much together, as we perceive these, in the sense of what they create as a byproduct... a state of ease, a state of acceptance. When you are confronted with or are before one of the step-stones of life's opportunity, and you have no straw with which to make brick, then perhaps that is a gift to you... that you must do something else. You can lament your lack of straw with which to make brick, or you can be thankful for this opportunity to sing and dance and to laugh.

Watching children can be very enlightening. All know this. It can also be a bit frustrating at times. If you watch the child within yourself from the perspective of the authority figure, the ruler (as in the analogy given) you can find a mixture of both within you – the laughter, the discovery, the potential to learn from the spontaneity of the child within; and/or you can be somewhat frustrated as you observe the child within and you evaluate it on the basis of your current perspective as the ruler, the adult, the authority figure.

Choice

It would be a good postulate to presume that somewhere between these two points – which are, in a manner of speaking, seen as poles or balancing points – to be some median of logic, some median that might be the best of all ways to live one's life. But is that Self? In other words, is that you? For if it's not, you won't be able to sustain it. You'll gradually begin to move back towards one of the other positions you previously held.

As you search each week for the better understanding of Self, you can also begin to understand that which is the nature of those about you. You can begin to understand the bond of oneness which is a part of the finite realms of expression. That bond of oneness is the thought-form, the belief mechanism, the hierarchy, the law of the land, the teaching and training that is a part of your society, your culture, your dogma, your creed. To the extent that you, as an individual, agree with this, is the extent to which you have oneness with the realm of your current expression.

Along comes a great Light, who recognizes, who even honors, this bond of oneness which is the finiteness of Earth; but offers to those who are willing to hear and see, that there are choices – that disease is a state of mind, of spirit, as much as of body; that faith, that attitudes of expectancy, can actually manifest; that being hope-full is by far the greater way to live, the more joyful countenance than not; and that forgiveness is freeing, liberating... most of all to Self, but also to others, and to life, and to the potential of the oneness which is in the finite realm of expression in which you dwell.

The reaction here, of course, can be diverse... disbelief and all that sort, just so as the Master did meet when He brought these gifts to His brothers and sisters in the Earth (and as others have done, as well).

FREEING SELF

When He came to the children, He stopped all else. And, whatever they were about, He joined them... whether splashing about at the seashore, building imaginary structures of twig and stone, or whatsoever activity they were about. Then only hours later, His hands would bring about healing to one whose body was twisted and deformed.

Knowing Self

Yet with each of these – playing, being one with the children, or bringing about the potential to be healed to another – there was the consistency of His spirit's light. Why? Because He knows Self.

In the works here, you have the opportunity to know your Selves. You might think of these works and begin them with some earnest, some dedication, and gradually that might fade. Perhaps this will be something you will remember when tempted to stray...

Knowing the nature of Self, being able to see the greater Self, and what's called the lesser self – and those forces, those influences which are between the spiritual Self and the finite Self – are among those pivotal keys which are needed to release Self from limitation.

Peter's work enabled others to be freed from limitation. The buffeting, the challenging, of your habit, of your limitations, is and shall be such so as to strive to continue to endure. Each thing that thou art, each thing that you have embraced, each aspect of Self that you have become, has been granted life, so to say, because you recognize and accept and then manifest the fruit after the seeds, the flowers of the seed of that potential.

Remind self: *This is a process which is empowering me. It is freeing me. It is that which can remove the veils of illusion and help me to claim all else.*

Life Is the Manifestation of Truth

"I and the Father are one," so the Master stated. And then He lived that, demonstrated it, manifested it, and still does. You can do this, and you can do it by knowing where you are in the moment.

We mentioned earlier that your soul chooses, and has chosen this current incarnation because it offers understanding, wisdom, knowledge that as you experience, you create understanding. It is the manifestation of your truth. It is the manifestation of your potential as it is in the moment. If you live your life in the Earth with the awareness that you are also the greater Self, the (capital S) spiritual Self, then you've built this bridge of communication; you opened this conduit, that, where there was previously a seeming separateness between the spiritual Self and the finite self, that this gradually erodes or dissipates, and the fruits of the Spirit can become expressed in the finiteness of self in the Earth.

Children's laughter is a liberating activity. It makes them feel good. Imagine how good your spirit feels when you laugh. Think about it. Contemplate it. Your laughter, being synonymous with your choice to be joyful, is a gift to your spirit. For your spirit is likened unto the granary of your soul's oneness with all of existence. This granary contains the harvest of many seasons or many lifetimes. And upon the liberating energies that are found in laugher, in joy, in the claiming of the moment, in the empowering of self, the potential harvest of that life and the resulting deposits to the granary of the soul (so to say) are greatly increased. See?

Valuing Self's Potential

Self has potential beyond comprehension (that is, unless you can in this moment totally comprehend God), because the potential of Self is of God and, therefore, one and the same.

And yet, life – the physical body, the reality of life's expressions, and all of the steppingstones therein – can take from this the truth of these words; because the intensity, the manifesto of finiteness, is so powerful, so seemingly real, in comparison to that which may or may not be, even among some of the more faithful. And yet, when these principles are enacted, when you live your life according to what is believed in the spirit and heart, it is self-evident that the fruits do appear, the manifestation does take place.

And so this continual to and fro, seesaw, push-pull effort is a part of the process of your soul's journey in Earth. And it's not a limitation! Don't claim it as such. It is, rather, a potential harvest of gifts, of fruits, seeds waiting to be sown, discoveries waiting to be discovered.

As you seek out to know Self in multiple levels of Self's expression, you will make other discoveries, and each of these may be quite unique to you. Or there might be a composite here of some that are commonplace, and others which are unique. Again, as you review your portions of life past, this life, and see when the ruler was in charge and when the children were in charge, you'll discover this even more. But for now, we shall leave you with these last thoughts and this prayer...

Knowing Self's Eternality

Self is indestructible... eternal... the intentional manifestation of your uniqueness by God.

The influences and resulting efforts on your part to subscribe to the influences dominant in your life can seemingly take you away from this powerful discovery and cast you into some sort of a mold, some sort of a pattern which is acceptable.

But as you look within and follow the steps (and others which will come to you and become apparent) you will quickly see that you have always been both ruler and child... that these are not separate but one... that you do not have to compartmentalize your life, allowing yourself to be a child here and insisting that you are of authority or a ruler there.

The objective, then, is found in this prayer:

O Holy Father-Mother-God, help me to be One. Help me to see the house divided within me. Help me to collect those aspects of self which are distant... which are not being nourished. And give me the wisdom and Thy light, O Father-Mother-God, to bring these into Oneness. I claim my Oneness now. Help Thou me to rise up upon the step-stones of my limitation. And with each one, to become greater and greater, according to Thy will and my uniqueness. I thank Thee, O Father-Mother-God. Amen.

The discovery of Self is likened unto an oasis in a great desert... Once you are willing to seek, to find, and to claim this oasis, the waters of Spirit will flow and nourish you eternally.

We are through here for the present. May the grace and blessings of our Father's wisdom ever be that lamp to guide your footsteps.
Fare thee well then for the present, dear friends.

GUEST LECTURE: Rebecca

Given April 22, 2000

REBECCA: Greetings of joy and love from these and other realms beyond Earth. I was called in past, Rebecca. I am a part of that group who tended to the Master as child… and later, as an honor and joy. It is not mine alone which is offered here, but mine the greater honor of being the spokesperson:

Consider, during these cycles, the importance of seeking out and claiming, what I shall call, the *Golden Silence*.

Each of you has a unique pathway, which can be supported and/or guided by the experiences and teachings of others… this is certain. But ultimately, each individual's pathway is unique, and that pathway leads to what I have titled the Golden Silence. Finding this pathway is a part of your spiritual journey, your quest, your purpose for being in the Earth, even as I am now speaking through this, my brother who channels these works. Seek you, then, to know of it, for it is pivotal in the process of claiming your potential.

The Golden Silence is synonymous with what some of you have heard through the works called PETER. But to be more explanatory here… it is the *quest* for, and the *discovery* of, and subsequently, thereafter, the *claiming* of the Christ Light within.

By naming the Golden Silence synonymously with the Christ Light within, some of you may find some reservation. I would say unto you, title this as ye find to your ease. Notwithstanding, it is one Light… of God. The intention here of calling it the Christ Light not only honors our Elder Brother and those who serve Him – then and now – but it also honors, you see, you. For this one Light, He has manifested, and elevated to a position where it can be seen and known and followed by many. Surely, they are those who have taken this Light and woven it into the fabric of their perception and understanding of it. But I, Rebecca, and my sisters, are coming together to join with this work, to present to you the opportunity, that you shall see this in the purity of its original source. Hence… the Golden Silence, as you would seek it. My brother, the Channel, and others here who shall assist him, will prepare for you the means by which to attain same.

The crux of this intent here, and my great honor to have been chosen to speak to you in this meeting, is simply this:

It is you who control the outcome. It is your choice, not another's, whether or not you shall attain your highest ideal... your greatest intention... the dream of your heart or spirit, for there is, as is carefully written, one Law above all else: the Law of Free Will.

Therefore, we here – as we are summoned joyfully unto this call and this work through our brother and sister... (our brothers and sisters – any, all, who would come unto this) we are with those. But you, individually, must choose.

Go within. Find the Golden Light. Listen to the silence. Hear your own soul's song. Claim it. And then, let your life be the expression of it. In your thought, in your word, in your action and deed, let your song be heard.

The Golden Silence is the place of the Eternal Self.

This we strengthened for the Master as a child and provided the foundation – some would say, the playground – in which He could see it for what it was, and know it to be good.

Wilt thou do the same? We are here for you.

I thank you in humbleness, and I thank my sisters... those who can hear these words, and those who know of them in other ways. I am come to be with you. Let us sing joyfully.

My honor to those who have permitted this work.

My love to my brother in Earth. Thank you.

STUDY GUIDE

Activities for Applying Self

Morning Activity

In the morning all throughout this month, we might encourage you, consider this simple prayer:

As I greet this day, O Lord God, help me to discover the beauty that I am. Help me to bring this beauty into the fullness of my comprehension and acceptance. And let it shine forth from me in all that I am and do in this day. Thank You, Father. Amen.

Evening Review & Exercises

In evening, review the day. Go into the day just past and feel it... not laboriously, but see yourself floating through the day, as though you are some beautiful winged creature who has absolute freedom, who knows truth, and can see through the eyes of truth, and notice, "Where have I reacted, perhaps even without thinking, from a pre-conditioned accepted level of limitation?" Did you like that reaction?

Each evening we might conclude the day with a prayer such as.

O Mother-God, here come I, seeking the nourishment of my spirit's light as Thou dost give this, ever, eternally, to me. O Father-God, strengthen me as I now come into spiritual oneness with Thee. Help me to see and know those things which are the step-stones of opportunity in this life here in the Earth, that my spirit's light shall grow, that my potential in oneness with Thee shall be enhanced through the understanding of the experiences in finiteness. O Father-Mother-God, give unto me as is my need, that I am awakened to know the beauty as is uniquely given and called (then place your name here...see?) Conclude with this: I now commit all that I am into the embrace of Thee, O Mother-Father-God. Guide Thou me. Amen.

Note your answers to the questions posed by Rebecca on P. 132.

NOTES:

_____

_____

_____

_____

_____

_____

_____

_____

_____

_____

Weekly Exercises for Self

Week 1:
Look at self and ask: What are my limitations? What are my challenges? What are the things that I have dealt with and am dealing with in this life? Am I fond of my limitations, (**The discovery** is the important work of this first week. Keep notes.)

Week 2:
Ask self: Is this the self I want to be? Why is this limitation truly a limitation? Is it something that is a comparison by someone else's standards? Is it something that is an evaluation? Why is this present? What is the under-riding force here? (Look all throughout from the standpoint of your family, your friends, your vocation, your dreams. This can be vast, so try to stay reasonably focused.)

Week 3:
What if I were to release these? What if I were to replace them, what would I replace them with? What if I were to focus upon something that brings me great joy, rather than something that brings me limitation? Remember, this is about Self as a tool, as a beautiful blessing, as a potential for growth. *What if I were to not think about it, to banish it from thought, from consideration, for an entire week?*

Each evening, review the day, and then use *"What if ...I had thought this way... or I didn't have this?"* Build the potential by contemplating what can be.

Week 4:
Week four is a week of empowerment: Consider the counterpoint of each of these things you have discovered - the offering which is constructive, something which, in the process of discovering it, will set you free. This is the week wherein you can know that you have the power to totally change your life, because you have chosen a perspective different than that which is the cumulative result of who and what you are in week one. Look for the emergence of the gifts that are the profound blessings of that which you previously adjudged as limitation. You can grow and learn; your soul can discover its creative potential, its unlimited **S**elf potential.

NOTES:

_____

_____

_____

_____

_____

_____

_____

_____

_____

_____

Further Exploring Self

NOTE: The thoughts listed here are merely suggestions intended get you started in further exploration of this subject. Use any portion of them as your personal guidance leads you.

POINTS TO PONDER:

- What is the "gem" of yourself, which you offer back to the All? What is that aspect of your self that adds your own special sparkle to God and to Life?

- The omnipotent nature of your Self is the heritage of your Source

- Why did Lama Sing state that "Self" was not really a "topic"?

- When, in your life, the child was in charge and when the ruler was in charge.

REVIEW:

You sought to discover that within you which was limiting you, empowering yourself to forgive and release and to be forgiven.

You looked at God as that Source of continual blessings and gifts, and gratitude empowered you, enabled you, so as you were willing, to *claim*, and to be released.

As you recognized and claimed, you received gifts by sending forth the attitude of joyful expectancy, of hope and hopefulness.

All of which brings you to a point of empowerment to see Truth.

You can now look within self without fear, without reservation, in a willing, open-hearted way, and see the aspects of your being, your personality... who and what you are. And in that quest for the truth of Self, came the willingness to recognize that this is unique to YOU.

NOTES:

_____

_____

_____

_____

_____

_____

_____

JOURNAL

_____

_____

_____

_____

_____

_____

_____

_____

_____

_____

_____

_____

_____

_____

_____

_____

_____

_____

_____

_____

_____

_____

_____

_____

_____

_____

_____

_____

_____

_____

_____

_____

_____

_____

_____

_____

_____

_____

_____

_____

_____

_____

_____

_____

_____

Step 6:

Faith

Given May 17, 2000

OPEN FORUM ON FAITH

LAMA SING: Yes, we have the Channel then and, as well, those references which apply to the topic as given hereafter. As we commence with these works, let us come together in this joyful prayer of oneness unto God.

> *We hallow Thee, O Father-Mother-God, in heart, mind, and body. From this claiming of Thee, help Thou us to know that all things are possible. Help us to see the potential in all challenges that we shall meet in this Earth day and those which lie beyond.*

> *And for those who are beyond the Earth, we offer this prayer: Here are we, the Sons and Daughters of God. We offer ourselves, in the sense of our light of God within, unto your every need. Look you... here is the Master, the Christ. His offering to you is His healing grace, love, compassion, and His wisdom. Take of these as you will, and bring them within self to the center of thy being. Here, let these ever be that light which shall guide you in all things and unto all needs. We call to those of you who have dwelled in the limitations of the shadows of your own choice. Hear our call, so as ye will. All these things and the greater do we offer to you as instruments of the One God. If ye will come forward from your shadow, you shall find joy, and we shall rejoice with thee. So as it is your will, these offerings remain for you to choose eternally.*

> *We thank Thee, O Father, for this continued opportunity of joyful service through this, our Channel, and his mate, in the Earth. Amen, and so let it be written.*

Capstone of the Second Triad

As we come together, dear friends, let us consider all those works that have gone before. In our last meeting, we spoke of the need to know self. We spoke of this from the perspective, not as one who has explored all the previous works and made many discoveries therein; but rather, to know Self as the eternal being that thou art. As you have sought, perhaps using the Channel's guided works, to know that golden silence within and to dwell herein, perhaps you have found a resonance that shall endure. This is our prayer for each of you.

Now, as you consider what might lie ahead, we would offer this as the sixth work in this project – for upon it is the capstone of this triad – and that would be, simply, *Faith.*

The Nature of Faith

Faith is the power which, when applied and lived, has no limitation. It is continually tested by the influences and (you could call it) status quo, of the realm in which one is existing or has consciousness. Faith is the light that you found in the greater Self – the spiritual Self... that being indicated in your communications with a capital *S*, as opposed to the small *s*.

Here, as one seeks from this golden silence within and claims and moves without, carrying some vestiges, some particles of that golden silence into the daily life, what wonders have you found? Many of you have discovered aspects of your being that you have either forgotten or neglected in one way or another for a time.

Faith is likened unto that pathway upon which the light of God can move freely, easily. Faith is like the channel of an ancient waterway... a waterway which has eroded all of the obstructions for the most part, and flows easily, broadly, gently, and comparatively straight along its destination to the sea. So is it, then, in many respects a good analogy, for the inner Self, along with the pathway of Faith, does flow unobstructed to the great sea, which is the symbol for God.

Faith is many things to many people, to many theologies, to many doctrines, and on and on. Faith is that light by which you measure, similarly to truth. But in this instance, faith is that which is not dependent upon anything without, in the sense of interaction with other forces. Faith is self-sustaining, for it flows from the inner conviction of one's (capital S) Self, in a sense of knowingness, a sense of trust, a sense of believing.

Faith, as one single word – or Faith-*full*ness – has so many aspects, and we do urge you in this time period to explore them... easily, gently, to flow with them.

EXERCISING FAITH

At the onset here, let us offer to you some works which we believe shall help you to explore these various avenues, and to discover even greater potential for faith and the application of faith-*full*ness in your daily life than perhaps you ever conceived. (This is our prayer, our attitude of hopefulness, and our joy for you.)

In the first week, consider what you believe in. As you arise in the morning, we might offer this simple prayer.

O God, here am I. I have been with Thee during slumber, and my body, mind, and spirit are in this moment unified in oneness with Thee. Let this be that staff upon which I shall lean, as needs be, through the challenges of this Earth day. Let me know my Faith, and let me know the Faith of the Christ spirit, as this, too, is awakened. I thank Thee, Father. Amen.

Throughout the day, practice the moment of silence. What we mean by this is, before you respond to conversation, to challenges, particularly in events that are energized with any particular emotion, practice the moment of silence by pausing after other entities have spoken. Give yourself and them a space. Look at them. Look around them. Notice any energies, any colors, any differentiations, that are offered to you in that moment. Now, the moment may be two or three seconds, or even more... y*ou* gauge, see. Then, remember that you are faith-full... *then* speak. See?

The second Earth week, we would encourage you in this way: *Who are those entities? Who are those people? What are those events and such, which are close to me, in which I have faith?*

You might have faith in your automobile, hoping that it shall ignite its engine and transport you to where you wish to go... that's an application of faith, is it not? You might have faith even before that, that your alarm clock will go off, will sound... that is an attitude of faith. You might, as you spring from your sleeping apparatus, your bed, energized with a wonderful night's sojourn with we and others here (loving humor intended) move to your bathing room and, with faith, turn on a water spigot and expect the water to be warm… there is faith that everything is aright, including the flow of water. And so on. We could pick many small things. But notice here, and this is our point… there are many things that you have faith in or put your trust upon and give very little thought to those.

So, in this second week, pause as you arise and think for a moment, perhaps still lying back, looking up at the ceiling (hopefully you have one) and consider what you are going to do when you roll and turn about and arise from your bed. What we've given is what you call a thumbnail sketch. Each day for this second week, think about all the things… you have faith that your heating or cooling apparati is working, and on, and on… all the little things. (Don't labor over this; have a jolly time with it, see.) Now, here is an affirmation for this second week:

> *I claim my Faith in all these things so oft unseen, O Fa-*
> *ther-Mother-God, and I give thanks for them. I give*
> *thanks, as well, for all those who have made the way*
> *passable and made it possible for me to have these*
> *things in my life. Throughout this Earth day, O Father-*
> *Mother-God, help me be aware of all of the subtleties of*
> *this life upon which I have trust, to which there is Faith*
> *flowing from me. I thank Thee, Father. Amen.*

Weeks one and two, we would recommend a review in the evening and a journey into faith itself (which, here again, the Channel will be guided to accomplish that work for you). But we do encourage you in weeks one and two to just think about the word or phrase faith or faith-*full*ness. Consider what has gone before in this Earth day. Consider all those things that have been a part of week one and then week two. Hold those thoughts, and just give this prayer:

> *I commit myself in spirit, mind, and body unto Thee, O*
> *Father. My faith is with Thee. I claim Oneness with*
> *Thee. And because I believe and have faith, I know that*
> *Thou will guide me to that which I most need. And know*
> *that Thou will heal my body, awaken my mind and*
> *heart, and unify me in all respects. Thank You, Father.*
> *Thank You, Mother-God. Amen.*

Week three, we would begin to look about in the broader sense, as somewhat the pattern of past works, and we'd look about… perhaps your country, perhaps your province or State or whatsoever it might be called… look for those things that are always there that you trust and believe and have faith that, when there is the need, this shall be available to you… your electrical current, the services of so many entities who gather your refuse, who prepare the foodstuffs, who perhaps provide the fuel for your automobile, and on and on… you can surmise these. They are outside of your abode, outside of your family, outside of self. Without their presence, perhaps any one of these, your life would be different. You are faithful that these will be here. A part of you can deal with momentary losses of these, but another part of you believes that they shall always be there.

Look around for those entities who have meaning, and who give life to your light… light to your life (that is, both are applicable, so it would seem). Those might be entities you greet each morning, or notice on your way to your employment or to your teaching work or any other journey that you are about on a regular schedule. Think about these entities for a moment, and allow your faith to flow through you to them. This is a practice which is opening for Self.

If you can, pause long enough that you can make contact with their eyes, or verbally, or both, look at them. Take that moment of silence again to smile, to nod. Just look. Hold their gaze. You will be amazed that they will reciprocate… at first, perhaps a bit awkwardly, but then the next day a little more ease. Give them your faith. Send it to them, as though you were a giant light casting a beam of radiance upon them, which is, in fact, what you are. Do this all throughout your Earth day. Look for those opportunities to let your faith flow… into things, into peoples, into events, and on and on.

I am faith-full, O Lord God. Help Thou me to open myself, that I shall find the comfort and joy in allowing my faith to flow. As Your gifts flow to me eternally, so then let my gift of faith and faith-full-ness flow to others. I thank Thee, Father.

In the evening of the third Earth week, consider the impact of your continuum of allowing your faith to flow… first, upon individuals and perhaps groupings… then perhaps upon events and happenstance in your daily life. You will find challenge here, for habit is strong. And in those things which you do not have faith or where you have doubt, we now encourage you to replace these with a sense of faithfulness. Perhaps not in the moment or not even in the individual's potential (if that is the case) on any time frame, but offer them faith-*full*ness. Not a word needs to be spoken. But that same moment of bonding, of connection, of eye contact... or verbally... think and speak as though you have faith in them, see... even if you don't.

The challenges will be met, one by one. We encourage you to note these: what things have you found so far, through this third week, which block or limit the flow of faith... which things yet remain that you have doubt towards or for or upon? It is not so important at this point for you to justify, *Well, this is simply not reliable.* Only identify the areas where you cannot place your faith. See?

Now, in the fourth week, we are going to encourage you to have faith in the broadest sense... again, similar to the pattern of previous works. In the global sense, think about all the entities whose thoughts, whose needs, whose desires, are very similar to yours, who have the same opportunities or challenges, who face the same opposition or doubts or fears – and send them your faith. And here is the prayer that we recommend to commence the Earth day of week four, consecutively.

> *I call to you, brother and sister in all lands. Here am I, (state your name). I am a Son (or Daughter) of God. I reach out to you, full of Faith, rejoicing in the knowledge that nothing shall be impossible, if we can just believe. I send to you my belief, my recognition of you as a Son (or Daughter) of God. Hear my call, for I call unto you in God's name. Listen, feel, and know that God and I and many others have faith in you. Amen.*

That is all.

Now, dwell for a minute or two and feel as though you are actually sending out this faithfulness... that you have faith in the Earth, for you know that all in the Earth are eternal. It matters not whether we or you shall evaluate the reaction, the result, of placing our faith upon others. For if we believe, then eternity holds the potential of the result of our faith... if we see no response (by our measure) in the first day, the first Earth week, the first Earth month, or whatnot, your faith needs to sustain itself. Put it there, and keep it there. See?

Here you will be called this way and that by the events of the Earth, and a portion of you will wish to question this. A portion of you will question to the extent that you might find it, at times, difficult to truly be faithful. Do it anyway, to the best of your ability. You do not have to be dependent upon a result.

Faith is its own force. It is not externally dependent. It flows from the center of Self... the connection, the place of the golden silence within, which is eternal. And the expectation of a reaction – whether justified or not – can be an impediment in the stream of your faithfulness. If you will do this to the best of your ability, you will see the results, the harvest, the fruits, of your faithfulness. For here again, Universal Law applies.

Faith is the connection of the small self and the greater Self into a oneness with God. So long as these two counterparts – the finite self and the eternal Self – can find a median point of agreement to simply let it flow, then wonders will unfold for you. See?

In week four, do not look to evaluate your Earth day before slumber. But instead, do this... reinforce your faith and your faith-*full*ness, and do so, perhaps, in this way:

> *I have had faith in Thee, O Father-Mother-God, for the presence of this Earth day. And Thou hast gifted it to me. I thank You for that confirmation and justification unto my faith. I also thank You for the many other things of which I have held my faith out as an offering, and to which Your law has brought me good return. Now, as I enter into this sleep period, I offer my Faith to You, Father, as Your Child. Let my faith and your eternal Faith be gifts to those in need. Here am I... so as Ye see those who can gain from my uniqueness and my faith, I shall attend to them joyfully. I surround myself with Your light, Father. I believe it. I trust it. I claim it. Amen.*

PARABLE: TRUSTING

Two men were walking across a frozen body of water. It was a bit early in the winter season, and one of the men spoke nervously to the other, "I'm not sure this is a good idea. It saves us several hours as opposed to walking around this lake, but I am hearing lots of little crackling sounds. Do you hear them?"

The other man, looking straight ahead and not even turning to talk to his colleague, states, "Nope... don't hear a thing."

The other man is waving his arms somewhat and sliding his feet along carefully, as though each step might be his last. "Come on! You surely have to hear that one. I think it echoed off the trees over there. Do you think we should turn back?"

The other man, his eyes transfixed upon something on the shoreline a distance ahead, does not turn, and simply states, "Nope. No need."

"Maybe I'd better move a little bit away from you. Walking so close together, we're concentrating our weight on one small area. That's right, I think I've read that. Uh... I'll just go over here about twenty feet or so and, you know, just to be safe."

The other man, striding along in a smooth, measured gait, eyes still transfixed on the distant shore, states, "Okay."

The first man is now truly nervous, for he can see some white cracks appear in the ice beneath him as he is walking. "Oh, my goodness. I think we've had it. Well, how is it over there? This ice is showing stress marks all around me."

"Fine here," states the other man, smiling a little and still gazing gently, easily, upon the distant shoreline.

"Oh, my goodness. Did you hear that one? I... I've got to go back. I... I can't do this. This is just not right. Something terrible is going to happen. Are you coming? Are... are you going to come with me?"

"Nope," the other man responds. And finally he turns to his friend, who is transfixed at looking down at his feet and the ice beneath him, and states quite simply, "Here we are. Saved two hours. And there's the chapel. I was wondering if she'd be there. I was hoping she would. If we had walked around, I wouldn't have had this opportunity. You need more faith, Frank. That's your problem."

Embarrassed because he's standing within several steps of the shoreline unbeknownst to him, he looks up and laughs nervously. "I think you're right. I do need some faith... but first, I need to find a bathroom."

The point here, friends, is quite simple. It is not so much so whether or not the ice is safe... even though some amount of what we would call good sense, or common sense, would seem appropriate here.

But the point is one's focus... both men were very vulnerable. Both men took the same (quote) "risk" (end quote). One became ill by the time he reached the other shore, out of pressure, tension, anxiety, and fear.

The second man joyfully searched for that one he loves... his face was beaming; he was glowing. The thought of the ice and the trek across the lake's breadth was not a thought in the forefront of his mind, but his love for the one he hoped to meet at the chapel's door. So he transfixed his vision, his thought, all of his being, upon his destination, his goal. And a nice one, too, for it is a goal of love and sharing.

80C3

FOCUS ON THE DESTINATION

Can you not see in this very simple little experience the parable of truth that it holds for you? Do you not walk across something that is akin to the frozen surface of a lake each and every Earth day?

Hold the Light of Hopefulness

For the most part, you keep your focus beyond that. You don't worry that something mechanical will happen to your automobile on the freeway, and that you could have a collision. You know that it is possible, always, for something to malfunction; but your focus is upon finding a parking place when you arrive at your destination, or what sort of biscuit or Danish to have with your beverage once you reach your destination, or you might be thinking and pondering work that lies ahead, and on and on and on. While these could be paralleled to the entity number two, whose eyes never wavered from watching the chapel door, even from the breadth of the distant far shore of the frozen lake. He held the vision of his destination, he held the focus of his love, his heart, within him. It could be said here that he was actually lighter because of it, couldn't it?

You have all tried to lift someone who is rigid, who is tense, as opposed to a small child's limp and limber body. You have all challenged yourselves with all sorts of potentials, and do so every day. But intensity has more density, see, thus, Frank *was* heavier... he *did* crack the ice as he moved across it. But not the second entity, for the light within him buoyed him up. See?

Focus on Being Grateful

Your light of hope-fullness can be used as a tool here, to bring faith to the forefront. If you are hopeful about something that lies ahead in this Earth day, dwell on it... find the positive, energized light of the day, and give it credence... think (as you are moving through traffic, or walking down the lane, or whatsoever you are doing) of the frozen lake:

Are you making yourself heavier and cracking the ice because of some fear, some doubt or concern? Did you apply faith as you arose? Did you think about the many things that serve you faithfully, because you have faith in them? Did you think about the entities who are involved, perhaps tens to hundreds of thousands of them, to bring you your expectancy of this day – the electricity, the water, the clothing, the food, and on and on? *Thankfulness*... remember? *You are welcome*... remember?

Truth is a virtue. Faith is holy. Truth is a tool which can clarify and make visible those things which are so oft obscured. Faith carries one through them, no matter what.

There are many tales of those who have been imprisoned... and, so often, those who are unjustly imprisoned... how they will build their faith through focusing upon some obscure little event, an insect, the building or designing of a home or dwelling in their mind, in their meditation... the writing of a book in mind, where they literally can see every page and turn it with their mind. It exists. It is their destination. Faith carries them to it.

GIVE IT LIFE

Faith needs your claiming to have life.

It is written here in many ways and in many realms that consciousness is for the building of faith.

Faith Opens the Way

Faith is the knowing of self and God that is empowering, and makes open the potentials which can otherwise be obscured, blocked.

All of your life in physical body in the Earth, aren't you like these two fellows walking across the frozen lake? Couldn't the ice break beneath your life at any moment, in any juncture? And that lifetime is concluded.

Many entities have a phobia... they focus upon all of the things that are about them and/or are in their life that can harm them. There are others who seem to have not a care, not a concern (some of these to a fault, of course, but we aren't talking here about the extremes, rather, those who have the faith to know these things and go beyond them). One who knows that the ice could be a bit thicker but has the faith to believe that it is sufficient for his need.

The ice of life will carry you far better when you have faith.

Faith Brings a Life of Joy

If you think about this and picture it in your mind's eye, you'll see that the movement of one through life who is faithful has a grace and ease which is fluid. It is almost as though that entity or those entities have no burdens, no challenges. And yet, upon exploration, you can find that, for the most part, all do. But their demeanor, their focus, their destination, is of greater joy to them than the focus upon the limitations. Thus, their focus is upon joy.

Joy is the embrace of God which is primordial... eternal... it effervesces omnipotently to you at all times.

DO YOU BELIEVE?

It is the paradox of life itself that one's choice... Just as a prisoner, perhaps in a chamber of confinement barely large enough for their body can find something to focus and build a path of faith, that their life is fluidic, moving, even though their body is confined and immobile.

Demonstrations of Faith

There are those who have limitations, in terms of the commonality of senses and their perception in the Earth... which are brought to them, which are offered to them, as opportunities (these are known by these entities prior to entry, and their soul knows all along the pathway of that life... that herein, is a potential gift). Those who have approached their challenges, their limitations, from that attitude of joyful expectancy and faith have accomplished wondrous works. Some who paint and have no mobility in hand or arm, some who write great works of literary notoriety and cannot speak, and on and on we could carry this.

But there is no need. For, if you will look around, as we gave in the weekly works, you will see demonstrations of faith as you open yourself... looking for your faith. Looking for your faith around you and what you have faith in, bringing the gift of faith into your work, to your life, all that you are and do. And then, in the fourth week, offering it globally, universally, as a gift to all your brethren and sisters.

Allowing the Flow

So here we have this point next to make...

The Master, the Christ, used faith as a powerful tool. He used faith just in the manner as we described of the ancient river channel, knowing that faith would allow the flow of God's grace to pass through to the needs of those who petitioned him, He asked of them as they sought from Him, *"Do you believe?"*

We have stated this as a suggestion to another son of God who seeks to do healing works, and to others in these ways and those; and so now, might we also, as a very precious gift to you, ask you as well: *Do you believe?* You have unburdened yourself, and you have worked at this very well...

FURTHER UNDERSTANDING WHAT FAITH IS

You have applied forgiveness. You have built and claimed with your gratitude. You have set the energy of expectancy and hopefulness before you. You have looked within to find your truth; you have listened to hear the truth of others. You have explored the dimensions of your finite self, also often referred to as the little self, and you have gone within to claim and unify your consciousness with the eternal... also called, greater Self.

Applying Your Understanding

How shall you apply this work in this lunar cycle? Shall you abandon reason? Shall you cast aside logic? We do not find that to be a very good idea, for reason and logic are also tools. You deal with events and happenstance in your life through reason and logic, in order to know them, to define them, to discern the breadth and depth of them, to (quote) "define their parameters" (end quote). So you cannot cast these aside... or rather, we should not think it wise, universally.

But when your senses, your mind, your logic, your reason, have provided you with as much as they can, then you look within, now that you are unencumbered – because you have forgiven, because you are grateful, because you are hopeful, because you know your truth and self – and you can state, *"My faith is in Thee, O Father. Guide Thou me."*

Look outwards, beyond the challenges, to the destination of your hopefulness. Look for your truth, and let it be your strength. Do not claim the truth of others, nor judge them; but forgive them, and in the process, free yourself. Your gratitude already manifests the result. All you have to do is walk across the frozen lake of life to find it waiting for you, symbolically, at the chapel's door.

The Holy of Holies is within you. And the Holy of Eternity is existence itself. The path from one to the other is non-existent in the literal sense, because they are both omnipotent. While you are in finite body, you believe that this body is the only vehicle which you have... and while in the Earth, perhaps there is, according to your logic and reason, some credibility to this. But remember the infirmed… remember those who have limitations, and how they went beyond them.

You are that power, so as you believe. Let us repeat this in several different ways:

You Are the Power You Seek

The power that you seek, no matter for what purpose, is always being offered to you. The limitations, judgments, expectations, and demands of others upon you have no impact upon your inner power. Remember the prisoners, enduring where endurance was seemingly impossible. Do you ever wonder whether your doubts of yourself are creating limitation for you? Have you ever stated, "I wish I could…" (this or that)? Faith is the power that makes these things possible.

Faith in God is claiming that which is self-evident, for life is eternal and, therefore, life is of God. You, as God's Child, are empowered at the moment of your spiritual birth. Shall we call it that? Then, as your spirit flows through experience upon experience, turning this way and that to explore something curious, because you've heard a beautiful call or sound… *Oh, look over here, how the light is twisting and turning, spiraling upwards. I must experience this! And here… other spirits, other souls, laughing. They are gleeful, joyful. I wish to share that with them.*

This is the counterpart that one perceives oft in meditation and movement to other realms, isn't it? What we mean here is that you believe by moving somewhere else, by doing something else, you'll have greater joy. If you have faith in self *now*, then why wouldn't you have that greater joy *now*? The illusion of limitation is a part of a balance scale. If you claim that side of the balance scale, off you go. Joy is making the way passable through one's faith. Faith is the *dis*claiming of limitation, and the claiming of one's unlimited potential.

Joy Is a By-Product of Faith

And one step more…

By defining that destination, by focusing upon the chapel door from the other side of the lake, you can pass through such challenges and limitations… and all the while, joy is flowing to you. Happiness and well-being are there, like beautiful fruit ripe for harvest on the tree of life.

Laughter is a tonic to the spirit. Laughter in the face of challenge depletes its energy. Joy and laughter are synonymous, though not mandated to be simultaneously present always. Heart-songs are songs of joy. Songs of limitation are discords. It's like having two radio receivers. One is joy and the other is limitation or opposition. And you have one hand on one control, and the other hand on the control of the other apparatus, continually adjusting the volume. Don't you?

Your Light Is of God

Or here's another one…

As you fill your bath basin, your bathtub, don't you manipulate (unless you have a lever apparatus. but even then, you move the lever left and right to find just the right temperature) or turn the right and left knobs until you have the right temperature water flowing out of the spigot? Isn't life just so? Who controls? Who controls the flow of your waters of life? Have you signed these over to someone else? Have you stated, *I do not want the responsibility of my faith. Here… I've written it down on this document. It is now yours. Take care of me* and so, you surrender your free will?

But here is the beauty of finiteness, of life in the Earth… the wonder and beauty is: The spirit can be occluded, it can be veiled, it can be obscured; but it cannot, nor its light, ever be vanquished… for it is of God. See?

FAITH THE GRAIN OF A MUSTARD SEED

The spirit within you, some day, some moment, will state something like this colloquial phrase: *Hey, wait a minute! This isn't joyful. Why am I doing this? Wouldn't I be better off without this seeming illusion of freedom and luxury, to be free and claim my own joy?*

You see… a bird flies through the air. First, it observes its parents from the nest. Again and again, they show it: this is how, movement here, movement there. Soon, the little ones are emulating, aren't they? And they grow, and their feathers flush out all over their body. And one day, on the side of their nest, they emulate their parents' wing movements and such with such vigor that they suddenly find themselves soaring through the air.

If they have faith, their flight continues, for they let go and focus upon some distant destination. If they have no faith but are fearful, they will look down and see their altitude, and fear their plight. In the process of looking down, they've lost their aerodynamic lift. They've lost their momentum, and they are a tumbling, fluttering spiral of feathered fluff, while their brother or sister feels the exhilaration and joy of the wind currents lifting, carrying, supporting.

Faith does not look for cracks in the ice of life as one walks across it, but looks for those joyful events and considers life, just so, what it is: *a wonderful opportunity to get from here to there.* See?

Faith Is Non-Proportionate

Power flows, unless one obstructs it. It is for these reasons that we have so oft given unto those who have sought from here our prayers of hopefulness, our prayers encouraging faith. If you speak a prayer for another, what should you do about that? Should you send it out with faith? *In other words, I believe that this entity is healed. I believe that this prayer is heard and answered.*

These things, those who have carried the light of God brightly within them while in the Earth, have repeatedly demonstrated. Our Master glorified the word Faith. *"If ye would have but the faith of this one grain of mustard seed..."* How can a tiny life form such as a mustard seed contain life? How can it spring forth from such an almost obscure tiny particle, to become such a vibrant, aromatic, productive plant?

Does size determine the validity and appropriateness of one's faith? Many great fruit seeds could hold thousands of mustard seeds on their half-shell. Because they are greater, is this then how one applies their faith... because the great fruit seed is of a size, of a dimension and property, to appear to be more valid? Try this. Plant one of each, and tend it, and see what happens.

Our point is not to encourage all of you to become gardeners or plant enthusiasts, although most of you are. It is, rather, to point out that the assessment of the intellect, the mind, the reason, and all that sort. The Earth plane conditioning measures and places validity or belief upon some thing, some event, some *any*thing, based upon the conditioned reactive thought-forms, which are preponderant in and about self at the time.

If you let your faith flow through these things, you can know them, you can be aware of them, you can acknowledge them... but you are flowing through. (This does not make you unproductive. It makes you remarkably more productive, at least in the potential sense. For joy is an energy, see... it energizes. See?)

Faith is the property of one's ability to claim that which they know spiritually, and live it in the world of finiteness.

You Choose the Harvest

Faith is the tree of life; thou art that one who chooses yea or nay to gather a harvest.

Some entities are likened unto one who, for a lifetime, walks 'round and about this great Tree of God's gifts... 'round and around, the entire lifetime. And we can hear them oft in their prayer (or in those times which are less than prayerful) calling out, *Where are the fruits? Where are the blessings? Where are the gifts? I am traveling and traveling and traveling, and I find no gifts.*

And yet, if the entity were to look to the left or right, they might find that what they are seeking is an arm's-length away on either side; that in fact, habit has them going 'round and about the bush without recognizing it is fruitful.

If you are in a challenge, you can equate it: *What are the potential ramifications of this challenge? Could I lose everything I have? Could I lose my life? Could I be imprisoned? Could I lose that which I love? Could I lose my material goods, my belongings, my abode, my automobile, perhaps my beautiful clothing or ornaments (or jewelry, as you call them)... could I lose these?*

You can question. You can think about these things and concern about them... and your forward movement is greatly impeded. You could be like the entity spending a lifetime walking around the Tree of Life, never noting the gifts continually offered to them.

Patience is a virtue, as well. Patience and long-suffering were given and spoken of through Edgar [Cayce] to considerable length, worthy of reference and review here. But faith... faith is the life of that soul who claims themselves as a Child of God.

Faith is like a light around you. Remember how we offered in our opening prayer for those dwelling in the limitation, the darkness of their own choice?

If one has a great mansion filled with brightness and color, sounds and light, those are synonymous with God's gifts to each of His children. Think about it. Standing in the vestibule of this great mansion, which is your life, and instead of walking into the mansion and partaking of it, feeling no remorse, no guilt... *Oh, I am not worthy. Oh, I must earn this. Oh...* this or that. Some open a door and walk into a closet, close it behind them, and dwell therein. We see so many who are in a chamber within the grandeur of God's blessings, and all that is required is to open the door and step out.

So, around you, like a great light, is all that you could ever seek and greater – wonders, joys, blessings, abundance. If you have locked yourself into a closet, like we've just described, faith is the key which will open the door and free you.

It could be offered here once again, with loving humor (apologizing to the Channel in advance)... but Zachary would state, *I am Faithful, I am Faithful...* [Sung to tune of Frére Jacque]. See?

Focus on Your Destination

If you focus upon what you are, rather than what you aren't... if you focus upon what you wish, what your joy is, what your destination is, your faith will take you to it.

Our Faith is with you, one and all, and our prayer for you is:
O Holy Father-Mother-God, here are Your Children. Here are the faithful. Help them, so as they are willing, to claim all Thy gifts, that the greater might be given. We pray this of Thee, Father, in the name of our Brother, the Master, the Christ, in the knowledge that, so as we do, You have heard and answered. This is our faith, and we are living it in You, O Father-Mother-God. Amen.

We are through here for the present. May the grace and blessings of our Father's wisdom ever be that lamp to guide your footsteps.

Fare thee well, then, for the present... dear friends.

GUEST LECTURE: Anna

Given March 23, 2000

LAMA SING: We find considerable honor and great joy to allow that one who is close to these works to come forward, to offer to of all of you that perspective and those suggestions which might, prayerfully, be of some purpose and service to you. And so we now shall communicate as clearly and as completely as possible from the entity who has been known by several names, but offers this work under the name, Anna.

ANNA: I greet you all in the spirit of kindredship... that which is the bond of God's spirit woven all throughout the fabric of each entity's being. I have been called by some according to that which is recorded, and by others who are closer perhaps by the name Anna, or Anne. It is the latter (Anna and Anne) that I have chosen to represent this work, which is presented to you on behalf of many here.

Each age of enlightenment and hopefulness is prepared by those who are of the faithful. Some who come into the Earth and who move to realms adjacent to it do so out of honor to that one who was known as the man called Jesus. Others enter similarly for the purpose of contributing to *all* of our brethren, brothers and sisters, regardless of their belief and the manifestation of it. I have in past borne a great honor to have served in several respects for the preparation of the Way. Some of you now in the Earth who shall read or hear these words were also present in one form or another. We have prepared these comments for you, but also for all who wish to partake of them as a lovingly neutral offering:

There must be that which awakens, in order for the truth to be known. There must be the summoning, before the banquet can begin. There is always the call, before the work is done, whether that be the call to service, to chapel, the call to the task at hand.

In each entity, there is that part which is always seeking. No matter how great the momentary joys, the accomplishments, what the possessions, the abundance, might be... do you not, each one, always have some part of you which *knows* the greater yet lies ahead?

As I was chosen to be that vessel for such works as would bring forth the calling and the awakening, so art thou, each one, equally blessed, for the greater is the coming and the awakening that begins within self. The call goes out. And the righteous are extending their light, gifting it to you on the wings of understanding, compassion, love, and forgiveness.

Some of you will focus upon that which is categorically defined as faith. Perhaps it could be said that faith is that small portion of self always listening, always seeking. In the sea of energies, the collage of expectations that are about you as you walk upon the Earth, there are those lights which are false; there are those reflections, which are the half-lights, or less. Never are you without the true Light, for that is always within you. And it is the bringing forth of faith, the summoning of the purification, the washing away of those things that limit… the baptism… the purification.

Faith is the heart of self, and all else can flow as a fount of light from it. The faith-full carry this, just so as one might, in the darkness, carry a torch brightly to illuminate the way for self and others.

Be thou of good cheer. Summon your faith. HE COMES. We come to tell you this… and that the Gift of Gifts is always within you.

I am honored, just so as I have been honored in past. A part of me is in the Earth even as my spirit speaks… and a part of my being, which shall ever be of me, is that through whom I speak. So shall it be, then, for you… that a part of you that is ever with God has the Way, has the Light. Look for the faith in all things that will empower you to pass through them.

We are returned in and about the Earth, as we gave just above, to prepare… to send the call… to support those of our sisters, our brothers, and all else who are in and about the Earth.

The Earth is in a state of change. This has been given to you. And the beautiful souls called the Elders are at the forefront, and brothers to my Son are with them. That there shall be Light… all will be given, that the Way shall be open and known, not one whit spared. Those who can, shall give it; those who cannot, are called to take of it. The flower of Life itself is the pulse of your faith, beating in simpatico with all of your sisters and brothers.

Oneness… claim it. It will empower you. But, think in terms of *who* you are, *where* you are, and *what your time is.*

I and we, thank you… and offer our prayer and our love, and those gifts which are ours to give to you. I thank those who have so honored me for this rare opportunity to speak to those I love, and those who are loved and embraced by so many here. God's Spirit is with you. See it. Know It. And it shall guide. Shalom.

STUDY GUIDE

Activities for Applying Faith

Morning Activity
Weeks 1 & 2: We encourage you in weeks one and two to just think about the word or phrase: faith or faith-fu*ll*ness.

Evening Review & Exercises
Weeks 1 & 2: Consider all those things that have been a part of week one and then week two. Hold those thoughts, and just give this prayer:
I commit myself in spirit, mind, and body unto Thee, O Father. My faith is with Thee. I claim oneness with Thee. And because I believe and have faith, I know that Thou will guide me to that which I most need, and know that Thou will heal my body, awaken my mind and heart, and unify me in all respects. Thank You, Father...thank You, Mother-God. Amen.

Week 3: Consider the impact of your continuum of allowing your faith to flow ... first, upon individuals and perhaps groupings, then perhaps upon events and happenstance in your daily life. *Amen.*

Week 4: In week four, do not look to evaluate your Earth day before slumber. But instead, do this: Reinforce your faith and your faith-*full*-ness, and do so, perhaps in this way:
I have had faith in Thee, O Father-Mother-God, for the presence of this Earth day. And Thou hast gifted it to me. I thank You for that confirmation and justification unto my faith. I also thank You for the many other things of which I have held my faith out as an offering, and to which Your law has brought me good return. Now, as I enter into this sleep period, I offer my faith to You, Father, as Your child. Let my faith and your eternal faith be gifts to those in need. Here am I. So as Ye see those who can gain from my uniqueness and my faith, I shall attend to them joyfully. I surround myself with Your light, Father. I believe it. I trust it. I claim it. Amen.

NOTES:

_____

_____

_____

_____

_____

_____

_____

_____

_____

_____

Weekly Exercises for Faith

Week 1:
Consider what you believe in. Throughout the day, before you respond to conversation, to challenges, to events, practice a moment of silence. Remember that you are faith-full, then speak. As you arise in the morning, here is a prayer:
O God, here am I. I have been with You during slumber, and my body, mind, and spirit are in this moment unified in oneness with Thee. Let this be that staff upon which I shall lean through any challenges of this day. Let me know my faith, and let me know the faith of the Christ spirit, as this is awakened. I thank You, Father. Amen.

Week 2:
Think about all the little things that you have faith in or put your trust upon, but give little thought to. Here is an affirmation for this second week:
I claim my faith in all these things I so often do not notice, Father. I give thanks for them and for all those who have made it possible for me to have these things in my life. Throughout this day, help me be aware of all of the subtleties of these things I trust, to which there is faith flowing from me. Thank You, Father. Amen.

Week 3:
Look about in your country, your city, your state for those things that are always there that you trust and have faith that, when there is the need, this shall be available to you. Look around for those who give light to your life. Think about them for a moment, and allow your faith to flow through you to them. During the day, if you can, pause long enough to make eye contact with them, or verbally, or both. Take that moment of silence to smile, to hold their gaze. Look for those opportunities to let your faith flow into things, into people, into events.
I am faithful, O Lord God. Help me to open myself, that I shall find the comfort and joy in allowing my faith to flow. As Your gifts flow to me eternally, so then let my gift of faith and faith-full-ness flow to others. I thank You. Amen.

Week 4:
In the global sense, think about all those whose thoughts, needs, desires, are very similar to yours - the same opportunities, challenges, doubts or fears - and send them your faith. And here is the prayer:
I call to you, brother and sister in all lands: here am I, (state your name). I am a son/daughter of God. I reach out to you, full of faith, rejoicing in the knowledge that no thing shall be impossible, if we can just believe. I send to you my belief, my recognition of you as a son or daughter of God. Hear my call, for I call unto you in God's name. Listen... feel... and know that God and I and many others have faith in you. Amen. (Now, dwell for a minute or two, and feel as though you are actually sending out this faithfulness, that you have faith in the Earth plane, for you know that all in the Earth are eternal.)

NOTES:

Further Exploring Faith

NOTE: The thoughts listed here are merely suggestions intended get you started in further exploration of this subject. Use any portion of them as your personal guidance leads you.

POINTS TO PONDER:

- Why has Lama Sing given "faith" as the capstone of this second triad of topics?
- Do the "triads" given so far relate to anything in particular? There was the triad of Forgiveness and Gratitude, capped with Hope-fullness. And now the triad of Truth and Self, capped with Faith. Consider why, of all the topics Lama Sing could have spoken to us about, given our invitation to them to speak to us about those things they thought would be most helpful to us in these times, they have chosen these – and in the order they have chosen to give them. What do you consider the significance of this to be to YOU?
- Consider how it is that Faith is the connection of self and Self in Oneness with God.
- Do you believe?

Remember this quote: "If you focus upon what you are, rather than what you aren't, if you focus upon what you wish, what your joy is, what your destination is, your Faith will take you to it."

When Lama Sing encourages us to have faith regardless of the challenges we might face, independent upon any results or lack of results of that faith, and then tells us we will see the fruits of our faithfulness for *Universal Law applies*, what is meant by that?

Ponder:
- Faith is that which is not dependent upon any thing outside of Self
- Faith needs your claiming to have life.
- Faith is self-sustaining
- Faith in God is claiming that which is self-evident, for life is eternal and, therefore, life is of God.
- You, as God's child, are empowered at the moment of your spiritual birth.

NOTES:

_____

_____

_____

_____

_____

_____

_____

_____

JOURNAL

_____

_____

_____

_____

_____

_____

_____

_____

_____

_____

_____

_____

_____

_____

_____

_____

_____

_____

_____

_____

_____

_____

Step 7:

Seeing

Given July 4, 2000

OPEN FORUM ON SEEING

LAMA SING: Yes, we have the Channel then and, as well, those references which apply to the grouping as gathered and those intents and purposes as are a part of same. As we come together in this joyful work, let us first come into oneness, offering this prayer unto our Father-Mother-God

O Lord, where art Thou? Help Thou us to see Thee, to know Thee, and to claim Thee. We are Thine, so do we proclaim unto eternity. Wilt Thou know us? Wilt Thou see us? Wilt Thou claim us? This is our call to Thee, O Father-Mother-God. We await Your answer...

We rejoice, O Father-Mother-God, for here is Thy light. It shines forth in the eyes, hearts, and deeds of those whose presence we claim in oneness. Here is Thy spirit in the birth of that which is new in the Earth, in the transition of those who are passing by, journeying to their soul's highest level. The bird in flight and its song are those messages from You. And here is the light upon the path – the Master, the Christ, surrounding us with His healing grace, love, compassion, and wisdom.

We have called unto Thee, O Lord, and Thou hast answered. Help Thou us, then, to see in all things Thy presence. This is our prayer and our gift unto those who are seeking of Thee. And as they are willing to receive same... yes, even those who have not asked... then their sight shall be opened, as well, and they might the better know the Way and be guided, supported, arm-in-arm, with those who are Thy faithful. We thank Thee, Father, for the presence of these beautiful souls of light who have gathered here and in the Earth to proclaim this and to accept it. For this opportunity of continued joy in service to Thy name, we thank Thee, Lord God. And our blessings and gratitude are the embrace of our hearts, minds, and spirits to this, our Channel, and his mate in the Earth, who are opening the way and making it possible that this work can be. Amen.

The Power of One's 'Sight'

It is important, dear friends, that each of us – whether here or beyond, in the Earth with you or elsewhere – recognize the power of one's sight. And as you have had, perhaps, many opportunities to study this aspect, to explore it in your meditations, your dreams, your prayers... and yes, even in your waking day's activities... still, the importance of this topic *Seeing* is so profound that we have, with good counsel here, chosen it as the topic for this work.

Seeing from the Physical, Emotive, and Mental

It is immediately recognizable that, in the Earth, one sees with sight. It is also known, to varying degrees, that what one sees is quite individualized. Even as one evaluates colors in the numerical value of same, just so as with sound and frequencies and their numerical value, the sense of receptivity of various visual stimuli are being explored continually. For the knowledge grows in the Earth that the mind, heart, spirit, and even the body's immunological system, all respond to the stimulus of seeing.

We shall, in a moment ahead, speak on this from diverse perspectives, of course. But we shall dwell on this point just a moment longer here, to remind you that sight triggers memory; that it is the perception through seeing that creates an attitude of mind or emotion, or of spirit; and that the cumulative effect of what one sees and how one interprets or reacts to this seeing is a conditioning factor in daily life. Examples abound here. Let us choose just several.

Some of you have certain favorite types of music, favorite passages within those musical pieces, favorite words that might accompany some such works. Isn't it curious that each of you have certain likes and, perhaps, also those which are either dislikes or lesser chosen? The point of this is, of course, obvious... that it is not the melody, the sound, the words, and all that sort, in and of themselves, but the reaction of these from within the perceiver.

If you look at a portrait with a collage of masterfully blended colors, depicting profound realism... that indeed, the subject of the portrait veritably seems to be there, looking back at you... each has a response to this inwardly. Some may think of an individual in the past, perhaps even well beyond the current life. Sometimes these portraits or paintings or any such variant of same, may open you and create a path through which certain emotions, memories, thoughts and attitudes flow. All of these things, and perhaps even the choice of the color of the clothing you are wearing as you hear this, was chosen with not too great deliberation, unless this is some special day or occasion.

Perception

Where does the choice come from? Just choosing to be random, to create a variation in what others perceive as they look upon you? Or does this certain color make you feel good this certain day? You see it before you put it on your body… you create a thought-form that all throughout the Earth day, without even looking down at your clothing, you (quote) "know" it. You have chosen or claimed it because it suits you.

Seeing, in the broadest sense, is very much like this… most entities will choose to see that which *suits* them (some humor and some loving compassion come with this statement, of course).

One of the values of learning to see, in the broadest sense, is knowing where you are at present; not only in this current time, as you hear these words, but in future, at any point. Having a reference point of knowing your own choice, of perception of *seeing*, places you in a position to recognize that which is beyond. It is the singular focus upon one object immediately in front of an individual, compared to the wide-angle or broad-view perception which strives to intake, so to say, all that is present.

'SEEING' ALL

A point of worthy note here is that a portion of your consciousness sees everything… in fact, sees so much that it cannot dwell for any significant time upon one singular aspect, or two, or three, or four, or twenty. Rather, the first thing that creates a reaction within you is usually that upon which you will focus in the primary sense. All else becomes peripheral.

In the works which we will suggest for you for the forthcoming Earth weeks, there will be several that will be intended to point this out to you. Sort of like a master technician who is being shown how to manipulate the controls, the mechanisms, with which they shall do their masterful work.

Seeing from Spiritual Sight

Seeing from the physical, the emotive, and the mental, is, for the most part, at least, passively discussed in the comments given just above. Let us shift for a moment to spiritual sight.

Here, in a comparison to the physical sight and the emotive consciousness reaction to same, most entities will, for the greater number of such occurrences, respond according to their memory, to their emotion and, as given, react to that which is to the forefront of their emotion and thought. It comes to the forefront, because there is some (quote) "living connection" (end quote) between the stimulus of seeing that object, thing, person, or whatnot, and their collective consciousness or collective *un*consciousness.

In the spiritual sense, of course, many of you have vast potential of consciousness. Indeed, all of you have this as a potential. Some of you are working on these levels over here, others over there, some to the left or right, and so on and so forth. Some of you are applying yourselves broadly, some more specifically. Neither of these is good or bad. They simply are. And each of these has an important part to play in the overall perspective of *Seeing*.

Seeing More Deeply Through the Five Senses

Spirit can see through the eyes physical... this, of course, is a common reliance on those who close their physical eyes, go into meditation or prayer, or even dreaming, and strive to (quote) "see" (end quote). Some may need this in order to feel that they have been connected, that they have accomplished an intended work. Others, with some considerable wisdom, may also or instead of seeing, strive to feel. Let us move back to the Earth momentarily and take a look at the five physical senses. We've spoken of seeing and sight.

Think about hearing. If you hear a child cry, an image will likely come to you, feelings will come to you. And you will turn to look to see the source of that cry. If you are in a female body and have borne a child of your body, the reaction may be an instantaneous remembrance along with a collage or peripheral memories and, perhaps, emotions and even opportunities for further growth and discovery. If you are in a male body, you may have quite the same reactions and you may follow these into differing essences. All of this triggered through sound.

Supposing you are handed a fabric, a bit of cloth, and someone states, "Just close your eyes and rub this between your fingers. Isn't it wonderful? Feel its smoothness, the depth of the nap on the fibers, the closeness of the weave." And you might think for a moment of something in past where a similar fabric was felt. And you'll see that, you'll feel it. You may think of who could have done such a work. Perhaps there is counterpoint of colors and fabrics of various hues and such woven into it, and on and on.

You may remember yourself standing in a meadow at a time earlier in your life present, and feeling the garment you are wearing. So, at the same time as you have your eyes closed and doing the rather common act of simply feeling something tactilely, with your touch… you might also hear the sounds of that day remembered… you may smell the fragrance of the fresh flowers, or perhaps new-mown hay, or some fruits blooming in bushes or trees nearby… or the call of others, the sound of water, cascading. All of these, as sights, as images, as re-membrances, can be triggered by touching a simple piece of fabric or cloth.

Of course, the sense of smell is oft, by many, considered one of the most powerful. As one can remember an odor, a fragrance, or as one might come across this in daily life, if you happen to observe the entity to whom or to which this is occurring, you will surely notice a few moments where their eyes lose their focus. They seem to glaze over with a mist of recall. They seem to be gone for a few moments, as they have walked back into some past life occurrence and are briefly re-living it… the smell of an apple which has been picked from a low-hanging branch from Aunt Agnes's apple tree, the smell of berries as you might have gathered them in a basket or tin along with other members of your family as a child, the smell of a freshly baked loaf of bread, cooling in some corner of the kitchen, or a pie, baked with those freshly gathered berries, the smell of newness in something just re-cently created.

All of these things give you *sight*. You can taste something and remember, and the sight comes to you. And you look about and state, "This tastes just like as (so-and-so) used to prepare it." Or "This taste reminds me of this event."

EMPOWERED THROUGH SPIRITUAL SIGHT

Spiritual Sight goes beyond these. And in the sense universal, empowers you. For within the dominion (so to say) of the wondrous potential of expressions that you can choose when you are in spirit form, there is that which is called *universal oneness consciousness*. It is the consciousness which is a gift given of God. And just so, in our opening prayer and affirmation we called out, so might you, as well, in your meditations, do the same, or even greater.

Spiritual Seeing Is Boundless

The point here, as relates to the topic of *Seeing*, is that sight is, literally, unlimited.

Sight in the spiritual expression of your being goes so far beyond physical sight, which is dependent upon a mechanism of the physical, finite body (leaving aside for a moment that sight triggers memory, see).

Seeing from Spirit Simultaneously from the Physical

In spirit, as one becomes aware of their spirit form, the potential for movement into and out of experiences is vast. It is without the boundaries, the limitations, of what's called time. It is even, as one rises into the state of oneness, beyond the boundaries of an individual. So much so that as one claims this, moves into it, and opens the sight...mindful here that we are not speaking singularly of sight as known in the Earth, but the sight of feeling as another might feel, knowing as another might know, based upon their uniqueness.

It is good for you to recognize that your sight is unlimited. And even as you walk about in this day's journey and see, doing all those things that you do almost automatically based upon what you see and so forth, set those aside for a moment and think about Seeing from spirit simultaneously as from the physical.

EXERCISING SPIRITUAL SIGHT

So in the first Earth week, our suggestion, humbly given to you, is that you know your own Sight. When you awaken, ask in this way:

Here am I, O Father-Mother-God. Before I open my eyes to let my sight guide me through this day, I first open my spiritual Sight, that I shall be able to see that which lies beyond the common, the norm. So in this day, Father, guide me to see on multiple levels. Help me to see in the manner as I am accustomed, and help me to know this. Then, thereafter, guide Thou me to go beyond same in all that I do. Amen.

As you open your eyes and perceive the room about you, the walls, the ceiling, perhaps the out-of-doors through a window or such, recognize the instant sense of belonging, of familiarity. Then as you go about preparing for your day, notice how you look about, almost as though you are making certain that things are as you remember them. In a manner of speaking, you are defining. You are claiming. You are identifying. And much more. As you have passed through the earlier works, beginning with forgiveness, you have found this to impact your sight, all of your senses, and your memory, your emotions.

Now, in this and the next two forthcoming works, our encouragement shall be for you to build upon this.

Take a moment here and there all throughout the Earth day. Pause. Look about you. See what is there. Look for those things that perhaps you've never truly dwelled upon in past. Simple things… the legs on a chair, the color of a certain background object, the knobs on a bit of furniture or the absence of them. See and think in the sense of the reaction that this perceptive exercise brings about. All throughout the Earth day, recognize the fact, here and there, that you *are* seeing, and how much of your life is dependent upon that activity.

Physical/Spiritual Seeing Also Applies to the Blind

There are those who are without physical sight in the Earth, but they see – and we know that you see, dear friends, so we ask you to modify our comments accordingly – so the true sight goes beyond the physical mechanism. See?

As you conclude your Earth day, take time for meditation, either just previous to slumber or at any point after your day's activity has reached a point of calmness. Visually and emotively, in that order, go back to the beginning of the Earth day. Notice how you felt upon awakening. This may have been conditioned by the memory of a dream or vision, but for the most part, your state of being upon awakening has some consistent pattern. That's a reference point. Everything else after that became the fleshing-out of the body of that Earth day, so to say… what you did with it, how you felt, who you interacted with. Draw the memory, try to re-create the sight of these things, these events, and such, even if but briefly, in mind.

This is a powerful tool and, thus, a powerful exercise. And you can do this, as we'll point out for the second week just ahead, in ways to enrich this potential.

But for now, see how well you can remember visually and with the feelings associated with same, some greater, some lesser, according to the activities of this Earth day. See? Then, finally, ask:

> *Lord God, guide me to understand what I have seen*
> *and reacted to in this day. Thank You. Amen.*

Very simple, very straightforward, but foundationally power-ful. See?

In week two, open self as suits thee for the Earth day, remem-bering the just-previous week, but not dwelling on those activities as in past. We might pray in this way:

O Father-Mother-God, here I am, coming forth into this new Earth day of this journey through my life present. As I strive to know, to see, to claim, help me to open myself that I can perceive more broadly than ever be-fore, that each day's activities shall increase my per-ception many-fold-over. This is the prayer and the thought-form that I place before me as I go through this Earth day. I thank Thee, Father. Amen.

Similarly to the first week, you will undoubtedly re-trace your steps. As you do so, do it more lightly than in the first week. It shall have become somewhat of a familiar event or happenstance for you. But throughout the Earth day, we would encourage you to do this...

Pause at times of your choice (and we would encourage you to choose some certain times... perhaps something like each even-numbered hour of the Earth day, and perhaps fourteen Earth minutes thereafter) wherever you are, whatever you are doing, take just a few moments and look about you, and choose the most beautiful object or thing that is within your field of vision at that time. Study it. Absorb the thought of it. Feel it.

But most of all *see* it. Look at it carefully, and then close your eyes and see it, feel it, in mind and spirit. Repeat this several times, until you can re-create it, so to say, or let it be re-created in the mem-ory or in the consciousness of your being. Try to do this at least three or four times. More often, if you are so inclined, and that would be the better.

Then at the conclusion of the Earth day, as given just previ-ously, take time to quiet self. Offer a prayer of affirmation, and go back to those objects you have seen. See how well you can see them again. And if there are three, can you see all three? In your meditation or quietness can you, in effect, still feel them, know them, sense them? If you can focus on something that has a connection through any of the other senses, this could add potential to this experience. For the more viewpoints you have of a thing – using touch, sight, smell, taste, feel, these sorts of things – the more you know it. This we would do. And conclude that work with a prayer similar to the former one:

Lord God, open me. Guide me to know – of these things and these experiences – the greater potential of my Sight on all levels.

In week three, we would commence the day similarly, modifying according to that which suits thee. Now we would ask you to see living things. You could include in this, of course, the first obvious one... other individuals (people, as you call them); animals, birds, plants, trees; water would be included here, for we consider water a living thing.

Here again, try to absorb the essence of it, first with your sight, and now adding your feeling of it. How does this person feel to you to you? You know what you see. But what sort of feeling is associated? You may wish to open and close your eyes (if it doesn't make you look too odd to them) and try to feel. What is the signature of their feel, the essence of them?

Do this little addendum to this: Notice their fingers; do their fingers match what you feel? Look at their eyes; is what you feel visible in their eyes somehow? In the sight of their movement, do their actions have a feel that is unique to them?

Explore Your Sight in the Fullest Sense

In other words, explore your *sight*. See? If it be a plant, look at the leaves... are they thick or thin, smooth or fibrous, do they have follicles or is it shiny, are the edges pointed or round, are there many leaves on a single stem or one on each truncation? See? You needn't become fastidious about this (humor intended); just lightly explore. Think about what you are seeing – get the consciousness and the emotion and the memory and the sight all active simultaneously.

This actually is a work which could span several weeks easily, for what you have being offered here can enrich your lives... the breadth and depth, the tenure of it... dramatically. See?

Now we would look about, in the tradition of past works, in the greater sense of the world (as you call it) at large. The clouds, the sky, the symphonic blending of the force of nature, the interactive-ness of the peoples, animals, creatures that you have observed previously, with the environ about them. Notice what they are noticing. See what they are focused on. Notice which entities are noticing those things beautiful, and observe them for a moment, if possible, when they are. And note again that there is that perceptible shift that goes beyond the consciousness of Earth.

Physical Sight/Spiritual Sight

This is the doorway into *spiritual sight*. These things acquaint you with the sight of spirit. And as such, then, we would move into this work which should be a part of the entire period of this Earth month, or longer... if not indefinitely.

Sensing Through the Physical What Spirit Has to Offer

The connection, again, between the senses – those five defined as such in the Earth, and those which are of spiritual essence – is very profound. Seeing from the physical acquaints you with what is being interacted with. If you want to choose someone to do a service or a work for you, you can use these methods to bring all of these perceptions into your spirit consciousness. And here you can feel the essence of their harmony, or lack of same, with your intent.

Now the wonder, the beauty, of seeing from spirit *and* from the physical, in the collage of ways we've given just above, is that spirit, your spirit, is not apart from what we have called in the exploration of Self-capital *S* versus self-small *s*. By acknowledging all of these perceptive events and stimuli (including, of course, the fact that they are felt, as well) and then moving into spiritual consciousness brings you the potential to, in turn, feel, know, and sense with the five physical senses and the emotive self/the mental self, what spirit has to offer.

This is a clear pathway as one opens self, so that in the scenario, as we have given it, where you are trying to decide on someone to do a service and you have multiple choices, the first collection of sensory mechanism input (as called, using your current terminology), then bringing this into spirit, and just letting go... relaxing... being. All of this will work for you, more or less in the background. You don't need to pick each sensory input item up and turn it all about and examine it. Once you've moved into spirit, that will all be done for you. Your spirit has comprehended all of what your consciousness has perceived through all senses, through the emotive feeling, and such.

Intention of the Eternal Self

But spirit is not conditioned by the singular, often powerful, emotive association that can be stimulated through the five physical senses. Spirit knows of these. Spirit can acknowledge this, and then set it aside. And more or less float, move, allow yourself to be guided. For your intention has gone before this, and your desire will guide you.

The important thing here is to get the small self out of the way. Its work has been done well. And now let the eternal Self sense and feel.

When you do awaken, you may feel this in the center of your being, the pit of your stomach as it's called, the solar plexi or plexus. You may feel a rush of heat or coldness that is, for all practical purposes, profoundly evident on the dermal layers of your body and the follicles and such. You may have a lightness, perhaps concentrated in the head or sight, or throughout the whole body. You may hear a soft ringing or some other sound. You may feel as though you are rubbing something very coarse or something very smooth.

We cannot give here, in the general sense, the specifics of that which will be the mechanisms for each of you as individuals. However, if you would look to what you (quote) "feel" (end quote) that is universal, the manifestation of that feeling can vary. Most will feel, clearly, something positive, affirming… or nay. Most will feel some response in the physiological sense of your body. At this juncture you may have consciousness, knowledge, that you have your answer. In some instances, however, you may wish to take these resulting reactions or stimuli and go back to the spiritual Self. Go back to see, once again, with this new set of criterion to base this on. See?

Seeing Simultaneously Through a Past Life and the Current

For those of you who wish to step beyond, here is another work that has great potential value and can be explored, in terms of the desire to see (or to claim seeing) that is quite profound. If you have the memory of a past life, no matter to what degree, do all that we have just suggested, go into your spiritual Self, and go back to that past life. Think of yourself as being in that past body. Think of yourself opening your eyes of that past body, and look about you.

Some of you may have a great ease to so do, for a certain lifetime is quite familiar to you. If you do not find this of great ease, it is important to recognize that a focal point, some keying mechanism, triggering object, is very good to be the focal point as one opens their eyes in a past-life body. This, obviously, could be discussed to great breadth and depth, but we believe that what we have just given can be explored joyfully and with great humor. See? Then just do as best you can, and try to look back through the perception, the sight, of who and what you were in past, at the event current in this life. If it is a decision, something you are striving to equate, to determine which direction to go, See what that expression of self can perceive it as. See? Go back, and See it from then, as well as now.

Seeing Through Another's Sight

The next step in this takes you even further. And that is to choose an entity to which you have an affinity, for whom you have great love. They can be in your current life, of course. But you may find considerable revelation if you would choose someone beyond this life. Why not, for example, even though you may not know these entities consciously too well in the present (some loving humor here), think about how this would look through the eyes of Elizabeth[10], as seen through Jacob's eyes. What if Anna[11], the great teacher, were to be seeing this? How about Josie? Nicodemus, whose valiant efforts to save the Master are widely known? Perhaps Samuel? Perhaps Peter? If you can muster it and find the joy that should be present, how would our beloved Mary see in this event or situation? And perhaps, with profound joy, ask of the Master: "Let me see this through your Sight. Let me know this as you know it." See?

If you open yourself...and it will, no doubt, be a joyful experiment, not ignoring the potential to see through the eyes of others in your life... a friend, a neighbor, a colleague, your mate, a loved one, a child, an elderly entity, any, all of these...what is their sight? And how can it give you even greater blessing?

Seeing Through the Spiritual Self

Seeing is the power of one's spirit. The physical body is the extension of spirit. It is on a journey through this lifetime. During this journey, you have agreed to be called a certain name, to adopt the habitation of a certain physical form. You have chosen, to the greater or lesser degree, your paths, your activities, and your interactions in this life. Your spirit is using this vehicle to see.

If what we have just stated is of truth, then going to your spiritual Self provides you access to all that you have ever seen. And if you can move your spirit beyond finiteness, that it can dwell in Universal Consciousness (also called God Consciousness), then all that has ever been seen is offered to you as you choose to know it.

Those who are called sensitives, intuitives, psychics, mediums, clairvoyants, clairaudient, healers, all manner of practitioners whose works reach beyond the norm as defined in the Earth, have claimed some aspect of seeing from the level of spirit.

A healer sees, literally, through their healing mechanism. If

---

[10] Elizabeth – an individual featured in the PETER PROJECT
[11] Jacob, Anna, Josie, Nicodemus – some of the more well-known of the Essenes

that is their hands, then their hands do the seeing and the reacting. The hands become the instrument through which they know. Those who use the power of oneness to heal through prayer at a distance, or with the entity present, it matters not, are seeing through the connection afforded in the state of oneness; and their energies flow through same, unobstructed, to the destination. For, so as it is asked, so is it given. And as this one or many choose to give it, it is a living essence, and flows, unabated, through the channel of agreement between them.

There isn't a moment of your conscious existence in the Earth when you are not seeing completely. You are always seeing in the total sense. What we are encouraging you to do in this work is to know that. The exercises are for you to explore and define, ever expanding this, until you reach the spiritual form; and once you do, to release yourself in terms of finite expectation, and to claim infinite expectation. The simple action of seeing through another's perception (not just physical sight) opens this.

PARABLE: PERCEIVING

Once again, we have a small grouping of entities traveling through a land which is harsh, rugged. They know that there is a destination that is worthy of their journey, for they have been told of it by those in whom they believe ad they believe their words to be of truth.

As they journeyed along a small river, winding, cascading over barriers, boulders, obstacles, and night descended, one of the grouping states, "We must stop, for we can no longer see."

The leader of the grouping who knew that in a short time there would be harshness of the environment, perhaps so harsh that they could be imperiled. Since their journey and the destination to which they were traveling was long and great, he stated, "I shall guide. Follow me." And to each, he instructed to grasp the hem of the garment of the one in front, forming, as it were, more or less, a chain of individuals which could be seen to be weaving, reptile-like, along the bank of this craggy river.

The one who had requested to stop and to make camp was right behind the leader. And try as he might, he could see naught, for the night was heavy with cloud and darkness.

And yet, the one who led, with only a simple staff, moved easily through obstacles, seemingly knowing of them before they were met. Finally, the leader, satisfied that they had traveled to the extent of their capacity for that day, instructed to pause, to make camp, in an area that was very hostile. And he stated, "Over there is a great plateau. There we shall make our camp." But no one could see to which he gestured.

Finally, with a bit of irritation, the one who had wanted earlier to make camp, stated, "I shall not follow any further. I shall not look for this plateau you speak of. But right here, in the safety of what I know and can feel, I shall rest for the evening." Without another word, he slumped to the ground and propped himself up uncomfortably against the angular forces.

The leader said nothing but reached back to grab the hand of the one behind this one, and handed him the hem of his garment. Silently and without any spoken words (though many were thought, humor intended) he led them a short distance. And, striking that to make flame, created it, and soon a small fire was glowing, illuminating a beautiful outcropping, almost perfectly flat, with an overhang above it providing shelter.

And the glow of the campfire reached out to touch the one resting against the abusive rocks. Reluctantly, he turned and arose and came, climbing with some effort, for he had none to lead and some areas were in shadow. And rising, finally, upon the outcropping, rested, was handed warm food. He looked down, consuming his meal.

The leader was seated cross-legged before the flames, a gentle smile on his face, the flashing, flickering, multi-faceted colors of the flames illuminating him in a mystical way. Or was it that this illumination was from within him?

Finally, feeling some awkwardness, the one who had questioned the leader spoke softly. "Please forgive me for not believing or not trusting. I can only say that I was weary and fearful. And as oft as I have seen you do those things which I cannot, this time I believed it to be impossible. And thus, the memory of times past flooded in, and I questioned and doubted. But I have learned and grown, and I hope that I shall in future have greater faith. But tell me, how did you know these things?"

Stirring the fire casually and watching the sparks rise up, the leader turned to respond. "I did not see them. I knew them. I did not look and perceive what was before me. I asked of my spirit to guide me, and I trusted. My body became the instrument of my spiritual Self, and I allowed this because I have faith. As I walked, my feet were guided by my spirit's sight. And each step made my faith stronger as my foot found secure footing. Did I question? Did I doubt? Yes. I tell you, yes. When and how? The first step. After that, never again. For I tell you, if you ask and it is given, and what is given is firm and secure, why would you doubt that the greater shall follow?"

80C3

Step Seven: SEEING

You see, dear friends, one can ask and say, as we did in our opening prayer, "Lord God, where art Thou? Let me see Thee. Let me know Thee." And all the while, our Lord says to thee, *"Sweet Child, will you not look upon Me? Will you not know Me as I hold you in your journey? Will you not take My outstretched hand to pass through obstacle and challenge? For I am here, and My love for thee is great."*

Interwoven Truths

In the wisdom of the example given of this leader of this grouping, the journey is to meet that one called Jesus. And the one who travels here with his colleagues was honorably called Benjamin.

Benjamin came to be known as one of great faith, and the greater he asked and the greater he believed, so then, in truth, was the greater breadth and depth of his faith manifested in the Earth. Benjamin, in gentleness, healed many, for the Master said to him, *"Your spirit is pure. Go. Let Me be with you. In your time of faith, our hands shall rest upon one another. And the Father shall doeth the work through us together. This is My eternal pledge to you, Benjamin."* And so off he went, some with him.

Benjamin is in the Earth, even as we speak. And perhaps some of his followers, as well. Our point for reiterating this to you is simple... Much of what one sees, or is a part of the process of seeing, is dependent upon faith. And faith is the purging through forgiveness... the affirming through gratitude...the knowing, by recognizing that self is unified... to see through the eyes of truth... to be hopeful and expectant. And now, to see, because the way has been made passable through these earlier works, that your Sight has potential to be unlimited. (We did not say that Benjamin was in male body. "Just to stir the pot a bit," Zachary states here.)

Open and Unlimited

What is faith, after all, if not the reliance upon what one perceives or sees and knows to be good? Benjamin affirmed his faith and empowered it because of the very first step... that one step. Thereafter, he knew that if he were to ask, to open, and to see in the unlimited sense, it was always answered and given.

Is your sight open and unlimited? Or do you only see what you expect? Do you see that which brings you joy in the personal and emotive sense? Or do you see the contrast, the definition brought about through the variation of colors, tones, essences? Your sight is, in truth, unlimited. Do these things. And those which you are guided to do, as well, for these are not the only paths... just those which we offer, that you might begin the journey.

In our next meeting, we shall offer to you that which we believe will carry you even further. But for now, see with the heart, see with the mind, with the eyes, the touch, taste, smell, and feel.

When you've collected all that, go to your spirit Self and expand your sight magnificently.

We pray of Thee, O Father-Mother-God, that Thy Spirit's light ever be that power which opens these, the faithful, and we, as well, Father. For each effort, we know... where we ask, the greater is given. We thank Thee, Father...

...and all of you, dear friends – in these... the Earth and other realms beyond – for joining with us in this wonderful work of oneness.

Fare thee well, then, for the present, dear friends.

GUEST LECTURE: Samuel

Given July 4, 2000

LAMA SING: We are prepared to attempt to convey as best we can, if not completely, that which is Samuel's intent. He is a very beautiful entity to behold, seemingly timeless. And from his timelessness there is the air of age and wisdom, and yet the sparkle of joy and love of youthful hope. There is the unification of the Principles which are a part of same, which are just so beautiful. Being in his presence, makes one feel good. We shall commence...

SAMUEL: What do you believe in? Do you believe in your visions and your dreams? Do you believe in what your eyes tell you exist? Do you believe in the sounds that your ears hear? Do you trust the faculties of your taste, your smell, your touch? These are, after all, extensions of your capacity to perceive. Are these those upon which one can rely? Or can they be muted or dulled? Is it possible that any one, or all, of these (under some circumstances) can be led to believe differently than what is? These are not questions I present to you seeking answers, for they are, I should expect, self-apparent.

Let us, if we might, humbly turn to those lesser perceptions. When you dream, when you have the vision, is this the byproduct of something ingested? (As the humor and traditional commentary is so given to suggest in the Earth... perhaps the most common, a pickle.) Or is it possible that your dreams and visions are gifts to you, are means of communicating with other sensory mechanisms, just so as with sight and sound, taste and smell and touch. Can you not feel, and thus, see? Can you not can feel something, know something, and thus taste it, smell it, feel it? Isn't it possible for you to recall a memory, perhaps from your current life (or even, if you so are open, from a life beyond) and when you recall that memory, recreate the sensory activities – the visions, the literal image of your favorite dress, your special plaything, the sound of something beautiful at a unique point in childhood or elsewhere – and in that moment *be* there, literally living it, experiencing It, as though it lives on?

Perhaps a dream, or vision, is an offering of something not yet born. Or perhaps the offering of something long forgotten. Perhaps as you look into your dreams and visions (those which come to you uniquely, and those which you seek along pathways of meditation and or prayer), perhaps all these might be as real as you are willing to believe. Perhaps you can even create from them. Perhaps they're guiding you. Perhaps they *are* you.

What is the importance, if any, of offering of these humble thoughts to you in this wonderful gathering of all of you beautiful Children of God? It is not to hear my own words; I have heard them before... very often... and for a very long time [said with much humor]. It is to call out to you. Just as I yet live, and each moment of eternity brings to me greater and greater blessings... and to all of us here, greater and greater realizations; so do we come to recognize that we are all one.

And *if* we are all one, if a part of that oneness dwells in limitation, it would be like some portion of your body being injured... you would direct your attention to treat it, would you not? We give to you in the form of dream and vision. We give to you upon the spirit of God, *in God's Name*. And we give to you of ourselves, of our own beings, because we too are a part of the oneness... equal, beautiful, and unique.

If you trust what you see, then if you see in vision, or dream, will you not trust in this? If you trust in what you hear, smell, taste, and feel, couldn't you take a fortnight and take these senses (the five of them, and the greater ones) and go within and activate them in the eternal sense?

As I turn to look about at all these beautiful servants of the Light who have gathered in honor of this occasion, I bow to them all. No matter what their gifts, no matter what their uniqueness, they are giving *themselves*... the greatest that they have to give. And as I turn to look upon you – each of you, for I see you clearly – know this: If you would serve another, if you would reach out to touch and heal another as some of you have (and some of you have seen me standing with you in that work) so do I pledge to stand with you. But do not rely upon nor believe singularly in that which is outwardly perceived. For each knows this, too, shall pass in its time. But what is within you – and what you claim as your dream, your vision, that which you embrace and balance with in this lifetime – is yours forever.

So our message to you in this gathering is to be joyful. If there is any thing in your life which is not of joy, go beyond it, go above it, go through it, go around it... but do move on. For often, that which seems to be an obstacle is (as has been given by this wondrous group so often called the Lama Sing group) nothing more than a stepping-stone, seen from the wrong perspective.

The Christ is our Brother. He has left a path of light for those who would follow it. There are others, whose names are honored here, too numerous to state in this brief time remaining. But I speak for all here and in this moment:

We urge you to allow yourself to hear, to see, to know, and to recognize, that the dream and vision given to you is the wondrous potential of that which can be... if you believe.

My gratitude, love, and honor are the gifts I wish to leave with you.

And to these, who have permitted this opportunity... I am with you. To this group gathered... we who are beyond hallow you, and shall come as you would have us, joyfully, with all that we are.

I am called Samuel, but this is not of great consequence, only for your reference. Those of you who remember me, those of you at whose sides I have stood often in service to another, and those of you whom I taught in times long past and who are answering the call in the Earth in body physical once again... my love is always with you.

I bid you farewell, and the goodness of God's spirit within you. Claim it.

STUDY GUIDE

Weekly Activities for Applying Seeing

Week 1
Morning Activity
Here am I, O Father-Mother-God. Before I open my eyes to let my sight guide me through this day, I first open my spiritual sight, that I shall be able to see that which lies beyond the common, the norm. So in this day, Father, guide me to see on multiple levels. Help me to see in the manner as I am accustomed, and help me to know this. Then, thereafter, guide Thou me to go beyond same in all that I do. Amen.
As you open your eyes and perceive the room about you, recognize the instant sense of belonging, of familiarity. Then as you go about preparing for your day, notice how you look about, almost as though you are making certain that things are as you remember them. In a manner of speaking, you are defining, claiming.

Throughout the Day
Take a moment here and there to pause, look about you and see what is there. Look for those things that perhaps you've never truly dwelled upon in past – simple things - or the absence of them. See and think in the sense of the reaction that this perceptive exercise brings about. All throughout the Earth day, recognize the fact that you are seeing (using physical, mental and emotional elements), and how much of your life is dependent upon that activity.

Evening Activity
Take time for meditation, either just previous to slumber or at any point after your day's activity has reached a point of calmness. Visually and emotively, in that order, go back to the beginning of the Earth day. Notice how you felt upon awakening - for the most part, your state of being upon awakening has some consistent pattern. That's a reference point. Everything else after that became the fleshing-out of the body of that Earth day, so to say. What you did with it, how you felt, who you interacted with. Draw the memory, try to re-create the sight of these things, these events, and such, even if but briefly, in mind.

Then, finally, ask, *Lord God, guide me to understand what I have seen and reacted to in this day. Thank you. Amen.*

Week 2
Morning Activity
(Open self as suits thee for the day, remembering the previous week)
O Father-Mother-God, here I am, coming forth into this new Earth day of this journey through my life present. As I strive to know, to see, to claim, help me to open myself that I can perceive more broadly than ever before...that each day's activities shall increase my perception many-fold-over. This is the prayer and the thought form that I place before me as I go through this Earth day. I thank Thee, Father. Amen.

As you open your eyes and perceive the room about you, recognize the instant sense of belonging, of familiarity. Then as you go about preparing for your day, notice how you look about, almost as though you are making certain that things are as you re-member them. In a manner of speaking, you are defining, claiming.

Throughout the Day

Similarly to the first week, but more lightly, re-trace your steps. Pause at times of your choice, certain times, but try to do this three or four times in the day. Wherever you are, whatever you are doing, take just a few moments and look about you, and choose the most beautiful object or thing that is within your field of vision at that time. Study it. Absorb the thought of it. Feel it. But most of all, see it. Look at it carefully, and then close your eyes and see it, feel it, in mind and spirit. Repeat this several times, until you can re-create it, so to say, or let it be re-created in the memory or in the consciousness of your being.

Evening Activity

Take time to quiet self. Offer a prayer of affirmation, and go back to those objects you have seen. See how well you can see them again. And if there are three, can you see all three? Can you still feel them, know them, sense them? Can you recall it through any of the other senses?

Conclude with a prayer similar to: *Lord God, open me. Guide me to know, of these things and these experiences, the greater potential of my sight - on all levels.*

Week 3

Morning Activity

Open self, again, as suits you for the day. Offer your own prayer and meditation, considering the world at large, and your desire, your intent, to "see" it.

Throughout the Day

Look about at the clouds, the sky, the symphonic blending of the force of nature, the interactive-ness of the peoples, animals, creatures that you have observed previ-ously, with the environ about them. Notice which people are noticing those things beautiful, and observe them for a moment when they are. Take note of the percepti-ble shift that goes beyond the consciousness of Earth, when someone is noticing something beautiful. This is a clear pathway as one opens self, so that the first collec-tion of sensory mechanism input brings this into spirit. Your spirit has comprehended all of what your consciousness has perceived through all senses, through the emotive feeling, and such. The important thing here is to get the small self out of the way. Its work has been done well. And now let the eternal Self sense and feel.

Evening Activity

Take time to quiet self. Offer a prayer of affirmation, and recall an event. See how well you can perceive it again. What new perceptions do you get now, looking at them from a more total sense?

Conclude with a prayer of your own, perhaps offering thankfulness for what has begun opening, and the fullness of hope for what yet lies ahead.

Week 4
Morning Activity
Open self, again, as suits thee for the Earth day. Offer your own prayer and meditation claiming your ability to see in the fullness of every sense.

Throughout the Day
Repeat the exercises of the past three weeks, applying, particularly those that bring you the greatest joy and satisfaction.

OR: for those of you who wish to step beyond, if you are able to recall a past life - no matter to what degree...

Prepare yourself in the way most comfortable for you, offer your affirmations for the work and your intentions that lie ahead, go into your spiritual Self, and go back to that past life. Think of yourself as being in that past body. Think of yourself opening your eyes of that past body, and look about you. If you do not find this of great ease, recognize a focal point, some keying mechanism, triggering object, as you open your eyes in the past-life body. Then as best you can, try to look back through the perception, the sight, of who and what you were in past, at the event current in this life. If it is a decision, something you are striving to determine which direction to go, see what that expression of self can perceive it as. Go back, and see it from then, as well as now. As you are able to open yourself like this, begin directing this ability to seeing through the eyes of others in your life - a friend, a neighbor, a colleague, your mate, a loved one, a child, an elderly entity - any, all of these. What is their sight? And how can it give you even greater blessing?

Evening Activity
Take time to quiet self. Offer a prayer of thankfulness for the fullness of your sight.

Further Exploring Seeing

PONDER:
- A portion of your consciousness sees everything, but the first thing that creates a reaction within you is usually that upon which you will focus in the primary sense.
- Some strive to see when they close their physical eyes and go into meditation or prayer and may need this in order to feel that they have been connected, that they have accomplished an intended work. Others, with some considerable wisdom, may also ... or *instead of* seeing ... strive to feel.
- What is meant by "One of the values of learning to see in the broadest sense is knowing where you are at present"?
- How would a blind person, apply the differences given in this lesson between physical sight and spiritual sight?

Begin acknowledging all of the stimuli - sensing with the five physical senses and the emotive self, and the mental self - and then move into spiritual consciousness to feel and know in the more total sense, what Spirit has to offer.

JOURNAL

_____

_____

_____

_____

_____

_____

_____

_____

_____

_____

_____

_____

_____

_____

_____

_____

_____

_____

_____

_____

_____

Step 8:

Knowing

Given July 30, 2000

OPEN FORUM ON KNOWING

[Due to technical problems, the prayer was not recorded. Rather than re-record the prayer, Lama Sing opted to begin with the following affirmation.]

LAMA SING: As we commence herein, dear friends, this we would suggest to you:

Reach out in heart and mind and open yourself.

Claim the light of your spirit, which is ever at one with God.

And embrace yourself with the affirmation of your spirit's presence in all that you are and do.

Do affirm your oneness with that which is holy unto Thee. And as you do, know that same embraces you in return, for the affirmation of Oneness with God and all those who are in service unto God, is to empower self unto every need.

UNDERSTANDING THE TERM 'KNOWING'

We have encouraged you to expand your sight. We have suggested that you do so in varying ways and on a schedule which has become somewhat of a tradition for these works (in other words, weekly).

In this new work which builds very importantly upon the just previous work – and, indeed, all that which has gone before – we should like to change the venue, the schedule, somewhat here. For this is a work which does not have separateness, in the sense of some of the previous works which lend themselves much moreso to strata, layers, and a progression of steps.

The topic here is *Knowing*. It is a topic which is very powerful.

As one hears that title, Knowing, the first reaction may be that one does (quote) "know, knowing" (end quote)… some humor intended here. But what our prayer shall be for this work, is to explore with you and to offer works for you that will take you into reaches distant from those, which in fact you do know.

Intimacy with a Subject

Let us begin here with just a recapitulation (we believe is your word) of the term *knowing*.

To know something is to claim intimacy with it. For the most part, it is suggestive of a very profound intimacy. Even Biblically you will find the use of the word *know, knew, knowing* and such, to be self-evident to imply very significant intimacy.

Here, in your daily life upon the Earth, you know things for the most part through the process of experiencing them, living them, and working your way through them.

In a general sense, those things which you know most profoundly have, for the most part, had profound impact upon you. That impact usually is of some emotive nature, for while mind is the builder/spirit the pattern, emotion is the substance, or at least *a* substance of which mind can build with considerable force and rapidity.

So *knowing* is, in the Earth, to say to someone that you have had an intimate interaction with that topic.

Deep Connections Through Knowing an Experience

How often have you heard yourself, or others, respond when someone is describing a significant event in their life, perhaps a challenge, perhaps a personal loss, perhaps some opportunity which is profound, perhaps a gift. If someone states to you they lament the loss of a certain entity and the pain is great, you will probably, if you have any tenure in the Earth at all, have experienced this yourself, thus you *know* it. And so you respond, "I know." True?

And in that moment, you might have a flashback to when you have lost someone who was dear to you. And from that moment forward, don't you have a bond of sorts with the entity who is currently grieving? Of course you do. And they look at you and they can see from the empathy, the compassion in your eyes, that you do indeed know. And you might embrace that entity in those moments, and you have bonded, in a sense of knowing. The bond is not necessarily physical, though it can be. But the coming together makes a connection, just as the words and thoughts also make a connection. Make a little note of this, as just given, for it will be important as we proceed, and as you journey through the experience of Knowing in the Earth month ahead.

These are bonds, bonds of light, bonds of affinity in terms of emotional experience, and all that sort; but they are also a bond of knowing.

Passive Bonds with Others Through Their Skill

Let us shift, then, from this to the casual use of this word. You might say, if you are a parent, to your child, "Do you know your homework? Do you know the material for your examination?" Someone might observe a skilled artisan, whether they be a stone mason, an artist with oils or canvas, music, dance, song, anything. And you have a colloquial term, "that entity truly knows their stuff". The knowing implies a great affinity and skill, with the talent being demonstrated, does it not?

The knowing, as you console a friend or a family member or what not, who has just endured a personal loss of someone who has crossed over, is a little different. That knowing is a bond, which can be shared.

When you look at the artisan who truly knows what they are doing, and they have a great knowing of their skills, you are now looking at something which may join you at arms length. You admire their work and therefore there is a subtle passive bond, but distant. See? You could say that it is moreso an affinity, shared between you both, for creativeness. But you may or may not know the artisan. You may or may not know the stonemason, and so on and so forth.

Now in mid-stream, between these two, we shall call them *peripheral* expressions of knowing, one is very personal and intense, the other is more distant.

Here, we might have someone who you encounter in daily life, not a family member, perhaps not even a friend, someone who serves. Remember our work in that area? And you thank them for their service, whatever it might be. But this is on a personal level, for they have served you, specifically.

In the moments which follow, as was in our earlier works of this nature, you might well look at one another. Even if you do not, there is a connection here – there is the giver and receiver and the affirmation of the receipt and the acknowledgment. Remember? "Thank you." "You are welcome." This completes a bond. There is the knowing between you that something has been exchanged that is good. And you acknowledge the knowing.

Now the intimacy of the first example stands at one peripheral point. And the admiration for a creative work, with the potential that neither artist nor yourself know each other, stands at the opposite. And here we have defined a midpoint, where there may be a moment of personal interaction, perhaps even a brief intimacy, though on a different level than the bereaved and yourself to be sure.

Various Depths of Knowing

Now we would like to suggest to you that you examine this. You do not have to use the scale, the points of demarcation we have used; we have given them for example. But we do encourage you to define a scale that you can order things, perhaps calling the mid-point 0, and the left +10, and the right, why not make it +10 as well, or −10, whatever is clear to you. See? You can use left and right, but just make a scale, see? It's a horizontal scale.

You move all throughout your Earth day to varying points on this scale. You may move from the mid-point, or median, which is the 0 point, balance between +10 and −10, if we were to use those points of demarcation.

The exercise here is: where are *you* on this? Do you know *yourself*? For in order to truly see, in order to truly know what you see, it is important for you to know what you know about yourself.

Now let us approach this from a different perspective, so that this is very clear…

A musician might have a pitch pipe; a piano tuner has tuning forks. They use these for reference, because the pitch, the vibrational frequency, is known and does not vary, especially, or exceptionally so, with the tuning fork. So the piano tuner might pluck a key, simultaneously striking the tuning fork, and evaluate what direction the adjustment should be on the piano string… towards the -10 or towards the $+10$. In other words, increase the tension or decrease it.

Knowing Self Is a Reference for Knowing All Else

When you *know* yourself, when you know what you know about yourself, you are given an instrument that is like the tuning fork for the piano tuner, like the pitch pipe for the vocalist, and on and on.

A reference point, which is the knowing of self, enables the understanding of what is seen. As you process your daily experiences, gathering up, so to say, a variety of stimuli input to your mind, what you know to that point in your life is what you are going to reference that stimuli against. This knowing then becomes the mirror – the reflective apparati, so to say – which then gives you your definition and understanding. Doesn't it? Of course.

What you feel, taste, smell, sense, see, hear, all of this is just, in your nomenclature of the Earth, raw data. Putting it all together in mind is, essentially, instantaneous. Processing it against what you know at that point… what you've experienced, what your emotions have been… is then the collage, or backdrop, from which you will select your thoughts, your actions.

You might want to re-listen to that several times… for it, too, is important.

Receptivity Expands the Depth of Knowing

Your life then becomes a reflection of what you know. Your experiences in life are continually offering you more knowledge, more knowing, more intimacy. And so you take these things, without truly thinking about knowing, all throughout each Earth day; and they become a part of you, including emotions, including rational thinking, and including, of course, learning and knowing from the experiences of others.

Now as we move into this, we expand knowing considerably. If we are open and receptive, if we are observing, if we listen, we can know much more.

OPPORTUNITIES TO EXPAND KNOWING

We can begin to know through the eyes and experiences of others. Just like at the onset above, your bond with the entity who is grieving over the loss of someone is multi-leveled, multi-faceted. Here, in the experiences, generally speaking, with entities whom you may or may not know (as in the −10 example, see) and those who serve you directly at the 0 point, are all opportunities to expand your knowing.

There are those traditions in the Earth, and teachings which center… which give as their *pillar of righteousness*, so to say… the primary support of their entire doctrine is based upon knowing. In many of the Eastern traditions, knowing is the ultimate. And some entities dedicate the majority, and even the entirety, of their life in a quest to know.

Knowing Expands God's Blessings Beyond Self

Knowing augments all else. In order to forgive, you must know what it is you are forgiving. For true forgiveness cannot simply be spoken as words; true forgiveness must come from *knowing* what is being forgiven. True?

Gratitude is an expression of claiming, of empowering oneself, by cementing the connection between the source and the recipient. Here, knowing is paramount. For if one does not know, it is difficult to truly have gratitude, is it not? Of course, one can have an attitude of gratitude all throughout daily life, and this is empowering. And it is essentially contributive, in a very similar way… with this distinction, to be noteworthy, a general attitude of gratitude, and stating,

Father, I am grateful for all that Thou art and have given unto me.

That is a wonderful prayer. It is a wonderful affirmation. It is a very fine demonstration of gratitude.

But if you know that you have received a very special gift in your life and you state an addendum to what was given just above,

And Father, I am so grateful and thankful for this special blessing, of this person, in my life. Thank You, Father.

In the knowing that that person is special in your life, and the affirmation and gratitude for that person's presence, you have here again rekindled the path of light between you. And you have empowered yourself, or claimed, sustaining and opening even moreso, the flow of God's blessings to both of you.

So now we have a specific expression of gratitude which comes about through the empowerment gained by knowing.

Knowing the Power of Being a Child of God

Back to you again for a moment. What do you know about yourself? Do you know what your blessings are? Do you know which areas of your life you would like more empowerment in? See?

Let us step for a moment, even further, beyond these two primary levels of knowing.

There is the knowing in the spiritual sense. There is the knowing, as we gave it, mentally, that a certain thing is so in the Earth and agreed upon, and that is so because it is agreed upon.

In the spiritual sense, the same is true. Two or more entities can gather and build a thought-form. Each can contribute to it from their uniqueness. Each can agree to the other's thoughts or ideas. And that thought-form is now their reality. The more they empower that thought, the more powerful is it. The more they know that thought, and know that one another know the thought, the greater is its power.

Knowing that you are a Child of God is to open yourself to *being* a Child of God.

Knowing the Power of a Group of Children of God

When two or four or twenty of you come together, and know that you are Children of God, the empowerment to all involved is amplified, greater than the number of participants. This we have given in past, oft times. When you know of a need among your grouping and you offer prayer unto anyone who is a part of that grouping, all of the entities in that grouping are contributing their prayer to the one in need... *all* of them, even if they do not consciously know of the need.

Example. You have a prayer group[12], which is blessed by our

---

[12] Prayer Group - The Watch is a prayer group with worldwide members offering prayers on behalf of thousands of people, resulting in countless miracles. For years, it was lovingly coordinated and watched over by Gisela Moeller, who sent out prayer requests to The Watch on a daily basis. The Watch continues to this day, but in 2007, Gisela made her transition, and the torch of her watch was passed.

dear friend Gisela. When a prayer message comes out from she, or perhaps one of her alternatives, you might read it today. Someone else may be journeying somewhere and have no access and not read it until a day or two later. Some may not have the opportunity to read it at all. But if you have agreed to be with one another in this work, and you *know* it, that knowing is a path for your prayer to continually flow to any need.

Now, here is a work for you. When you next hear of a request for prayer, know that you are empowered to offer the prayer of your entire group. *Know* it.

A beautiful work was done and is now completed, and we shall speak to it in times ahead, where simple little swatches of colored cloth were sent about for each entity in the grouping dedicated to prayer for others. And now each in that grouping has a bit of this cloth, which has been held by all others, and everyone knows it. If there is a need which does not come to the grouping, and our sister Gisela has not sent it to you, you can still employ the power of your entire grouping, because you know that you are one with them, and the cloth symbolizes this. But again, more shall be given on this in future. Our point here is to illustrate knowing.

KNOWING THE FULLNESS OF YOUR POTENTIAL

You know that you are born into the Earth in physical body. You also know that you shall lay the body aside, and resume your journey elsewhere. These things you know. This knowledge you share universally upon your sphere of Earth. So you could say, very clearly, that all know this.

Latent Knowing/Eternal Knowing

Now here's a distinction, which we hope to make very clear to you: that you can know something and not acknowledge it; that you can know many things and ignore them. That there are those forces which will, by their nature – through habit or whatnot, the dictums of the Earth, tradition, and all such – turn your head, so to say... that you don't acknowledge what you know. You've all heard entities state, with hopefully humorous frustration, "How many times do I have to learn this lesson before I know it." See?

In the Earth there are those events which appear to be paramount. There are those events which clearly seem to preclude Knowing in the eternal sense. So that birth and transition (or, as you call it, *death* in the Earth) are not given a lot of thought, nor are they intended to be except when it is appropriate. So you could call this a passive knowing. You could call this a knowing which is latent, but it is there and it is known by all. This would probably go beyond a –10 on that scale, which means quite clearly, that there must be something which counterpoints that and goes beyond a +10 on the other side of the scale. And there is – that is your eternal Knowing.

Eternal Knowing is the claiming of the sum and substance of your soul's experiences to the current point.

Universal Consciousness Knowing

You can even go beyond this and know beyond your own experiences. You can know from the experiences of others, collectively, spiritually, eternally. You can now from Universal Consciousness. So the point here is, there is actually an expanse through Knowing that is perhaps almost incomprehensible to most entities whom you would meet upon your byways, upon your journeys in daily life.

So what's the point of all of this? It is quite simply, that as you take information, experiences, subtleties, the sensory input, the dreams, the meditations, and on and on, and you process these, inwardly, and you learn from them, and you know them, these can lift you up. These can bring you greater and greater potential (power, if you will) to claim, to know, and *be* to the fullness of your spirit's potential. To know a thing is to be one with it. To know an entity is to have been one with them, on some level. To know an emotion is to have experienced it and have, thusly, been one with it. The harvest of knowledge comes to you as you apply it. Knowing is the processing of experience. And you can carry this to become wisdom. See?

We might suggest that as you awaken each morning and all throughout this Earth month, this simple prayer might precede your Earth day:

Lord God, help me in this day to better now Thee. Help me to know the way. Help me to know, through my senses, through the words and deeds and energies of others, to better know. Help this knowledge to move into wisdom, that from wisdom, I might act. Thank You, Father. Amen.

Throughout the Earth day, pause here and there. Close your eyes, and just state these words: *I know.* You will feel them. You will feel the after effect of energy moving all throughout you.

I know. Of course you know. You are a Child of God. If you claim it, you can know that which is unto your need; and if you are willing... beyond this. Often state, *I know.*

KNOW AND ACKNOWLEDGE THE GIFT OF OTHERS

When you take food into your body during that Earth day, each Earth day, think this. Close your eyes a moment, and think these words: *I know the many loving hands that have labored to bring this unto my need.* See?

What have you just done? You have gifted them. You have recognized their gift to you. They may not even think about it; it's just a job to them... but not all of them. See? And even those who don't think about it will feel the impact, the energy, of your knowing.

If you see someone on the byway, or street, as you call it, and you can see evidentially that they have a need, take the seeing into yourself and think this: *I know your need.* Think about it. The entity may not have anyone else. But now they do... they have you. *I know your need. Here's my gift of prayer.*

Knowing is the Bond

See? Knowing makes the connection.

You have a custom in the Earth, which is in many countries and traditions, to clasp one another's hand when you meet someone anew. In that moment you know them... perhaps not well, perhaps only cursively. But you do know them. In this process, the knowing comes from having felt their energies, held their hand, looked into their face, their eyes. And now you know them.

You might, several of you, refer to an entity and state, "I've heard of them but I don't know them." In fact you may have heard a great deal about them. Perhaps their works are of some renown like the artist on the −10 scale. See? But even here, as you might know someone for no particularly outstanding artistic accomplishment, no labor of particular achievement, you know them. And that is another bond, which falls somewhere on that scale. And it's important for you to define that scale, and to also associate it with yourself.

When you felt the compassion and you brought forth the memories of your own experiences, when consoling the one who has just had a loss of a loved one, you are connecting all that together. The energies involved here can flow freely, insofar as all involved know it.

Knowing Makes Healing Possible

The Master walked about through the Earth and healed entities that came to Him, because He knows the Law. Knowing, He asked them, *"Do you believe?"* In other words, *Do you know that I can heal you? Or that through me, your healing will be given?*

Yes. I do know this. I do believe. And so they are healed.

Think about this. Don't just hear the words and let them pass. Think about the many ways of empowerment that are yours, lying before you as you walk through daily life.

Knowing Makes the Journey Flow

We know an entity who created a work of art, thinking that the work of art was intended to bring entities into a greater attunement with that artistic work's focus. But in the process, the work of art took *her* into the process. And she found the Path, and walked upon it. She did this because she knew the need. She did this because she saw the truth. She felt, experienced, heard, knew and became a part of that knowing and the works flowed through her as well as to her. And she moved with the knowledge, with the knowing and journeyed upon it.

So then, here is our suggestion for eveningtide:

Lord God, as I come into this time of rest and oneness with Thee, I affirm that which I know. Take me into Thy knowing and gift me with Thy wisdom. Help me to know, to see, to claim. Help me to know my greater Self, and Earthly self. Help me to know truth... mine and others.

In all of this, see, you are asking to know.

So again, in this way, more concisely this time:

Lord God, as I come into oneness with Thee during sleep, help me to know as Thou knoweth. I bring my knowledge from the Earth and I place it upon Thine altar. See it. Awaken me to it, and guide Thou me unto Thy wisdom. Amen.

IN SERVICE

Knowing is a part of the purpose for being in the Earth. The souls come to the Earth and indeed petition to enter therein, that they might know it. Souls come to the Earth, that they might come to know themselves. Souls move from the infinite into the most finite of expressions, that they might know themselves and others from this perspective.

Knowing the Purpose and Truth of Others

When someone asks of you a certain thing, do you know them? Or do you merely process the words, evaluate the request, and then respond according to what you think is best? But do you know them? Do you know why the request comes to you? Certainly there is the outward knowing. But what is the inner knowing?

When someone is attempting to explain to you, to give you their understanding or their position on a certain topic, do you open yourself to know their position? Or at the opening commentary, have you simply shifted to your position, and merely wait for them to finish speaking out of courtesy?

Knowing another's position, Knowing another's emotion and perceptions does not mean that you must embrace them. To the contrary, often you should not. But to know them, to see them, to understand them, progresses you. If you deny all these opportunities in daily life, then your growth for that Earth day is just that, your growth. And your growth could be accomplished without external stimuli, without the finiteness, without interaction with others, couldn't it?

So you could leave your physical body, move to a beautiful realm of choice, dwell there and simply know yourself, much as in many Eastern philosophies is done in the Earth. Of course you can do this. But you are in the Earth, surrounded by a myriad of opportunity to Know, much more rapidly, much more completely. (No disrespect to those who follow the path of inner knowing. *Please*. For both are equal. But it depends so much upon the individual and their dedication, to follow that path in what we have, categorically, called Eastern teachings.) You can do both in fact. And that is very empowering.

But the point here is, you are in the Earth, surrounded with this collage of wonderful *tuning forks of opportunity*. Remember the piano tuner… strike the fork, and listen to the string's vibration… *Do I need to move a bit to the left on the scale, or to the right?*

Knowing Self Through the Reflection of Others

Isn't everyone you are meeting in daily life, every event, and every situation like that? A looking glass… (this we have given often) the mirror of what one sees in others may be just that… a reflection.

All that is in the Earth is offered to you always. The degree to which you have a certain thing or a certain way of life in the Earth has to do with your willingness to claim it. In that work which we performed with groupings in past, called *Abundance*, we looked at all these things. We asked the group to look within themselves and ask, *Am I truly willing to receive abundance, or are there some reasons that I am holding, that are preventing me from being abundant?* And there were, for many. And many changed these, and their lives changed accordingly.

You have an abundance in life itself, to perceive, to see, to know, to experience and know the truths of others. You have the power to set people free, through gratitude, through forgiveness. If you can see another entity's truth, you may be more likely to be able to forgive them than if you are just trying to forgive them from an emotive level or superficial point.

As you examine, after hearing this work... what's going on in your daily life, who are you interacting with, what is it that they are offering to you in terms of discovering yourself? If an entity chastises you or states that they are not pleased with your work or anything, it is an opportunity to know yourself. It is, of course, an opportunity to know the quality of your work through the eyes of another. But that is not at all the point here. Do you know the entity who is chastising? Or are you simply reacting to the emotive content of the event? Of course, that is to be anticipated. But knowing the entity who chastises you, as much as you would see to know the entity who loves you, gives you polarity... gives you a definition of who and what you are, through a reflection of who and what others are.

PARABLE: OPENING

There was once was an entity who did live in an Eastern land and who was quite a skilled artisan, a wood carver actually, and for many, many years did fine works, and gained some reputation of renown. Entities would come unto him and state, "Your craft is superb. Your knowledge of the flow of the grain of the wood, and your sense of knowing how to create in harmony with the wood, is masterful."

The entity would simply nod, but inwardly he knew... he knew that this was a talent, an ability. And he knew that he could feel the flow of the creation which was to be simply by holding the wood, pressing it, touching it, *knowing* it. See?

Then, there came an entity who was representative of one of

extreme power... indeed, such power so as to be able to have considerable impact upon the life and well-being of the woodcarver. The emissary stated, "My master wishes to commission you to do this work." And unrolling a lengthy scroll, there was a beautiful, ornate headpiece to be mounted over the portal to his private chamber. It was glorious. The emissary looked pensively at the woodcarver, and down at the scroll and the sketch of the work of art to be commissioned. "My master asks me to ask you, do you know that you can do it?"

The woodcarver, studying carefully, finally looks up and states, "I know I can do it".

The emissary smiles and states, "I shall return. I am to convey this message to my master."

A day or two passes and the emissary once again presents himself to the woodcarver, and states, "Here is all that is for your need, and greater. My master states this should tide you, and provide you with all your needs until this commission is completed. He states to you, 'Do no other work until this work is complete.'"

The emissary summons two bearers, who bring great wealth and place it before the woodcarver, who is simply in awe of what is being given to him. "Now," the emissary states, "you know you can do this. True?"

"Yes," the woodcarver states from a bit of a dazed state, for he has just become wealthy.

"Good. Then this area here," having taken a wand (a saplet actually) and is pointing at the sketch, which is now rich with color, "here, this should blend. And my master wishes these colors, and here," and on and on.

All the while the woodcarver is standing, mouth agape.

The emissary finally looks up and states, "Very well. I shall take my leave of you. But we shall have emissaries confer with you from time to time, to determine your completion date."

And the emissary turns to leave, but the woodcarver states in a stammering voice, "Wait. You do not understand. I am a woodcarver. I am not a painter."

The emissary stops, without turning about, his back to the woodcarver. "You have told me that you knew you could do the work. I repeated this to you, and you reaffirmed it. And I told you I would tell my master, which I did. Now, what shall I tell my master? I tell you, he will be filled with rage."

The woodcarver is getting distraught. And there is silence.

And the emissary states, "Do you know you cannot place the color upon your work?"

"No," comments the woodcarver. "But I know I haven't tried."

The emissary turns about, looking very stern, and states,

"Then if you have not tried, how do you know you cannot?" And he turns and departs.

How do you, dear friends, know that you cannot do a certain thing, if you have not put forth an effort to do it?

How do you know that your prayer won't make a difference? Do you *know* that your prayer heals, or nay? Do you think your prayer is a good thing, but it has only *this* degree of power? Where would you place your prayer power on that scale of −10 to +10? Where would you place your spiritual progression? Where would you place your joy? Do you *know* your joy? Do you know the joy of others for whom you care? Do you affirm what you know, and empower yourself to meet that, and go beyond?

For months the woodcarver toiled, all the while grieving that his very life might depend upon the completion of the work as commissioned... now, with color.

And because of this, each great piece of wood that he began, fell prey to some flaw, some mis-stroke of his cutting implement. And again and again, he commissioned others to find a certain block of wood, a timber actually, and he labored and labored. Notice, this is an entity who is renowned for his skilled talents in woodcarving. And now, three attempts... all failures.

His mind is focused; his heart is heavy on those things he believes he cannot do. And because of this, those things which he previously did with excellence, neither can he do these.

Think, dear friends... if your disbelief of a thing is powerful enough, how far does its shadow reach into you, and occlude your other potentials?

On the fourth attempt, the woodcarver, careful, finally began to evolve a work which was every bit worthy of the sketch, the artwork. And finally, the carving was done, and he sat and looked at it for days... sometimes weeping, sometimes angry, sometimes frustrated. The gamut of emotion passed through him. But never once did he pick up paint and brush, for he knew he had never done this before. Therefore, it must be that he cannot.

He went out into his little village and wandered, very sad. And he passed by a young entity, who was, of all things, painting a scene before him... odd little containers, strange-smelling and looking pigments. But the work of this young entity was beautiful to behold. You can anticipate what transpires.

So the young artisan came, and studying the wood said, "I can do that for you."

And the woodcarver stated, "Are you sure? Are you certain? I have labored heavily for long, long days, weeks, months to produce this. You could ruin it within a stroke, or whatnot."

The young entity simply looked at him and finally said, "I know I can do it."

And so he did. And the work was finished and the great leader was joyful and all went on through their lives with abundance.

But the woodcarver still does not know if he can paint.

ഇ൦൩

OPEN TO UNIVERSAL CONSCIOUSNESS

Can you *paint*, dear friends? Or is your woodcarving talent obscuring your exploration of your other potentials? Or would the shadow of dominance of this man of great authority have precluded and caused you fear, and so you wouldn't have even tried?

It is not to minimize the excellence of the woodcarver's talents. It is to point out that it was his spirit in that work. And we are certain that, had he tried, he could have done a magnificent work.

If you are as a woodcarver, who calls upon someone else because you believe their talents, their abilities to be greater than yours, this could be thought of as cooperation, of harmony, of working together. But do not do this because you are afraid... because you have not explored your potential to the greatest possible depths.

That painter will never carve a block of wood. Do you know why? He has no interest. No one will ever ask him to, perhaps. But if someone does, don't you wonder what he'll say?

Open or Pre-Adjudged Potential

If you wonder about that, then ask yourself this question, "Have I allowed myself to know the breadth and depth of my potentials, or have I so pre-adjudged these that they cannot flow? Have I turned away those who have come to me with a need or a request because I do not know myself?"

Lord, God, help me to know myself. Help me, as I slumber, to claim Thy knowledge. And let me combine these into wisdom.

The Ultimate Measuring Rod

The Master knew that one of His disciples was sleeping against a tree and in telling this disciple, impressed him. "Lord, how did you know this?" And the Master merely smiled, and said, *"I Saw you."*

You've worked on seeing. Now, take what you've seen, and know it. But know yourself, for you are ever the reference point, see, against which you shall measure all in this life.

Look to the past – in this life and beyond – and your knowing will be expanded considerably.

Again, listen, observe, and hear from others who are in your daily life. And you can know them, and you can know yourself.

Oneness with Consciousness

What is *knowing*? It is a spiritual state of oneness with your consciousness, so powerful that you are able to see the consciousness of others and know that as well.

In order for one to have wisdom, as the Master, one must be able to see and snow.

We thank you, dear friends, for this opportunity. You have come far in your works. There is no rigidity intended in this topic, for to know is to be open.

To become one who knows, is to become one who has opened themselves to experience… from themselves, from others, from life itself, from ideals, purposes and goals, from works, from past lives, and from Universal Consciousness.

Knowing builds upon Universal Law. If you know the Law, and know the events and circumstances, know your desires and needs and the same for others, then all of this combines itself into wondrous empowerment. Open yourself to know, and you are following in the footprints of the Master Himself.

We are through here for the present. May the grace and blessings of our Father's wisdom ever be that lamp to guide your footsteps.

Fare thee well then, for the present, dear friends.

GUEST LECTURE: Sophie

Given August 3, 2000

SOPHIE: I greet you all from the openness of my heart and spirit. May your days be filled with joy and wonderful opportunities of service.

As you travel along the pathway called life, you are continually brought before numerous crossroads. Indeed, in each day's journey, there are crossroads of the mind, of the heart, of the spirit, and of course, of the body. So many of these come and go, for the most part, scarcely noticed.

It is wonderful for one to take time here and there, to be aware of the many small choices that are made in each day's journey. As you do this, you become more and more aware that many small events in your daily life are opportunities for you to strengthen your spiritual intent, your ideal. For as you see these small choices, you empower yourselves to apply your spiritual truth in making the decisions.

It is true that perhaps your choices will change very little… perhaps not all. But what you are doing is claiming the power of these decisions, rather than relegating them to the subtleties or influences of Life itself. This is *knowing*. And you are working upon this topic in your current lunar cycle. But this small facet of your life's activities can be very significant.

In conjunction with this, recognize too that in the little things, the small events, the chance encounters, you have an opportunity to bear a gift to each of these; as you know these and see them, you can then *choose* to give your gift unto it. You might never do this in any tangible way… then again you might. But the objective here is to know of the opportunity and to *intend* – with your spirit, your mind, and your heart – to give the gift that is your uniqueness to give.

The splendor of potential in each step of one's journey cannot be underestimated. And yet so many move throughout each day of their journey, in Earth and elsewhere, with rarely a moment's pause to observe such subtleties. But these are as the grains of sand mixed into the water of time, and are that which bind together the greater events that you do note and that you do have reaction to. It is this mortar of knowing, in the moment-to-moment journey of your soul in Earth in this body that can be of such power, such magnificence so as to enable you to do all things. The strengthening of self comes through these small, continual, repetitive opportunities to use, to exercise, to explore, and to know.

And thus our gift to you, in this wonderful opportunity to speak with you all, is that we shall be with you in those works… so as you ask, and so as the Father grants us that great blessing, we, or others who continually walk with you, are at the ready to help you.

But remember:

A few moments can change one's life. A few moments can change the lives of others. It is the perceiver who claims those moments, and strips away the boundaries which contain them into mere moments, that they might flow and undulate, ebbing all throughout the lives of many, as a ship upon a great sea. Bearing what to them? You and your gifts.

We thank you for this opportunity to bring you this message.

I have been part of these works in past, the preparation of the Way. And it brings a song to my spirit's being to be with you in this work once again. As I look upon you, I know many of you very warmly, for your image is in my heart and ever shall be.

And the others of you, I see your spirit's light, and how pure it is as you come forward seeking to know yourself and to be one with the flow of God's light as it moves into the Earth now.

I was called Sophie and my favorite blessing is:
May the beauty of your own being so shine forth that your path is ever illuminated by it.

My love… *our* love… to you all.
Fare thee well then.

STUDY GUIDE

Activities for Applying Knowing

Morning Activity

Lord, God. Help me in this day to better know Thee. Help me to know the Way. Help me to know, through my senses, through the words and deeds and energies of others, to better know. Help this knowleage to move into wisdom. That from wisdom, I might act. Thank You, Father. Amen.

Evening Activity

Lord God, as I come into this time of rest and Oneness with Thee, I affirm that which I know. Take me into Thy knowing and gift me with Thy wisdom. Help me to know as Thou knoweth Help me to Know, to See, to Claim. Help me to know my greater Self, and Earthly self. Help me to know Truth - mine and others. I bring my knowledge from the Earth and I place it upon Thine altar. See it. Awaken me to it, and guide Thou me unto Thy wisdom. Amen.

Know your desires and needs. Know your joys, and those things for which/whom you are appreciative.

Define a scale for KNOWING that resonates for you. Begin placing people, experiences, your understanding, etc, somewhere on that scale of plus and minus.
Consider the worth and power of your prayer. Where, on your scale of Knowing, do you place it?
Where do you place your spiritual progression?
Where do you place your joys? Forgiveness, Gratitude, Hope-fullness, Truth, Self, Faith, Ability to See, Ability to Know, Self-Worth?

Weekly Exercises for Knowing

Throughout the Month

- When you next hear of a request for prayer, KNOW that you are empowered to offer the prayer of your entire group.

Question yourself: "Have I allowed myself to know the breadth and depth of my potentials or have I so pre-adjudged these that they cannot flow? Have I turned away those who have come to me with a need or a request because I do not know myself?

- Throughout the Earth day, pause here and there. Close your eyes, and just state the words: I KNOW.

- When you take food into your body during the day, close your eyes a moment, and think these words: I KNOW the many loving hands that have labored to bring this unto my need

- If you see someone on the street, and you can see that they have a need, take the Seeing into yourself and think this: I KNOW your need.

- When someone asks something, don't merely process their words - KNOW the person

- When someone is attempting to explain their understanding, or their position on a certain topic, open yourself to KNOW their position. Know their Truth. Know who you are interacting with, and what it is they are offering to you.

- Employ Sophie's advice: "It is wonderful for one to take time here and there to be aware of the many small choices that are made in each day's journey."

NOTES:

_____

_____

_____

_____

_____

_____

_____

_____

_____

_____

_____

Further Exploring Knowing

NOTE: The thoughts listed here are merely suggestions to get you started in further exploration of this subject. Use any portion of them, or not, as your personal guidance leads you.

POINTS TO PONDER:

- Knowing experiences through the instantaneous processing of the senses, without truly thinking about them or knowing them

- Knowing things, but not acknowledging them

- Knowing about something through the agreed upon elements and experiences from others

- Knowing people and things profoundly, through the emotive impact of an experience with them

- Knowing your talents and skills

- Knowing the path of Light that exists between you and the events and people in your life; knowing the connections

- Knowing in the spiritual sense, beyond your personal experiences and from the experiences of others

- Knowing from Universal Consciousness

- Knowing the spiritual state of Oneness with your consciousness. Becoming One with all, through KNOWING. Carrying Knowing beyond, to Wisdom.

When the Master was able to heal, because of knowing the Law, what do you suppose Lama Sing is referring to?

NOTES:
_____
_____
_____
_____
_____
_____
_____
_____

JOURNAL

_____

_____

_____

_____

_____

_____

_____

_____

_____

_____

_____

_____

_____

_____

_____

_____

_____

_____

_____

_____

_____

Step 9:

Claiming

Given September 2, 2000

OPEN FORUM ON CLAIMING

LAMA SING: Yes, we have the Channel then and as well those intents and purposes as are a part of this work. As we gather together in this joyful intent, let us offer this prayer of affirmation.

> *O, holy Father-Mother-God, in the semblance of Thy presence, do we know that we are ever a living part of Thy spirit. In this, which we see, is the promise, the hope, and the light which is, so as we claim same, that which shall ever guide us in every moment of need, upon every pathway. We call upon Thee here, now, to enlighten all who are gathered about this work, knowing that so as we ask, Thou shalt answer. We seek of Thee. We see in that called the semblance of Thy presence, all things, for there is naught apart from Thee. Here are we then, O Lord God, following the path of He who has gone before. As we do so, we find many gifts offered. Those of His healing grace, His love, His compassion and His wisdom. As we gather these and take them unto ourselves, so shall they multiply therein. And as they do, these are the fruits we offer unto all who come upon us in need. As we see those needs, we claim Thee and the gifts within, and together in oneness, we answer that as is their call.*
>
> *For those who are dwelling in the illusion of their own separateness... here are we, awaiting you, calling to you, offering to you, ever, that which is our gift to give.*
>
> *We thank Thee, Father, for this continued opportunity of joyful service in Thy Name, through this our Channel and his mate in the Earth. Amen.*

Choosing the Gifts of God

In the process of seeing one's self, there are ever to be found new aspects, new perspectives, new combinations of potentials which are ever growing, unfolding, reaching out to claim the experiences of this current Earth day; and to take from them, as surely as one takes building materials from the stores, to create that which is unto thy need and intent.

Many Pathways

As you *know* and *see*, you find many things possible, many pathways appear in terms of choices, and much of this has been spoken to. But as one assesses the choices made, and finds from these, learning, growth and potential, there is always that which awaits thee, which calls to thee: *Claim me, know me, take me unto Thy being.*

For in the presence of all experience, is also the presence of the promise of God. And these are His gifts. As you claim them, you can the better, truly, know and see them. It is difficult to truly believe unto that which thou knoweth, without claiming same for self.

Knowing is the process of gathering information, experience. It is also the process of assimilating through interactions with others, sharing, exchanging. It is the process and experience of offering one's self unto a work, together with others, that the greater number empowers each, far beyond the nature of the individual. All of these and so much more are ever present about you in the Earth and beyond, as continual invitations: *Come unto me, see me, know me, claim me, and I shall serve you well.*

The Act of Choosing Can Be Challenging to Others

The power of claiming has similarity to all that has been given in the works past. The power of claiming challenges many of the tenets in the Earth. For as one claims and becomes empowered, through this there shall be that change in self, about self, and in all that you shall do. And this shall surely be evidentially noted by those about you... perhaps first and foremost, those closest to you. Those who witness or interact with you daily will be the first to know and be impacted by the changes through your claiming.

As this moves outward, beyond those closest to you, there well may be impact and reaction on the part of those who are clinging to limitation, to finiteness, to habit, to the way things are and should be...

by the accounting of many.

This is known, and it is perhaps one of the greatest opportunities that stands before you as you consider claiming. You may think in regard to that, *How shall others regard me? What will they think of me? How will they react?*

These are commonplace. We oft see them in the Earth. There is the sense of looking at self through the eyes of others that so often predicates, results in, a limiting ability to accept.

If others would chastise you because you touch someone and heal them, should you pass through their intent to limit you and heal no more? If in your prayer you find marvelous, wonderful joy... the result of which frees you, breaks you out of molds and habits, and thrusts you into a joyful state of ease, and you, yourself, become empowered... shall their evaluation of this as being inappropriate cause you to give up your state of ease, your state of joy, your oneness?

The Vessel of Spirit

Many of you look to the example of great teachers who have gone before, and of course, we (as so oft here) shall point to the Master, the Christ, as the Example of Examples.

Noting, as one reviews His life and works, that He was continually challenged... that those who were about Him, chastised Him: *Who art thou, that you speak in the name of God? It is blasphemy. Why do you do these works on the Sabbath? It is a disrespect to God. It is a violation of Law. Who are you to say that those who follow and believe unto your word, shall be free, and unto they, all things shall be given. Art thou greater than God to say these words? How can you, a man of flesh, standing before us, say that 'my Father and I are one'? Is this not treason against all that is good, blasphemy against the sacredness of God?*

And each He answered, and the works He continued to do in spite of this. And to the end of that pathway of exemplification of truth, the ultimate chastisement was to take His life, in order to give to you – and to we, and to the all – the Example.

Our recounting of this is not to minimize the wondrous beauty of all of the other teachers who have gone before, and who have followed the appearance of the Master. It is to point out through this – which has such clarity, such beauty and truth – the validation of all the others. Not a one do we stand apart from; but with Him, we embrace all of the others, for we are also one. But here is an example which lives on and to which we are, of course, in oneness.

DIVINE HERITAGE

The Father and you are one. The presence of the Spirit of God – sometimes referred to as the Holy Ghost, the Great Spirit, the Force of Life and on and on – is within you.

You are the vessel which contains the potential of that very Spirit. If you could truly see this, if you could actually know it and see the truth of it... not just rhetoric, not merely words which are repeated in almost all teachings and exemplified by the Master, but truth... would you then be hesitant to claim it?

Is your claiming of this an edification of self, as was given to you? Or is it the passage of transition into righteousness, and the claiming of your heritage?

What Others Will See

If you know this, and see it as a truth within... that you are a Child of God, and then you believe unto this and claim it... what is it that the others, whom we spoke of above (first those closest to you and those a bit more distant) will see and know and perhaps respond to in varying degree.

They will not, if you are following the truth within you, see you bedecked in radiant robes of gold and satin and silk. They won't see you weighted down with wondrous medallions, crosses, ornaments that outwardly symbolize your special-ness. They won't hear you professing aloud to any and all who pass by the things of truth that thou knoweth, again and again, with emphasis and effort... though we would not judge same, see.

But what they will see is the change in and about you. Some will see it as a light, a glow, a radiance. Others will hear it in your words, your voice, see the light and sparkle in your eye; the renewed vibrancy and energy of how you go about your day's activities; a wondrous capacity to hear and see, and to be able to evaluate without becoming a part of any aspect of that which limits; to be able to offer counsel, support, encouragement and the wondrous power of prayer.

Overall they will see, perhaps, that which is similar to what they might see were the Master Himself to stand before them. It is a matter of degree, we might suppose, and that degree is directly relevant to how much you actually claim.

For if you believe, and you know His words, then it must be so: *"These and greater shall ye do."*

Where the Choice Begins

Let it begin with self.

If you wish to be of service, as all of you do… if you wish to contribute in a way that you know is filled with righteousness, purpose, joy and honor to God… through what shall those blessings of God flow, if not through self? Can you go out and command the potential, the heritage, the abilities of another entity?

It is self who is under your direction. And the Law is perfect. If you claim it, it is yours.

PARABLE: EXEMPLIFYING

In an ancient land, there was a custom when entities reached stages of adulthood that they had to demonstrate their ability to be recognized as adults and no longer be looked upon as children.

There were certain things that were expected to be known, and to be demonstrated. There were those which were the customs, the teachings, the tenets, which were for the female entities, and others for the males. But together, both of these were expected to know certain things, regardless of whether or not they were male or female.

Among some of these things that were expected of them, not by recitation or merely by word, but it was that at the point of ceremony of adulthood, their progression to this point in the years past must have demonstrated this. Those who evaluated this, were the very ones who walked with these entities, who guided them, who taught them, who offered them the tenets of all these aspects as were to be known in order to be considered an adult.

Now, this passage from adolescence into adulthood was very important. Without this, the gifts and the rights of these peoples would not be given. And the entities would be considered adolescent until these were demonstrated.

There is value in knowing some of these tenets for they have not changed. Even as we speak, they could well be tenets for your times in the Earth now….

There was the tenet of honor. And this honor had to be demonstrated, not only inwardly but outwardly. It was observed, whether or not the entity honored themselves as well as others.

There had to be the exemplification of the capacity to forgive, inwardly and outwardly. Those who continually lamented, and who became burdened by their own judgments of themselves, were given special tutelage. Often two, three entities of the elderly grouping would assist them and offer them challenges… games if you

will, at some age groupings. Until forgiveness was not only an outwardly given blessing, but an accepted one within.

There had to be gratitude. And the gratitude had to be expressed for all that they were and did in the day which had concluded... as a part of this, the attitude of oneness with God, the
viewing and knowing that God is a living part of them, that in all
things that they were about, God is with them; in all words and actions, deeds done for others, to others, with the remembrance that
God's Spirit did those things with them.

There were the tenets upon which they were tested...

Doest thou love self, thy neighbor, and all, as one... equal?

Is there the compassion to see and know and to release, because it is seen and known; not only by way of the event, but that
the seeing was built upon all of the other aspects. And just so as it
was seen without, so was it considered a gift and seen... searched
for, and seen... within self.

Truth was considered *the* tenet upon which one tested all
else. The truth was designed to be individualized by the perceiver.
And thus, outwardly expressed through that perceiver in a manner
of uniqueness, intended to bring out the individual beauty as a gift
to the entire community. For it was known that, as one sees the
unique beauty within self, thus are they capable of also seeing it
without. And if it can be seen without, this strengthens the claiming
of it within.

And all of these things were empowered through the final
ceremony, perhaps which lies yet ahead in these teachings. But it
is called *Righteousness*. And the portal through which one passes,
to begin the journey in righteousness, is claiming.

Who were and are these peoples? They were called the Expectant Ones... the Essenes.

80C3

YOUR PURPOSE IN THESE WORKS

As we look about your grouping, gathered near and far, we see
you and know you, many of you to be one and the same grouping.
Why have you gathered? What is the purpose of your search? How did
it come to pass that you are a part of these works, which we are honored and humbled to offer to you... not from we alone, but moreover,
from those of great wisdom and righteousness who are here with us,
and with you, in these and the works which shall follow. Perhaps you
have come unto these works because your spirit has guided you. Per-

haps you have heard a call, a beckoning, which you know not the source of, but which has been such that you have answered. And now you are a part of these works.

Your Coming Rite of Passage

In that action, did you begin to claim; and perhaps, most assuredly, long before that. But here, that decision, that choice and that action began the process of claiming. And has made this way passable for you to emerge into the ceremony of oneness, just as the Essenes had their ceremony, their counsel, for this rite of passage.

Claiming cannot be dependent upon the acceptance of others outside of you. If you believe that you cannot claim because others around you – perhaps even those whom you love dearly – are not ready to claim, this is not a valid criterion.

Claiming Your Inner Truth

The claiming of one's inner truth is an important gift. It is perhaps one of the most wondrous actions given to you under Universal Law – the right of Free Will.

Some of you have seen, in other works of late, entities that have chosen… and therefore claimed… limitation. And you have seen the lot that this has brought to them. You have also seen what can occur, when even a small light of hope is brought to them and illuminated before them. Of course, those about you are not dwelling in realms of darkness as those who are within the Borderland works[13]. But is it a matter of degree? Shall we judge limitation to be serious or not depending upon the degree of it, and the fruits of that choice?

The death of joy and the death of a body physical, to we here, is a comparable event. Indeed, difficult to equate in the sense that the death of joy, as one lives on in physical body, can oft be worse, far worse, than experiencing the process of death, knowing full well that what lies beyond has the potential of wonder and joy, love, compas-

---

[13] The Borderland Works – Following a night of horrific lucid dreaming, and after giving a reading the next day, Al was met on his path on the "way back to his body" by a large group of individuals, who we later came to know had escaped from the Shadowland (the name given by Al and the readings to that realm of consciousness that lives in the shadow of the Earth where discarnates dwell whose lives are dominated by fear and utter hopelessness, out of which is born heinous aggression). What followed was a gripping recounting of events that explained Al's dream and led to the series of readings called, THE BORDERLAND PROJECT. It is an incredible look into those forces that seek to hold us in our illusions of finiteness, and, through that exploration, offers us new hope for how to break the hold.

sion and freedom. It is that one who walks about in physical body, who has not the light of joy, who well may be enduring the greater burden.

Service Through Claiming

Your claiming could give them back their joy. Because you will know them, you will see them, you will feel their need. And perhaps all it will take from you is a certain smile and a light in your eyes, an encouraging and supportive word at just that moment when they are making a decision, that shall lift them up, that shall show unto them the way to recover their path of joy.

There are those in the Earth and other realms who are in conditions of dis-ease. Some of these you have seen in prayer. Perhaps some you have offered your prayer for. As you speak your words of prayer, as they might offer their own, is this done from completeness? Is this done from the perspective of what you would call a victim consciousness? Is it a plea for intervention and grace? Or is it a call from a daughter or son of God, asking for their heritage?

It might be well then, rather, they should pray:
Lord God, I come before you. See my condition.
Awaken me to claim Thy righteousness within. Show me
the path, that I may claim it. Help me to see, to know
that I am ever one with Thee. I claim my right to be in a
state of joyful ease.

Some say, "Lord God, why hast Thou forsaken me? Why hast Thou visited this inequity upon me and mine?" Is it the Lord God that bringeth this? Or is it an answer to your call?
Father-Mother-God, guide me. I seek to know myself,
my spirit. Help me to claim the gifts and fruits of Spirit.
Let me be the greatest that I might be in this life and in
the works therein.

It is possible that challenges bring to you the step-stones upon which you can rise to the perspective of seeing and knowing. And from this higher perspective (if we might call it such) attained through the claiming of each opportunity – whether joyful or nay – and seeing within same, knowing, and thereafter searching for the gift of it, the gift in it, and the gift which it calls forth from within you, to see, know and claim.

WORTHINESS

Are you worthy?

What sort of a question is that, after all? Could you walk up to anyone in your day's activities and state to them, "Excuse me, but I was wondering... are you worthy?"

If you saw someone dis-eased would you go to them and state, "What a shame... you've lost your worthiness."

Denying, or Claiming, the Power Within

What is it that you do to yourself when you deny that which is ever within you? Your right to laugh and be joyful. The power to claim, to know, to be a Child of God. Aren't you saying to yourself in those moments, *Gosh, what a terrible thing that you aren't worthy. If you were, you could have these things, and your life could be filled with the fruits of them.*

Do you believe that because something has been in your life, it must always be? Are there aspects of your life to which you are familiar, and that familiarity builds a degree of comfort? And that comfort and familiarity denies you venturing forth, beyond? Of course, for that is the way of the Earth.

And those who do reach beyond the familiar, who do expect... and thus, through the expectation, find, claim... these are those who are given, in answer to their expectation. And what they are given becomes theirs, as they claim it with gratitude, as they release themselves through forgiveness and are able to love themselves and know their own worthiness, empowering them to claim the gift being offered.

We recommend, humbly, in your first week of exercise, in striving to truly claim, that you consider some of these little examples and look for them within you.

You might begin your Earth day in this way:
Lord God, in this day, show me my worthiness to be a son or daughter of God. Help me see it. Help me know it. And help me claim it. Amen.

In that day, look to others, look to life itself, to reflect this back to you. Look at the little things that you would otherwise do... without thought, without consideration... and see where and how your worthiness is doing a good work. Look where you have been supportive, encouraging; where you have given a kind supportive comment, perhaps to one you do not know well; where the simplicity of your spirit's light has simply radiated forth and touched someone who may not have even acknowledged your presence, and feel the response from their spirit, and claim it as your worthiness.

Evidence of Worthiness

In all these things – in the smallest areas and the greatest – look for the gift you bear… that can be seen as a worthy work from one who is worthy.

At the conclusion of the Earth day, in meditation and prayer, take a few moments. It need not be long, but review the Earth day. Do a bit of accounting for all those little things of worthiness that you have seen in self, reflected from others back to you. And look for those areas where you might have given more, if you had been able to claim for self, for these things. Do this the first Earth week.

In the second Earth week, do this, humbly suggested. Begin with a prayer:

Lord God, I have seen my worthiness. Open me now, in this day's activity, to see the worthiness of others. To know it and to see the oneness between us.

Growing Worthiness

Obviously, look for this. Exemplify it in return and as you do, notice that as you find a gift of worthiness being given and you respond to it and reciprocate, how it grows between you and becomes a light. Collect these lights of accomplishment throughout the Earth day.

At the conclusion of the Earth day, examine these as treasures, as one who might have gone to gather some harvest as a day's work, might at the conclusion of that day, rest and sort out the harvest of that day. Treasure them. Take them unto self. Meditate and pray and ask this:

O, Lord, as I enter into slumber, show me the examples of these events that I might claim them for self and bear the fruits of same for others. Guide me. Help me to know and claim my oneness with Thee. Amen.

In the third and fourth weeks, look for the worthiness in all things about thee. In the third week, look for it in proximity to your life (in terms of distance, that which can be perceived and known) but look for it all about.

In the fourth week the focus should be beyond the immediate, to look for the worthiness being demonstrated, no matter where you might find it.

In the third and fourth weeks, we would begin the day as such:

I have claimed, O Father-Mother-God, my worthiness as Your Child. This has empowered me. It has opened my sight and my knowing. Guide me to see this all about me, in this world in which I am living and experiencing. Let me see the gifts of others, the demonstrations of worthiness, that I might claim the power of this, and offer them the power of my own worthiness. Amen.

Seeing Worthiness Striving to Be Expressed

In the evening, before sleep, meditate upon the worthiness that is known. Have a care not to judge it, or evaluate it too intensely, too finitely. But look for the subtleties of intents of worthiness, in all that you know and experience.

Have a caution not to look for result, but for the intent. That will open you to see and know worthiness as it is struggling to be expressed, as it is striving to be a part of another entity's claiming.

Send your prayers then, to that entity or entities, knowing that, as you have in the first two weeks, seen and claimed your righteousness and that of the righteousness of others about you, that this is a power which is expanding. And you have the right because you have claimed it, to offer it to others, to strengthen their intent.

TRANSFORMED

What would be the result of this? If you will do these things, you will find yourself in that fortnight having been transformed.

We do recognize here, and we have Zachary present, as may have been detected, to emphasize, "That is no idle comment." But even Zachary would state to you, " If you do this, you will change."

Looking for It Without, Finding It Within

You cannot find worthiness within yourself, without finding it without. You cannot see worthiness without, without finding it within. The claiming of it is the key.

If you have an automobile whose tires are good and inflated, and the fuel reservoir is filled, and the power plant functions wonderfully, and all about it, the automobile is good, if not perfect... You could stand and admire it. You could walk about it, touch it, sit in it and then walk away and state, "That is one fine automobile." And you have known it. Haven't you? You have seen it. Have touched it. You are fully cognizant of its availability, its presence, its potential and all that sort.

But only when you operate it, when you use it to transport yourself from where you are to where you wish to go, have you truly claimed the potential of it.

All of the things that we have spoken about and shared with you to this point are similar to the automobile – claiming is the action of commanding it, directing it.

Claiming Is the Empowerment

Claiming is the key, which when placed in the ignition switch and turned, is the empowerment. It can't take you anywhere if you merely sit and look at it. It can't bring you to a new accomplishment or destination, you can't make a new discovery, see a new piece of beauty in the Earth, until you claim it and turn the ignition key and direct it to your intent.

Truth is this way... love is also... compassion, forgiveness, gratitude, great Self, little self, on and on... they are as beautiful potentials, and the key for igniting them to begin to function for you, is found in claiming.

CLAIMING ONENESS WITH GOD

Two entities, born into the Earth in similar circumstances, in similar life events, equally bestowed with blessings, may arrive at totally different end-point destinations in that life. More oft than not, the one who has arrived at their destination joyful and fulfilled, in a state of peace and/or ease, is the one who has claimed.

The one who denies himself and does not claim, is continually searching, continually believing, *There must be something better. Why have I arrived in this less than joyful circumstance?*

And you know it is because of choices.

The most powerful one of which is the claiming of oneness with God.

Claiming Dominion

Is it such a great action? Yes, it is. Is it a difficult action or work to accomplish or do? It would appear so, for so many do not do it. Is it selfish, a grayness of ego, to claim in such ways?

We ask you, whose thought is that? Who has decided this? And is it a mandate? Is there somewhere where you have signed an agreement that you will never in your lifetime, step out of these perimeters of being a finite, limited, expression of God?

The birds you see soaring about with ease, in song, joyful, have no concept, no idea that they aren't supposed to be able to fly. They just do it. They claim it and do it. The beautiful sea creatures which you see moving with grace and ease in the waters of the Earth, can be a source of inspiration if one were to observe them. For the water is their domain and they claim their oneness with it. They live and breathe it, and those above on the land, cannot. And their movement, with surprising speed and grace, is their claiming of dominion of their environ. They don't equate it. They don't evaluate it. They don't ask permission. They simply do. The insects, whose body weight is so much out of proportion to their wing span, they cannot fly. According to the laws of physics, it is nearly impossible. And yet they do. Did someone give them permission?

Choose with Intent

We know the counterpoint to this only too well. But the fact remains, they do it. They choose with an intent, and that intent empowers them. If you would claim these inner potentials, these outer awarenesses, perhaps you could do even greater than is conceived of by those who cling to habit.

Why else would great souls who enter the Earth to demonstrate this, be so edified? Why do we continually point to the Master as the example? Because he exemplifies and urges all to follow this, and to claim. And beyond that is the promise of movement into righteousness. And it is righteousness that is the empowerment, the claim, the rod and staff of God.

One who is called Judith is ever with the Master, was with the Sisters[14] who loved and nurtured, guided and taught the Master and

---

[14] Judith – This is not the Essene, 'Judy.' This Judith, Lama Sing has told us, has never incarnated, but, as the soul mate of the Christ, is ever at His side. The Sisters were also known as the Holy Maidens, of the Essene community, who nurtured Jesus, and the other children.

many others… indeed some of you, who are here and read these words, were among that number.

And of all the teachings, the beauty of this eternal expression of God – called Judith – ever gives… it is to claim.

Supposing versus Knowing

If you suppose you are worthy then we could respond, "We suppose that's so."

But if you state, "I *know* I am worthy," we would answer, "We *know* you are worthy."

What is the difference between supposing and knowing? Claiming. If you claim, can you go forth on the next day, see a diseased entity, put a hand upon them and state, "I Claim my right to heal this entity," and remove your hand and expect them to rise and be diseased no more?

Our answer may surprise you. It is yes. And that is that.

Now the entity who is to be healed… there is a responsibility here. And we have given much on this here and in other works. The greatest of all examples is from the Master's own words, *"Do you believe?"*

And those are the keys, the claiming. Through knowing, through seeing, through garnering wisdom, through looking at all of the steps which bring you ever closer to oneness with He… Lord God.

Not as though you were distant from Him, and climbing some great mount to reach where He sits upon an ornate contrivance or throne; but to raise your thinking, your consciousness. Those are the step-stones and that is the process of ascension to oneness… lifting your thinking, your belief, your willingness to accept that which you already have.

LIVING WHAT YOU BELIEVE

What is Claiming? Claiming is living what you believe, knowing what you know, seeing what you see, loving self and others equitably, having compassion within and out, looking for and seeing truth; knowing truth as others see it, their truth; ever opening self to grow, to release in order to receive; to expect, rather than to lament and deny; to claim abundance, and thus honor God and open self that it might flow to and through you; to complete the cycle, always through gratitude, which is empowering because it sees, knows and affirms.

United Aspects of Self

The little self and great Self can no longer be, for that implies division; in claiming, they are united into oneness. The Master was not an exemplification of the little self, for the little self and one who is the greatest among us, are also one with the All. And so the Master, as might be expected to follow the pattern of the Earth, should have been seen in a duality, and yet there was none, there is none, there shall not be any. For He has claimed. See?

You could say that, to your spiritual being, your little self is a child you are raising. Just as if there is a part of you which is a parent who has a child journeying in the Earth to whom you can give counsel and guidance, just as you would a child who is of your physical body. And as Zachary points out here, "You might find that little-self child doesn't listen any better than your physical children do." (Humor intended here.)

The Cycle of Opportunity

It is not a lesser-than/greater-than scenario. It is a wonderful, magnificent opportunity to put a portion of your consciousness into a classroom called Earth, from whence great growth can come forth. Wondrous understanding, perspective, and all that sort, can be a wondrous harvest that shall be yours forevermore.

What happens, though, if you can't claim that? Then the gifts of that lifetime go for the most part unopened. And if you are given the blessing (and most wait anxiously for that) you will turn back to the Earth and strive to do it again and again. And that is, as called, the Wheel of Life, or the Wheel of Karma, which is no more than the cycle of opportunity.

So we would leave you with these thoughts...

We shall, during this work, do a special work here. We shall pray for your empowerment. We shall give all that we are permitted to give to empower you, to claim – as a wellspring of love and light, inexhaustible – from which you may draw. You must choose, and all else will follow. See?

We are through here for the present. The grace and blessings of God await you.

Fare thee well then, for the present, dear friends.

GUEST LECTURE: Judith

Given August 20, 2000

JUDITH: Each of the qualities of discipleship are found within the works which are being given. Each has borne an essence which shall resonate within the spirits, hearts, and minds of those who have ears with which to hear.

But do know, as well, that the qualities of your eternal nature are not merely some aspect of you waiting to be awakened; they are, rather, as the flowers afield only awaiting their time... that the blooms which are held within might gently, but gloriously, burst forth under the Light of God as flowers afield burst forth in bloom under the sun's light. What nourishes you as a spiritual being is likened unto these flowers afield – while they have their root in the Earth itself, the root of your being is in the heritage of your spirit's journey. You can bring the Light of God to shine upon those blooms awaiting it within, and that Light of God is claimed through the power of your faith, your believing, your seeing, and knowing.

We are here, so it would seem, some distance from you; it would seem to you that you must prepare in certain ways, and journey in mind and spirit to find us and to be one with us. And yet, dear sisters, dear brothers, we are at your sides each and every time you would ask.

There are aspects of the opening of that Light within which are ever offered to you. Indeed, Life itself, through the embrace of the Earth is continually offering these to you. But so many know these not. And so these and other works – many of them elsewhere, through others – have been and are being given, in the loving prayer that these might be an offering which is acceptable in your sight and knowing.

Are not the thoughts within your minds, the emotions and memories and all that sort which you feel, which rise and flow all throughout you... are these not all opportunities which bear gifts of potential joy?

For no matter what the challenge, nor how frequently it might visit you, each time there is another step... each visitation brings to you a slightly different perspective to understand, to know, to rise above.

You are holy. You are sacred. You are the work and the workers. You have the Light in your hearts, in your minds and words.

Do we edify you? Yes, we do. Do you not edify He who has gone before… our Lord Jesus? Do you not edify Our Lady? Have they not themselves told you that even greater shall you do? Then if we edify they, can we not find honor in also edifying you? For they have said it, and we believe unto them with all of our being.

The supposition that such edification is exclusionary is a part of the illusion. Speak to it first within yourselves. For if you cannot claim, if you cannot know and see yourselves as sisters and brothers to we, to Our Lady, to our Master, to our Lord God, then what have you to give in honor to His words? How shall you respond to those He will send to you? How will you serve them? Can you stand before the Master and state, "I am not worthy. I am sorry but I cannot do Your work because I can't accept my worthiness to so do"? Shall He send them to another?

It is a joy to know one's self in the beauty of one's own uniqueness. And so you have forgiven… outwardly and inwardly; it matters not, for if oneness is truth, then all is of the same, and the work is everywhere, and within.

And as you acknowledge through your gratitude, are you not affirming His very word?

And so we have come forward in the honor of this opportunity and our sweet brother who permits this work to continue in the Earth now as in past, and our sister who stands at his side contributing.

And those of you of our sisterhood and brotherhood who equally so stand shoulder to shoulder with they… we honor you. We are with you. Our love and the qualities of our grouping are ever offered to you. You have but to claim them.

When the teachings of *Righteousness* come forth, look you with a care upon them, for these shall be works of meaning, of hope, and truly gifts – question not so much so that you limit yourself; let the Way be passable within you.

Thank you.
We do love you.

GUEST LECTURE: Shem

Given September 2, 2000

SHEM: I am come to this gathering to offer, what I shall pray to be, a gift to you all.

In the process of one's evolution of experiences, there are those which are equated here and there to have goodness and worthiness, and others which are considered unfortunate or less than joyful. It is the collage of these interactive and contrasting experiences that offers to each who knows them or who has dwelled within them a very precious gift of contrast.

In the multifaceted contrasts which are a part of life in the Earth, is the crucible into which one's soul may journey, within which the tenure of life expands and contracts, according to the experiences which are visited upon that soul.

Upon departure from that called life in Earth, there is the shifting and expected period of adjustment as one begins to reclaim their unlimited self and looks back over the happenstance, the events, the collage of contrasts that were a part of the just concluded walk in the Earth. In the process of that review, many things are suddenly realized through the loving guidance and support of those who are in attendance to the newly departed.

One of the most common responses to that process, that is agreed upon by all those who lovingly serve as guide or council to the newly departed, are these words:

If I had only known.

And so, dear friends, I am come to this gathering to lovingly encourage you to *know*.

You can know and awaken yourself, and through that knowing and awakening, claim the knowledge... claim the contrasts, as neither good nor bad, nor claim them to be a burdensome part of you; but *see* them, *know* them, *claim* the knowledge from that knowing: these are those things, *the very reasons*, for which you have petitioned to enter the Earth.

If you are in a state of joyful ease, the gift that bears to you may seem apparent. But if you are in a state which is neither joyful nor filled with ease, are you among those who could be called *denied by God*? Or is, perhaps, your gift in the lack of joy and ease in those moments a far greater gift? Perhaps it is so... if you had only known.

If you had known...

- that challenge inspires the best to come forth

- that *need* necessitates a search within self to find that which is greater than the challenge before thee.

There are so many who have come forward to be a part of your search. In these times in the Earth, those who are honored all throughout these and other realms are with you.

Those who are in physical body, whose lives have been a gift to the Work, who have been challenged and met challenge, who have returned goodness for that which is less than same... those who have searched for, found, claimed, and walked upon a path which leads clearly to righteousness are there for you, as they are here as well, awaiting your call.

Those who walk with you whose love never wavers, those who are at the ready to help you as you are willing to claim, to strengthen you as you offer yourselves in prayer and service, are the same as you. Your places, your positions, are different in this moment in this time. But consider you well that in the next cycle of the Wheel of Life, it well may be they – dwelling in the crucible of purification, seeking that which is pure and eternal within, through the challenge and test of the contrasts of Earth – and you may then be that faithful one ever walking with them, hand-in-hand... if they only knew.

Do *you* Know?

The message here is a part of the next work. For what shall follow the process of seeing and knowing, and the visitation of all the tenets that have been lovingly and humbly offered, are to bring you to the point in this current work of claiming, as though you are opening a portal, a doorway... beyond which, is *Righteousness*.

Worthiness is the mantle which you must don to begin the passage into righteousness. And you can only wear it through claiming.

Let not one day's activity pass in the period which follows, wherein you are without the empowering wonder of claiming yourself to be a Child of God.

No force is greater than this.

No illusion can stand before it in dominance.

No challenge cannot be met through the eyes and words, actions and deeds, of the righteous.

So in this precursive work to the first steps into righteousness, the urging from here is ever claim, know, and be.

Live it. Take it, as life itself, and let it flow through you in all that you are.

When your thoughts, as they shall surely do, strive to lead you back into the familiar, the comfort of what is known and called *status quo* – or more accurately, *limitation* – throw it off. And claim this wondrous voyage into eternal righteousness.

In times past, I stood with Him. We called to our brethren and they answered. And we stood with one another in equality. We looked for joyful works, and varying members of our grouping would step forward and do them... not one, but all. And as we gathered in celebration, there was not one only who would bless the bounty before us (that meal, or whatnot) but each and every one did so equally and was honored by all the rest.

How could such a wondrous state of equality, loving oneness and all that goes with that, ever come to be? Because each and every one of us claimed. And in the claiming, the beauty of the uniqueness of each was seen as the beauty of a great bouquet of flowers... each one ingratiating the other by its uniqueness... each one assuming its rightful and intended position of giving glory to God and to all of their brothers and sisters.

So then, do I, Shem, offer you my glory. Will you not gift me with yours?

My spirit is with you in this work and the preparation of the Way. My prayer is with you. I thank you and those who are serving this work for permitting this opportunity to speak... may the glory of God's spirit be known and claimed within you.

Come, and be one with us. We invite you. We call you.

Namaste. Shalom.
Fare thee well then, for the present, sweet brothers and sisters.

Step Nine: CLAIMING
246

STUDY GUIDE

Weekly Exercises for Truth

Week 1:

Morning Activity

Lord God, in this day, show me my worthiness to be a (son or daughter) of God. Help me see it. Help me know it. And help me claim it. Amen.

Throughout the Day

In that day, look to others, look to life itself to reflect these back to you. Look at the little things that you would otherwise do, without thought, without consideration, and see where and how your worthiness is doing a good work. In all these things, in the smallest areas and the greatest, look for the gift you bear, that can be seen as a worthy work, from one who is worthy.

Evening Activity

At the conclusion of the day, in meditation and prayer, take a few moments to review the day. Do a bit of accounting for all those little things of worthiness that you have seen in self reflected from others back to you. And look for those areas where you might have given more, if you had been able to claim for self, for these things.

Then, ask, *Lord God, guide me to understand what I have seen and reacted to in this day. Thank you. Amen.*

Week 2:

Morning Activity

Lord God, I have seen my worthiness. Open me now, in this day's activity, to see the worthiness of others, to know it and to see the oneness between us.

Throughout the Day

Notice that as you find a gift of worthiness being given and you respond to it and reciprocate, how it grows between you and becomes a light. Collect these lights of accomplishment throughout the day.

Evening Activity

At the end of the day, examine these as treasures. Take them unto self.

Meditate and pray and ask: *Oh, Lord, as I enter into slumber, show me the examples of these events, that I might claim them for myself and bear the fruits of same for others. Guide me ,help me to know and claim my oneness with Thee. Amen.*

Week 3:

Morning Activity

Open self, again. Offer your own prayer and meditation, in this sense, considering the world at large, and your desire, intent, to "see" it.

I have claimed, O Father, Mother, God, my worthiness as your Child. This has empowered me. It has opened my sight and my knowing. Guide me to see this all about me, in this world in which I am living and experiencing. Let me see the gifts of others, the demonstrations of worthiness, that I might claim the power of this, and offer them the power of my own worthiness. Amen.

Throughout the Day

Look for the worthiness in all things about, but particularly, look for it near you, that which can be seen and known.

Evening Activity

Meditate upon the worthiness that is known, not to judging or evaluating it too intensely. Look for the subtleties of intents of worthiness in all that you experience, not looking for result, but for the intent. (That will open you to see, and know, worthiness as it is struggling to be expressed, as it is striving to be a part of another's claiming.)

Week 4:

Morning Activity

Open self, again. Offer your own prayer and meditation, claiming your ability to see in the fullness of every sense.

I have claimed, oh Father-Mother-God, my worthiness as your Child. This has empowered me. It has opened my sight and my knowing. Guide me to see this all about me, in this world in which I am living and experiencing. Let me see the gifts of others, the demonstrations of worthiness, that I might claim the power of this, and offer them the power of my own worthiness. Amen.

Throughout the Day

In this week, the focus should be beyond the immediate, to look for the worthiness being demonstrated, no matter where you might find it

Evening Activity

Send out your prayers, knowing that as you have in the first two weeks, seen and claimed your righteousness and the righteousness, that this is a power which is expanding. Know that you have the right because you have claimed it, to offer it to others, to strengthen their intent.

NOTES:

_____

_____

_____

_____

_____

_____

_____

Further Exploring Claiming

NOTE: The thoughts listed here are merely suggestions intended get you started in further exploration of this subject. Use any portion of them as your personal guidance leads you.

POINTS TO PONDER:

- "These and greater shall ye do". How much are you actually willing to claim?

- Let it begin with self.

- Ponder the tenants the Essenes had to demonstrate, claim, before they were "granted" adulthood. Evaluate yourself using these tenets.

- What is the purpose of your search?

- What about this course, if anything, is equating to your search?

- What, if anything, is not?

- Are you worthy?

- Claiming Oneness with God

- "Do you believe?" How much do you believe?

LAMA SING: "We would leave you with these thoughts. We shall, during this work, do a special work here. We shall pray for your empowerment. We shall give all that we are permitted to give to empower you, to claim - as a wellspring of love and light, inexhaustible - from which you may draw. You must choose, and all else will follow."

NOTES:

_____

_____

_____

_____

_____

_____

_____

_____

JOURNAL

_____

_____

_____

_____

_____

_____

_____

_____

_____

_____

_____

_____

_____

_____

_____

_____

_____

_____

_____

_____

_____

_____

_____

_____

_____

Step 10:

Truth, Honor, Love, and Compassion

Giver October 2, 2000

OPEN FORUM ON FOUR SACRED TENETS

LAMA SING: Yes, we have the Channel then and, as well, those intents and purposes as are a part of these works. As we come together, let us join in humble oneness, affirming unto our Lord God by way of this prayer.

> *Holy Creative Force of Oneness, we are with Thee ever. Guide Thou us, then, that we shall know of Thee in all that we are and do. We call upon those aspects of Thy being, Thy awareness, and that of Thy presence, that these shall gather 'round us now, here, in these works and ever. So as we know ourselves to be one with Thee, then too, guide us to know the All to be ours, as well. We thank Thee for that pattern and light which goes before us in all that we are and do and sets the way aright, that we might know and claim our heritage, our eternal potentials as Thy Children. In Thee do we see our Father and our Mother, each of which is, as such, a part of our being. So do we unite these in this work which now lies before us, as we claim and know our oneness with Thee.*

> *That pattern which is perfect within us is awakening. As it does, we know it, we see it, and we call to it by that name called the Christ Spirit within. As we do this, here are the gifts of healing grace, love, compassion, and wisdom upon which we can build eternally that which is righteous; so do we turn to those who have asked of Thee, O Lord God, and offer these as we know we are offering them from You. To those who have guided themselves through fear, doubt, or those things which limit, here are we to guide you out of that which is your own choice of darkness and limitation. We thank Thee, Lord God, for this continued opportunity of joyful service in Your name through this, our Channel, and his mate in the Earth, and through those forces which are now awakening in all realms and those who are willing. We thank Thee. Amen.*

The Crown of Oneness

We welcome all of you to these works, which we would consider to be as the crown of oneness upon that which has gone before, that you should know of the wonder and joy which is present here as we have gathered to present this, the first of the final three works.

There are those who have gathered to sing, literally and also in spirit, that you shall hear their song, united, and calling to you... *Come, join us. Be one with us.*

So as we are cleaving unto that same spirit and intent, so is our power in this form of oneness enhanced, and brought to the fore.

There are those who have gone before you in the Earth. Some of you have walked with these and looked upon them as great teachers, great workers of the light, whose works have manifested in many diverse forms. These are here, even as we speak. And not only we, but that Force Universal which is the connecting fabric or filament unifying the All, is also a part of this work.

So as we look upon that which has gone before, each one, as a step, can bring you into the realization that, while you are a beautiful creation, existing within the bosom, the embrace, of that called the Earth, you are so much more. And you are eternal.

The process of claiming that which is eternal is challenged every step of the way by the finiteness of expressions found in the Earth. Indeed, even so, within self are those challenges to be found, perhaps the greatest of all. So in this work, then, as we commence it, we would offer to you in humbleness, but certainly in love and encouragement, these things which we find have been given to us, to be presented to you...

Empowering the Path

There is within the context of discovering self to be an eternal Child of God, the need to recognize that thou art worthy.

The worthiness of self cannot be measured against the scales or tenets as are found in the Earth, though, to be sure, you will attempt to do this. As you do, recognize that if one is considering from the eternal perspective one's own nature, it follows, certainly, logically, that the eternal cannot be measured by a finite or singular perspective or measuring rod. But rather, that the Eternal is measured by that found within self. And as this is discovered and claimed within self, your sight is opened to see this as well in others, and perhaps in all of existence.

So as you look through the spiritual sight, then, this is the path and these are the works which will empower you, so as you do.

GUEST LECTURE: Michael

We have that one who is the guardian, the protector, so to say… that expression and emissary of God who goes before those who claim His righteousness. And that one here, known to you as Michael, comes forth to offer you this humble prayer.

MICHAEL: Hear, all of existence. I am come… Michael, Lord of the Way.

Unto each who claims that which is eternal, that which is righteousness, do I raise this, the signet of Eternal Righteousness, before you upon your path. Here then, in the symbol – of this sword of Righteousness – do I offer to you each my shelter, the very love and compassion of God. See it. Know it. Claim it as your own.

For even so as I come before you, it is the Father whose spirit has sent me. It is the Father whose power and righteousness are symbolized in this sword. See yourselves as arm-in-arm with this sword before you… and fear not, but love; deny not nor question, but have compassion; stand firmly and aright, through your honor; and ever look, quest for, and claim, Eternal Truth.

For these are the foundational points upon which all else shall follow. And so as thee seek, it is given.

The blessings of our Lord God are yours, offered to you. And I, as His servant, bring them to you now.

FOUR SACRED TENETS

What is worthiness, then, dear friends? As Michael has indicated here, it rests upon four sacred tenets. These tenets can be found in all teachings. In some, they are bright. In others, other facets may overshadow them and yet they are ever present.

Some would think of these in terms of the balancing points of all existence and that which you call the positive and negative polarity, and which has been defined, for the purpose of spiritual works in the Earth, as the Masculine and Feminine. And yet in truth, they are, as such, neither and both. For the essence of eternity is built upon itself through the quest, the search, the discovery. Therefore, again as Michael has given, one can find the foundational points of all else to be these pillars of righteousness:

Honor and truth, representing then that which you call in the Earth the Masculine... Love and compassion, as is found and represented in the Earth as the Feminine.

These are not separate. And yet, as you are manifested in the Earth, you are defined as either masculine or feminine. Should you then, because of this, claim only two of these, and to your uttermost attempt to manifest those two, knowing them to be, as you are, in feminine body or masculine body? It is a good work to recognize that these qualities in the natural sense of order of finiteness do flow through you with a heightened propensity, according to your gender, as it's called.

This, then, may be thought of as the gifts which you bear, in the primary sense. But in truth, righteousness is the unification of these. It is the bringing together to a point of incredible solidarity... balance, if you will... midpoint harmony, if you prefer... or as the Channel so oft uses in his explanations, that point of truly loving neutrality.

Truth

Truth is as its first letter... the cross upon which all things are meted out.

In order to claim truth, the symbol of the cross is at the forefront. For often, truth requires, in finiteness, a sacrifice. For to be a part of the illusion which oft beckons unto thee with comfort, with shelter, with the embrace of familiarity... and yes, with the agreement and comfort of general mass-mind thought. And yet, if it is not truth, what is its purpose in terms of service to you as a Child of God?

Therein may so often lie the sacrifice, to give up that which is commonly accepted and subscribed to. Whether known as truth or nay, it is the force, the pattern, the intent which goes before so many in the Earth. To truly claim truth, you must be, in the most explicit sense, willing to sacrifice the shelter of the illusion.

Honor

Honor is as its first letter, as well... solid, four points upon which the letter "H" seems to support the upper and the lower, a bridge, if you will, a step-stone. For Honor is claiming that which thou knoweth to be in accord with your ideal.

Here again, one must travel back and forth between truth and honor to find the strength to carry on in the face of challenge, question, hardship, pain, sorrow, and all that sort that will be the reaction of those forces in place, as they seek to perpetuate their tenure.

Honor is as the pillars of righteousness; and truth and honor, together, form two of the columns that support true righteousness.

Love

Love is as its first letter… it is as one would extend an arm to embrace. It is as one would extend their thought, their encouragement; that upon which you can rest or rise; that which looks to the potential within and sees not that which is the limitation, the finiteness; that which has been claimed because there is not knowledge of claiming it not.

Love is not an expression which is symbolized, enacted, or brought into creative force through physical bodies…

Love is the willingness to stand at a distance and hold good intentions for another, while they may know not you are so doing. Love is the willingness to release those who have wronged thee, that they might find their own righteousness. Love is the compassion of one's spirit reaching out, stating, I know you. *Thou art a brother… or a sister. We are all one.* Love is the power through which great wondrous works can be accomplished. Love and compassion are inseparable. And yet…

Compassion

Compassion… in its first letter is the comfort of knowing. It is that which surrounds and holds, and yet leaves a way open for the uniqueness, the individuality, to explore, seek, and grow.

Compassion is the pillar of one's soul. It is that which seeks to know causal forces, to embrace them and to see them as an energy in motion, so to say. Compassion is the understanding of another's needs, wants, and uniqueness; and bringing the force of love within same, to love one's self sufficiently to, as such, allow compassion to flow.

Grace in the Center

If we were to place these – all four of these pillars of righteousness – upon a piece of paper, you would first start out perhaps with one or the other at the top… the north cardinal point, as you call it in the Earth, and another to the south, and yet another to the east, and the final to the west. If you were in the absolute center between these four, equi-distant on this paper, to place one word: *Grace…* that would be the pivot point upon which these four would find their balance.

Now you would, in your individuality, choose one of these four to be uppermost, perhaps somewhat influenced by the order in which we have given them… though that would be, as you will see in a moment, an illusion. For as you take this piece of paper and perhaps thrust some axial implement (a pin or something) through the center directly through grace, you could now spin this piece of paper. And perhaps whatsoever comes to rest at the very top might be that most appropriate for you. Perhaps this might be that which you most need to focus on in that Earth day or that moment.

A Wheel of Righteousness

But you could take this and develop it, perhaps make a circle of more sturdy substance with a center point, and put these four, as given, with grace in the center. And you might, for your own personal discovery, take the earlier nine steps we have given and shared with you, and put them wheresoever you find appropriate on this wheel of Righteousness, as we might now call it.

Where you place these might typify the uniqueness of who and what you are. Does forgiveness, for example, fall moreso between love and honor? Or would it be between truth and compassion, or any of the other quadrants. What about self? Where would this fall? And so on and so forth. You can create for yourself an ever-changing wheel of life, the wheel of righteousness, upon which you intend to ascend, ultimately, into your true eternal nature.

TWO IMPORTANT UNIVERSAL LAWS

There are two very powerful Laws among the many… which are, in fact, equal… and yet, we call these two so very powerful because they are so often overlooked by those who are expressed finitely in the Earth and, to be sure, in many other realms.

The Law of Free Will and the Law of Grace

The first, of course, is as you might surmise. It is the Law which grants you each your right of uniqueness… the Law of Free Will (or Free Choice).

The second of these also of such power, and yet so often forgotten or overlooked, set aside for varying reasons, and that is the Law of Grace.

The Right of Choice and the Right of Forgiveness

The Law of Free Will and the Law of Grace could be thought of as handmaidens to Righteousness. For in the first is your assurance, your guarantee, so to say, from God, to the Right of Choice.

Holding its hand is Grace. Grace is that statement, if you will, from the Creative Force – God – that you are forgiven. Hence, we gave forgiveness as the first of the steps.

But *you* gave the very first step, embraced by the first Law (the Law of Free Will or choice) by choosing to follow this path in this course of oneness.

Here, in the choice to participate, and in the awareness found through exploring forgiveness, you opened the doors to the Law of Grace and to the Law of Free Will (personal choice).

As you have passed through these portals, you have made many-fold discoveries. And these, to be sure, continue to unfold and shall, into the future and beyond.

If you were to take this wheel of *righteousness* (or *life*, dependent upon one's view of it) and to spin it, you would arrive at a truth, a pillar of righteousness, which can never be over-explored. These are the foundational premises, building blocks, truths and such, upon which we shall begin this, the first of the three… we might call them, *jewels in the crown…* of righteousness.

Sacred Number of Three

It is of no small coincidence that this number, three, is sacred and has such diverse meaning. For thou art spirit, mind, and body.

Here then is the body of righteousness. It is that which you tend, just so as you tend your very physical body in the Earth. The foundation of righteousness must be nourished through your own grace. It must, first and foremost, be your choice, not the choice of others which are, as a result, influencing you.

Feel the call within. Hear it. Bring it forth. Look upon it. Claim it. And live it.

We shall now offer you what we would call a brief visit to a time long past, and offer in that the example, as given lovingly by a great teacher of the past to his children.

Parable: Soaring

It is a very beautiful day, and the sun shines brightly at its low angle of mid-morn, across several small, gracefully twisted, thick trunk, branches, and shiny, waxy leaves. They are few but staturely. The rocks and terrain around them, to some who see this, might be thought of as harsh. To others, merely the structure, the foundation, upon which life itself flows.

A short distance away, through an array of large boulders, a broad stream cascades down, creating a sound and an atmosphere, as the water moves from rock to rock, coming to rest in a pool of water, which then courses, following a stream off into the distance. Here, seated by this pool, is Shem, and his children and wards.

Shem states, in answer to one of the questions placed before him, as some rest, dangling a foot or hand in the coolness of the morning water, the sun's rays reflecting off it, illuminating Shem, as though some great light of sorts was focusing upon him as he speaks. "You do honor yourself when you honor others. You do not honor yourself if you dishonor others. Honor is a force which must be ever in balance. You are responsible for your part of that balance, and not that of any other aspect of it."

"How then, dear father," questions one of his children, "can honor ever have any true expression, if only I am upholding it?"

"The seeds of the earth," responds Shem, "do not depend upon the earth for their sustenance, do they? In other words, the seeds of each of these plants which you see about you, they are not dependent upon the earth, are they?"

Of course, the children look at each other.

And one boldly stands and states, "Dear father, of course they are dependent upon the earth. A seed cannot grow without earth in which to place its roots. It cannot flourish unless it has such as this water which flows by us here. We do not understand your meaning. Please, explain to us."

"You have explained it," responds Shem. "In the obvious is truth. The earth loves each seed and strives to embrace it, and give it that of foundation upon which it might grow and flower. So is it, then, your honor, just so as the earth. If you expect goodness in your life, you must be as the earth… willing to be honor where none else is manifesting this. You, then, become the good earth in which the seeds of beauty, of abundance, of hope, of nourishment, of love and compassion, may root themselves and grow."

"Oh-h," comments that one who has just spoken, "then honor is as the earth… it is that which nourishes all else?"

"It is as such," responds Shem.

"How can I know if my honor is aright?" questions another of Shem's children shyly.

"You know it by the measure of that which you consider to be aright."

Puzzled, the young lass looks at Shem, shrugs her shoulders and smiles, then responds, "But how do I know what is aright? Some would say to me, 'No, don't do this certain thing… do this, rather. It is right.' And yet, when I do as they say, the end result is not a good one."

Shem, smiling broadly, for he indeed loves this child dearly, responds softly, "Think of yourself as this pool of water, dear child," turning to gesture to the beautiful mirror-like surface of the pool of water. Reaching down, he picks up a small pebble and tosses it to the mid-point of the pool. "See how that pebble has caused ripples which reach out in every direction, finally coming to the shore, which is the earth? Honor, if you will… it is absorbed by the earth, itself.

"Truth is like this. It is the pebble which you toss into the pool of life, the ripples of which reach out and embrace, touch, caress, and are, if they are willing, absorbed by those who receive same. The truth of others is like the surface of the pool, which is now calm. Note that the ripples are gone and the pool is tranquil again.

"Your truth is like this and, as such, cannot be thought of as something tangible which remains eternally. You are the source of it. Truth rises up out of your honor. Or perhaps we could invert this and say that honor is supported by truth. But the fact remains, all that you see reflected in the pool are the individual perspectives, teachings, needs, wants, that are a part of the Earth. But truth is as the pool itself… perfect, reflecting back that which is given to it. And yet, the water is constant, pure, and always in motion, always seeking to know itself and to come together."

The young lass pauses for a moment to reflect, and then follows her father's words with this, "But others speak that which is aright in their word with such authority. And I am but a child. How can I speak to them my truth, when theirs bears such power and authority and presence? How does the child speak to the elder, and there remain honor?"

Shem chuckles aloud and states, "That is as the pool of water… a reflection of what *is* in terms of the transitory… that in motion. It is only time that separates you from the elder, is it not?"

And she nods vigorously.

"Then in your time, shall others hold their truth because you are then the elder?"

"Oh, no," she responds. "I would always want to hear the truth of others."

"Then should you assume that because this one is an elder, that they would not wish to know your truth?"

"Well, with some I would," she responds vigorously and with a smile.

"Then there you have your answer," smiling back. "Truth is yours. It can be offered, and that is the end of it. You live your truth. Just as honor nurtures the seeds of all that is good, so does truth, like this pool of water, reflect what is. The water, as you look upon it, speaks not except for its sound of movement. And yet, it ever is present to nourish, to refresh, to replenish the finite. But it is also the symbol of Spirit, and truth is the symbol of Spirit. Thus do we ever, children, look to the symbol of water in the Earth as the symbol of Truth, of Spirit, of that which is Eternal.

"Your test, then, will ever be this: 'Is my truth something which I would to be eternal? Does my truth meet the need of the moment and that alone? Or can it stand eternally and reflect to all with loving neutrality, with openness, with compassion?'"

Another stands, waving her arm vigorously, and Shem nods, smiling with equal love for this one.

"They won't love us. They won't care about us, if we hold to *our* honor and *our* truth, dear father. And I grieve, I am sad, when they are not loving, when they are not kind to us or others, because we are holding these sacred truths and honor, as you give them to us." And she settles back down, to sit cross-legged before her father, erect and bright-eyed.

"Do you look, dear child, to others for your love? Is it important for you to see in them their embrace of who and what you are? For if you do, all that you are is in the Earth and dependent thereof.

"Look you upon this rock upon which I rest. Touch it. Come... Gather 'round me, children... be with me on this great rock," which they do, giggling, scampering, climbing all over Shem as they do, who simply smiles. "This rock has long endured, has it not?" And they all nod and affirm this. "And here are we, perched upon it. It did not call us. We did not call out to it. And yet, here we are, one with it, upon it. Place your hands upon it and tell me, dear child, what do you feel?"

The questioner does so, closes her eyes, snuggling up against Shem as she does. And she states, "Well, this hand in the shadow feels cool, soothing. It feels good. Here, where the sun's light has hit the rock, it is warm. It feels dry. And it, too, feels good. It feels very solid."

And the others giggle at this.

"Then let this be your symbol of what love truly is. It is the rock of foundation within you, your very heart... which has the capacity to know darkness, the cool embrace, the good feeling that comes when one finds a cool place to rest and the sun's light is high and intense. And it has that part of its being which warms... which is in the light, which brings to you such a sense of oneness, the warmth and light of it passing all through your body, embracing it, holding it, permeating all of the aspects of who and what you are.

"Two seemingly different aspects found within this rock, which cannot move, which simply is... always here to support one who would come by and seek to rest upon it... surrounded by the waters of truth," gesturing again to the pool and stream, "nurtured by the force of honor, waiting for you to root your intentions as seeds into it.

"You might not think of matters of the heart as a rock. But if you do, your love will always be, and it will surround you, cooling you when needed, warming you when needed, always solid, always present.

"Look you now upon this," and he bends to grasp a handful of sand at his feet. He holds it out and gradually opens his clenched fist. And as he does, the grains of sand begin to trickle out of his great hand and down to the earth again. "This is the love of others. Once as this rock, but transformed in so many ways by the challenges, the needs, the wants, the desires, the fears, all that sort of the Earth. Just as the elements of the Earth have taken this once great stone and wrought it into many small grains of its former nature. Isn't it still the great stone... similar to the one we are resting on?"

One young lad is shaking his head very seriously, and Shem nods at him, and he speaks, "No, not at all, dear father. This is tiny. It's only fragments of what it was."

"Ah, yes, very astute," chuckles Shem, and all of the children chuckle, as well. "But you see, that is your perception of it. If you look here, and there out over the distance... isn't the Earth comprised, in fact, of all these tiny granules? Aren't these tiny fragments of a once great boulder now that which is the honor of the Earth itself? You will decide this. You will decide which of these is truly worthy of claiming. You will decide what   of love is outside of yourself to which you will interact... sometimes very intensely, other times more openly, with less need or want.

"But if you do this – recognizing this great, solid, permanent love which is within you – you are ever capable of knowing these tiny fragments to be just a different form of what is you."

"Are you saying, Father, that these tiny grains of sand are the same as this great boulder?" questions the lass again.

"It is true, for if you look upon love in terms of its size, then you are not seeing. Some can give to you such as this great stone upon which we rest. Others can only give a grain of sand. But love is love. They give what they have to give. If your love is like this in-side you, you will never... *never*... be without the presence of love. And you will see the love of others as within their capacity, their ability, to manifest."

"Teach us, Father, how we can understand these things. How can we look upon truth and honor, love, and truly know them, as we know them when we are at your side?" squirming up to embrace Shem as he speaks.

"You know them through the capacity of your own knowing of self. If you can know yourself, and do as God has asked us to do... forgive... then that opens the way for you to know others. If you cannot forgive yourself, you cannot know that which is the aware-ness, the truth, the life of others. But when you can forgive yourself, you have opened a pathway upon which the needs and wants, the sight, the teachings, the understandings of others can travel back and forth easily, unobstructed, upon the path of compassion.

"Look you over here. See?" pointing up into the sky. "See that great bird? Watch it for a moment as I speak to you. It is not ex-pending effort to remain aloft. It is simply soaring in great circles, riding the forces of the Earth. As the sun warms the air, it rises... and lifts this great bird up. In the evening, even on a moonlit night, we do not see it. For it knows in those times that that is a good time to rest, to re-balance itself, to find oneness.

"Just so as this stone, dear child," patting the questioner on the head who spoke, invoking the parable of the stone, "night is as the cool side, and day is as the warm side... that was an example of love which has many profound aspects to it. Compassion is the understanding of what is. That great winged creature," pointing up aloft again, "knows compassion. It knows that the forces of nature respond predictably. In the sun's warm rays it can rise easily, with minimal effort. At times during the eveningtide, it must, too, take flight, but only as it must. During those times, the effort is much greater.

"So it is with compassion, then... as you open yourself with truth and honor and love, and let these shine upon this inner path of understanding, then can you rise as this great bird, easily, and soar, spiraling, through the levels of consciousness and under-standing of others. But if you do not hold love, honor, and truth as the lights upon your inner path of compassion, then you must labor. You must be as the bird flying in evening, with no warm currents to lift it, no light of love under its wings, no strength of currents of air borne by truth and honor upon which it can move easily.

"The test of compassion, then, is simple: *Am I looking upon these things – these works, these thoughts, these deeds of others – in the light of love, truth, and honor... not theirs, but mine?*

"And if you are laboring to find compassion, if you must struggle to reach out and understand, then you are in the darkness of the eveningtide, and your love, truth, and honor are not shining. Neither can you shine these upon another, without them first being illuminated within you. For these four, dear children, are the pillars of righteousness upon which all else can be built. And at the core of it is the promise of our Lord God – that even if we should go forth and error, by the judgment of ourselves or others, or the comparison to our truth or honor have fallen short, God knoweth this and we are forgiven.

"You must, ever, each day, forgive yourself. How do you do this?

"Touch the Earth and claim it as that which nourishes, symbolically and literally.

"Bathe yourself in the spirit of truth, and be cleansed of limitation, illusion, and doubt.

"Rest often upon the rock of thy love within.

"And oft, ever oft… be in joyful prayer and meditation and soar upon the currents of the Spirit of God, knowing that He shall lift thee and lead thee."

8003

APPLYING THE FOUR TENETS

In these teachings, lovingly given by Shem to those whom are ever yet, even so, with him, can you find the answers to all your questions, dear friends.

But perhaps you should do these things: Make a wheel of life, place upon it the four tenets, place the other nine as you would see them, and move them about. Look to the Earth and remember Shem's teachings, and the rock upon which you might rest and know it to be as eternal as your love and God's love for you. See through your truth with compassion, thereby enabling you to know the truth of others. All of this is made possible through grace.

Grace is that power which assures you worthiness. Begin, then, with your own worthiness, asking yourself, *What is it that might come between me and my righteousness?* Define it.

In the first week, pray as follows:
Lord God, show me my worthiness. Light the way with the spirit of Thy grace, that I can know these things to have been my quest for oneness with Thee. Amen.

In the second week, from your own worthiness, try to see the worthiness of others in the same way.

During the third week, try to see the worthiness of those who are not known to thee... casually met in your Earth's journey through that week, those who are distant, removed. Know their quest and understand through your own worthiness.

In the fourth week, look upon all of existence, and perhaps offer this prayer:

O Father-Mother-God, the intent and force of life itself creates according to those choices and needs of those who are creating... help me to see and understand this. Help me to know the nature of that which is their need, that I can, in that knowledge, know its worthiness. For all things are as step-stones to Thee, Father-Mother-God, and I am upon these steps. Let me see them as such, and not as a limitation. Amen.

Appreciate All That You Are

Each evening all throughout, offer a prayer, asking to see all that you are. Whatsoever you might have denied or set aside, bring it forth. Know it. Empower yourself to see it as a part of your journey from spirit to finiteness. Whether adjudged good or bad, error or wisdom, know it. You take the power from it and place it, permanently, as a step-stone for the ascension of your own spirit into righteousness.

All those who are gathered here are with you. Not a one of you walks alone. Not a one of you is without guidance. All are equal in the sight of God. Each of you in this lifetime in the Earth – and each of you who are aware of these works in other realms – are expressing a unique facet of your true potential. You might think of your body...or the manifestation as you now bear it (should you be beyond the Earth) as that which *is*. And that is truth. But it is not all that is. See?

All Is of God and All Is a Gift to God

You honor God by honoring self. If that is truth, then what happens when you dis-honor self?

You love God when you love yourself. What then happens, what is your gift to God, when you do not love yourself?

When you hold your truth upright, you are holding the truth of God before you in all that you are and do. If you do not claim your truth, what then goes before you in testimony to God?

If you hold yourself in compassion, you are embracing compassionately the existence of All, which is God. If you cannot have compassion for yourself, what is the nature of your gift to the All and to the Spirit of God?

Grace is *the* cloak of righteousness that is worn honorably and in truth that is embraced with love and compassion by those who would walk with He – the Teacher of Righteousness. Wilt thou not do the same?

Mind is the builder, so it has oft been given.

What is the pattern to be? As Shem told his children, "Oft be in joyful prayer and meditation and soar as the great bird," then, too, dear friends, can we not all soar together? Rise up, claim, and be joyful, free, and soar upon the very Spirit of God.

In all of this that we have given here, our prayers are woven all throughout. So many here – whom you love and know from the past… who were with the Master as the man called Jesus, who were with Shem, Anna, Sophie, Jacob… who were guided by the beauty of Judith, who were held in the embrace of Rebecca… whom Miriam held and embraced with her love and wisdom… whose inspiration was nurtured by Hannah, who found in all the potential for joy and goodness.

In the prophecies as given by John that He would come, were the tenets of the Maidens of Righteousness as love and compassion… were the teachings, the rod and staff of the Disciples, the Apostles. These he wove into the promise:

"He comes. He, who is the greatest of all, and bears the keys to righteousness, approaches. Make the way ready. Open yourselves. Come, let this simple symbol of transformation – the waters of truth with which I baptize you – let them awaken you."

So then, dear friends, baptize yourselves in your own truth. Walk upon the Earth of your own honor. Feel the strength of your love. And open the way to soar, freely, with compassion in all. Let God's Grace embrace you.

We are through here for the present. We thank all those who have come forward… and our dear brother, Shem, for his gift here. And those of you who are his children, who are now in the Earth… awaken… remember his teachings and his love and those of all gathered here.

Fare thee well then for the present, dear friends. Om Shanti.

GUEST LECTURE: Judith

Given October 2, 2000

JUDITH: From the heavens of eternity, upon the winds of light of God's very spirit, I come to you as the spokesperson of those who bear His light.

I am called Judith, and I have dwelled through eternity at the side of the one known as the Christ.

In the teachings which are being offered to you in this conclusive segment of these works, there is the presence of a wondrous hope... a promise, if you will, that has been as a child asleep.

We who are of God's service and dwell eternally in His light beckon to you to awaken this sleeping Child: the promise of God within.

In those journeys wherein my Lord has sought to bring light to the dimensions of expressions of finiteness – and, of course, that being especially so, the Earth – I and my sisters and brothers have seen much. We have seen the beauty of those things which have flowed through the minds and hearts and skilled hands of artisans who have opened themselves to the creative force of God. In so many instances, these creative forces have been directed towards needs in the Earth. And as these creations have filled these varying needs, the expression which is called the Earth and those within it are seen to have progressed.

This progression, as it is looked upon from the Earth, is seen as the growth of enlightenment, the advance of knowledge and science, the progression of medicine, the birth of technology.

It is, as well, the birth of spirit... the call to awaken the sleeping Child of promise within you.

So as you see these as contributions to your need, see them, as well, as the spirit of God – His love, Her embrace, our Oneness – answering the calls of your needs.

As I have dwelled in and about my Lord's very being and have known Him and do know Him, the vehicle of words cannot express to you, nor am I so knowledgeable in them so as to be capable of using them, to give you true insight to the love He bears for you.

The quest for what you consider to be of import in your life – the search for meaning and substance to who and what you are, and what you do in daily life – He loves these, because He loves you. We have come forth to speak, with I as the spokesperson here, to tell you this and so much more.

It is the truth of your heart's greatest desire, your highest ideal in spirit and the step-stones which lead to it, which are ever held in His being… His heart and mind, as well. And He knows these.

But as you would look upon these now (in the light of the beautiful teacher Shem's gift to you, and that of the steadfast, untiring, unwavering service of Lama Sing and those with him) you do not, in these expressions in what we are conveying to you and that which you know by example, know how profound this body of love and compassion and oneness is for you.

There are brothers and sisters in the Earth who have journeyed long, whose challenges have been great, whose burdens have oft bent them low. And yet, they have endured. Could you ask why this is? Are you one of these?

It is because the very things dear Lama Sing has given, and Shem and the others, are of eternal permanence within those of whom I have just spoken. These are the examples you have about you, and they are reflections of what you have within – the sleeping Child of promise within you.

I have not known the limitation (as it might be called) of finiteness, by wearing it, by being in it. But I have known it through the heart of the Christ, through my Lord's own understanding and compassion. So perhaps it could be said, while I and my brothers and sisters have not worn the mantle of flesh, nonetheless we know it, as all can know through He.

And where is He? Distant? At the throne of our Lord God? So far away that the repetition of prayer again and again must be as a continuum of a call unto He, because He is distant?

Fall not into the illusion of separateness, for He embraces thee, even now as I speak.

I am with our Lord by choice. His light and mine are as one… and with you, as well, if you awaken the Child within.

I and my brothers and sisters thank you for all that you are and that which you intend. And we are with you. The peace of God and the glory of His grace… may these embrace and keep you.

In the love of the heart of our Lord, there do I dwell, offering same to you every step of the way.

Love to you. Fare thee well.

GUEST LECTURE: Jacob

Given October 2, 2000

JACOB: I am called Jacob. I have walked with the sisters of righteousness. And held the hand of the babe called Jesus, and John, and many others.

As I looked into their eyes so often at twilight time when we were gathered, I would see the vibrancy, the light of their hope, the promise of it for humankind to come... then and in future.

And as the ladies of righteousness would encircle us and gift us with their song, I would hold these (and others... as many as I could) embracing them and looking into their eyes and hearts.

It was such an inspiration, for I could see the vibrancy of new life, the exhilaration of their hopefulness, unfettered by the illusions or limitations that is placed upon those who journey through a lifetime in Earth. And just as one would fan the embers of a small flame to bring forth the evening's cook fire, so did I reach out to fan the flames of hopefulness within these.

Their questions were as a torrent of rainfall, bringing to my heart the delight of those who seek. And as the Lord God would guide me, so did I speak unto their inquiries, and gift them with the gifts given me by the Elders... the teachers, those who have loved the Law and placed it before all else, even before their own lives.

As I held them and embraced them, and they me, I opened my spirit to flow to they, and took from them, equally so, the light of their hopefulness.

Each, I knew, was to go a different pathway.

Each, I knew, was to come to journey's end with the greatest of all challenges of Earth... that called death.

One, I knew, was destined to journey for the most part alone. I embraced him. I gifted him with the spirit of all that I am and all that had been given me. And the sisters did the same. Thus he, though outwardly appearing alone, was rich and embraced with these... and greater – for the spirit of those who are the truth of God walked with him... and, indeed, the angelic host never left his side.

And this one upon my right knee would have little time alone. Throngs would come to Him to hear the Word, to receive the gifts from the fruits of His tree of life as Jesus. What can I give to Him? For

I could see… He is the Son of God! What might I, Jacob, in my aging years, give to one of such Light?

And an ancient one came and spoke to me. "Measure not, Jacob, against the rod of illusion, but against that of the staff of God of truth."

And so I gave to He, as to John and the others, equally. And He took of it equally. And it was good.

I knew then, as I know now, that each of us has that which is precious, which is beyond the measure of those qualifiers of Earth or eternity itself. For it is the intent of God, given unto each, that is the gift within.

I knew in that moment from the ancient one, as I was embraced by these many children of such light, that I must ever honor this – the incredible majesty of the gift within.

And so do I, then – as called, Jacob – give to you all of my being. The greatest that I have to give is who and what I am. Take from this, as ye will. Look upon it in a moment of need, and see that the process of claiming can be joyful and filled with love and compassion if you will receive my gift to you, the gift of these beautiful ladies of righteousness who are gathered here, even as I speak.

But more than this, know it to be from your Father-Mother-God. How can you, then, deny it?

Peacefulness descends upon those who know themselves to be Children of God. This peacefulness opens you and makes the way passable, that all things might thereafter follow.

In this time, as you hear or read these words, know this as a truth. That is my prayer for you.

Joyful journey, dear friends.
Peacefulness of God be with you.

GUEST LECTURE: Abraham

Given October 2, 2000

ABRAHAM: What can I bring to thee, O Children of Israel? What is the message, the gift, that I might bear to you, following those splendid gifts of love and compassion as have already been given? Perhaps this small example of a time past of an experience of my own as Abraham might be the token of my love and blessing to you all.

They were times that were harsh in the Earth, and all about us were famine and pestilence. They were times wherein the newborn cried out, for the nourishment from their mothers could not flow. They were times when the seeds, placed so lovingly in the earth, bore not fruit but came forth and withered and perished.

We traveled and journeyed and searched... I, and my peoples. And yet, the hardships worsened. We struggled, even so, only to find the barest of our needs, the sparsest unto our desires. Here and there we came to find small pools of water, and as we took from these, the source closed and they were no more. And so we journeyed... and journeyed. But each evening-tide and morn we gathered together. We did not lament, though certainly just cause was present for so doing... even so, some wept, silently, hoping the others would not hear or see. Some were left behind as we traveled.

And yet, each morn we gave thanks. And each evening we came to prayer and service. And we held out our hands, all of us, palms up together and said these words:

Lord God, here are my hands outstretched to Thee. If there is that within them and my life which Thou would have, this I give to Thee openly. Take of it and me as Ye would. If Thou seeth, Lord, another whose need is great, bring them unto me, and I will give unto them as is mine to give. I thank You, sweet Lord, for the gift of this day and for Thy guidance within it. I am ever open to that which Thou would have me do, and that which Thee would guide me unto. Thy will, not mine, O Lord, is that which I seek with all that I am. Amen.

Such a prayer was the closure of each day.

And we trod on. More fell, in need and in hardship.

And we journeyed.

And one day we could go no further. Many turned to me, and their eyes questioned. Their hearts had grown heavy; their sorrows were many... these things I knew.

And I spoke these words unto them… in the distance was a small mount, and I said to them, "I go forth now to that mount. Do not follow, but wait here until I return. I wish to be one with our Lord God and ask of Him for guidance."

None spoke, but simply looked… their hunger, their pain, sapping them… yet, I could see a bit of a light in each as they looked upon me.

And my heart, in that moment, grew heavy. The thought came from the Earth, calling to me as the shadows of night would, *Abraham! What hast thou wrought? God has abandoned thee. Look at your children. Look at their want. Look about you. Everywhere, there is need. God hears you not. Turn back.*

It was in the sea of such temptations that I strode, my staff in hand, with naught but my garments and staff.

When I finally reached the mount, I settled and looked to the evening sky as the sun slipped away.

And the voice said again, *Look you, Abraham… it is the promise of God slipping away! Soon I will come and embrace you. Turn back. Turn away.*

I bowed my head and sought out oneness with our Lord, and I spoke these words:

"Lord God, it is I, Abraham. I come to You not of my own need, but those of Thy Children who are in my care. I have called to Thee again and again, and I have heard You not. If Thou must forsake me, I accept this. But forsake them not, for they are innocent. My faith is strong. My heart has not wavered. Even in the voice of the shadows of darkness, my love for Thee remains. Take me, O Lord, if there is this as a penance for wrongdoing. But give unto our Children to meet their need. This I pray Thee."

As my head bowed with fatigue and hunger, my faith grew within. And in the place of the darkness following twilight, a light surrounded me, and I was uplifted. It was as though some force of God lifting me up in great hands, carried me back to look upon my children. And as I looked down, I heard these words: *"Thy faith endureth all. Your prayer is heard and answered."*

So great was the power of that spirit that I could see no more. I slipped away and fell into the light and danced the dance of life… of love, compassion, honor, and truth.

When upon the morn's first rays I awoke, I turned to witness these first rays of light and offered my prayer. I rose and strode with renewed hope, and promise burst within me.

And as I came to my peoples, I heard their song. I was puzzled for a moment, until I remembered the vision and the promise.

A group of herders and their flock had come down from the hills, mysteriously finding our encampment, and they were of our faith and belief in the One God. And the children had meat unto their need, and the babes could again suckle and find nourishment of a mother's love. And that evening, as we all gathered, we sang mighty praises unto God. But this, too, did we sing out: a prayer of gratitude for our oneness. For as surely as God heard my prayer and knew my faith, so did He speak to those herders and send them joyfully to us, their distant brothers and sisters.

And so, from that day forward we traveled together, helping one another, loving one another, singing songs of joy. Faith was the strength, the rock upon which we rested.

Let then this be my gift to you and the gift of my children, many of whom are you, hearing, reading these words:
The promise of God is ever, ever with you.
Faith is the key with which you can unlock that promise.

No matter how great the hardship might seem, go a step or two beyond it. Look for the summit, ascend it, and be one with your Father-Mother-God, and the answer will be given.

God's goodness is my prayer for you. And the call to your faith to claim it is my request.

Thank you all.
Shalom

STUDY GUIDE

Activities for Applying the Four Tenets

Evening Review & Exercises

Each evening all throughout, offer a prayer, asking to see all that you are. Whatsoever you might have denied or set aside, bring it forth. Know it. Empower yourself to see it as a part of your journey from spirit to finiteness. Whether adjudged good or bad, error or wisdom, know it.

NOTES:

_____

_____

_____

_____

_____

_____

_____

_____

_____

_____

_____

_____

_____

_____

_____

_____

_____

_____

_____

_____

_____

_____

_____

_____

Weekly Exercises for the Four Tenets

Week 1
Begin then with your own worthiness, asking yourself, "What is it that might come between me and my righteousness?" Define it.
Lord God, show me my worthiness. Light the way with the spirit of Thy grace, that I can know these things to have been my quest for oneness with Thee. Amen.

Week 2
In the second week, from your own worthiness, try to see the worthiness of others in the same way.

Week 3
During the third week, try to see the worthiness of those who are not known to thee, casually met in your Earth's journey through that week, those who are distant, removed. Know their quest and understand through your own worthiness.

Week 4
In the fourth week, look upon all of existence in the same manner.

Perhaps offer this prayer:
O Father-Mother-God, the intent and force of life itself creates, according to those choices and needs of those who are creating. Help me to see and understand this. Help me to know the nature of that which is their need, that I can, in that knowledge, know its worthiness. For all things are as step-stones to Thee, Father-Mother-God, and I am upon these steps. Let me see them as such, and not as a limitation. Amen.

NOTES:

_____

_____

_____

_____

_____

_____

_____

_____

_____

_____

_____

_____

Further Exploring the Four Tenets

NOTE: The thoughts listed here are merely suggestions to get you started in further exploration of this subject. Use any portion of them, or not, as your personal guidance leads you.

POINTS TO PONDER:

How would you define Righteousness?

How would you define Grace?

-You honor God by honoring self. If that is truth, then what happens when you dishonor self?

-You love God when you love yourself. What then happens, what is your gift to God when you do not love yourself?

-When you hold your truth upright, you are holding the truth of God before you in all that you are and do. If you do not claim your truth, what then goes before you in testimony to God?

-If you hold yourself in compassion, you are embracing compassionately the existence of All, which is God. If you cannot have compassion for yourself, what is the nature of your gift to the All and to the spirit of God?

Given that "mind is the builder" what is your pattern?

Which of the pillars of Righteousness do you consider to most closely relate to your individual uniqueness?

Why do you think all these "guests" are stepping forward now (as they have never before done) to take part in these works?

NOTES: _____

_____
_____
_____
_____
_____
_____
_____
_____

JOURNAL

_____

_____

_____

_____

_____

_____

_____

_____

_____

_____

_____

_____

_____

_____

_____

_____

_____

_____

_____

_____

_____

_____

Step II:

Grace

Given October 26, 2000

OPEM FORUM ON GRACE

LAMA SING: Yes, we have the Channel then and, as well, those references which apply to the intents and purposes of those who are gathered about these works. As we commence herein, let us come together in this joyful prayer of affirmation.

> *O Lord God, in what ways might we call upon Thee, that within our being we shall know that Thou hast heard and answered our call? What words, thoughts, actions, symbols, might we employ, that we shall know ever that it is Thy Spirit which guides us, that it is the light of Thy promise which gives life itself?*
>
> *This answer we know, O Father-Mother-God, is borne in the example of that called the Christ. For in the gifts which are His to give do we find all that is needed and greater. For He gives unto us His healing grace, His capacity and power of love, the wonder, the joy, of compassion; and above all else, here, Father, is the grace of the Christ Spirit, moving before us as that light of opportunity... the eternal gift You have given and which He has claimed. So then do we pray Thee, as we accept this gift from He, help Thou us to be the example and follow in the pattern and way of the Master, the Christ, that we, too, might impart these and the greater gifts as are unique to those who Thou would bring before us. We turn in this prayer, Lord God, to those who are lost in the illusion, the darkness, of their own doubt and fear... we send to you this, our prayer. And those who are in Thy service, Lord God... we bless you, as we know you are a part of those works of light, moving, offering, traveling into the very realms of limitation and darkness, to bear this... our Lord God's light. So do we thank Thee, O Father-Mother-God, for this continued opportunity of joyful service in Thy name through this, our Channel, and his mate in the Earth, and into the very spirit and heart of all those who have ears with which to hear and who are seeking. Amen.*

THE ELEVENTH HOUR WORK

It is appropriate, dear friends, to consider this work now before you to be similar to that called the eleventh hour, for it is that time of determination of so many aspects that are borne within self as the product of the journey through life in the Earth. (And for those of you here – who are from realms beyond the Earth – all of this and so much more is offered and applies to you, as well.)

Might we share with you, dear friends, and you with us, the memory of that time when those gathered with the Master – knowing (some) to detail, others with doubtfulness – that this would be the last meal shared in physical body.

A Call of Assembly

Is it you, then, that calls the others to this gathering, to partake of the nourishment of the earth in the symbolic definition of it being also a spiritual nourishment?

Is it you, then, who has gone out to spread the call that all are welcome at your table? Shall it be you who raises the chalice, the cup, and offers it into eternity... calling to those who would seek, who are lost or weary? That, *Here is the cup of life, here is the bread of spirit... I give this unto you.*

If you contemplate what was just stated to you, then take it within self, for here there are the vestiges similar to those who might be thy neighbor in a village past, who might be a distant traveler passing along this route to some unknown destination. And all of these are aspects of self.

Send that call, then, out to these. Call them to the table of thy spirit and sup with them, give unto them that which thou knoweth to give, that which is, by your measure, the greatest of all. For in each entity there can be found aspects which are likened unto a community of sorts, complete with travelers passing here and there along their way through the expression of your life or consciousness.

What is the meaning behind this? What purpose would there be for us to offer such as opening commentary here?

It is a call to unite. It is a call of assembly. We have heretofore offered many things, humbly and with loving grace, that you might be, in your current consciousness – whether in the Earth or beyond – re-awakened to the power and simplicity of those things as have been given. And now, in this eleventh hour, as you move unto that called the Christhood, can you call upon those which are the aspects of self still standing to the side, observing, looking, questioning, asking... yes, and perhaps even doubting and fearing?

The Call to Worthiness

This is that eleventh hour call. It is the call to worthiness. The table is the table of righteousness in your own spirit or heart of hearts. And upon this is bound those tenets as are eternal. These are those promises of God which are the unique essence and spirit of you, yourself. As you claim these in the unison of your being, you are prepared. And that which shall follow shall be yours to claim, smoothly and with ease and joy.

But if you deny one aspect of self, if one neighbor – which is a part of self – is not invited to thy table to sup with thee, then is not that of the final movement strained? Is it not in so many ways to be looked upon as incomplete?

Some of these aspects you might perceive and make judgment in regard to whether or not they are worthy, whether or not they are appropriate. And yes, perhaps even is there guilt, doubt, shame, remorse, fear, or any such associated to that aspect or, perhaps, a memory of an event past. Some might look into the cup of their own spirit and see here and there that which they would have not present.

The Great Gift

So might we remind you, as the Master has – personally, to each of you again and again – the spirit of Self is that which is precious and eternal. So as you would see it as a golden Child within... knowing it to be in need of honor, of truth, of love and compassion... then remember as just given, the center of all of this is grace.

As you seek, in daily life in Earth and in your sojourns beyond the Earth to apply those nine steps as were given, and as you begin with forgiveness as it was given as such, can you not now, having passed along all nine steps, see the import of the great gift of grace?

It is not that you must decide. It is not that any here or in any realm should or shall equate, by the balance scale of anyone's definition, that this or that is worthy of grace, and this or that is not. It is to be seen by those who approach the altar of God that such experiences, such thoughts, even deeds, have been forgiven; have been seen in their true nature, as the quest of one Child of God to know, to understand... to struggle through the passageway of darkness, which seems to limit and yet, all the while, embraces… to pass through the light, covering themselves out of concern or even fear, that some inner attitude, action, flaw, or whatnot, might be seen by those of light.

YOUR SPIRIT'S SONG

Stand within yourself and look all about. See the village of your being in the personage of the past. See the travelers who come and go as new ideas or old habits seeking to gain residency once again.

But in all of this, you are the power. You are the presence of God's Spirit made manifest in the profound uniqueness as is our Lord God's intent for you.

Determining Worthiness

Some of you have asked about worthiness; and how is it possible, while yet in Earth, or in these nearby realms, to truly know and claim one's worthiness.

It is, clearly, to begin now – where you are, whatsoever you consider yourself to be as you hear or read these words, and know this to be the moment of truth, the eleventh hour of your spirit's song.

Do you know of anyone who is more worthy than you? Do not answer quickly, but pause and think about that. And when you do… and perhaps you shall come forth with one or more names or identities… then the next question is, quite simply, *why*? Is their worthiness greater than yours because they are more visible, that their actions, words, or deeds have been perceived by the greater number than your own? Have you offered an act of kindness, of charity, of compassion, of forgiveness? Have you extended understanding and truth to another this day?

If you have so done, then does this not equate to anything else? For know this: Our Lord God perceives all. And it is not by the measure of the perception of others that a deed, an intent, a thought, a word, an action, is considered to be great. Your kindness to a passerby in the form of a smile and nod might be transformative, changing a day otherwise barren and bleak of recognition and compassion into one which is now offered to them, if they will accept it. For in that, the connection and the flow of your spirit's light must be recognized, must be known.

Witnessing, then, the Master demonstrating this, *"Dost thou believe?"* followed by *"Thy faith has restored thee."*

If you believe that you are worthy, then your faith will bring about complete worthiness.

Worthiness is not a comparative nor competitive thing, as so common in the Earth. It is not by the measure of that without, but only, as such, wherein the fruits as self offers without are measured against that of the potential within. In other words... What you have to give, is this your gift? If the measure of what you give is one-half of what your potential is, are you only half worthy?

It is not to be misleading nor cryptic, but to evidence to you that these are the measures used so often in the Earth to determine one's worth and one's worthiness.

Those whose appearance in physical body is adjudged by the standard of that time of measure to be beautiful, are oft considered desirable, worthy. They are edified by the materiality and its intents of the Earth. And then comes one whose beauty is within and the outer is not so much so, by the measure of the Earth, considered as such; and yet, as their words, their actions, their deeds, come to be known, their beauty can be seen. It is not quantified nor qualified; it is simply the outpouring of what is.

GRACE IS NON-EXCLUSIVE

And here is one of the keys that is intended to be our humble offering to you in this meeting: Turn away from that which is defined as a limited or exclusive measure of worthiness; turn, rather, to that state of worthiness which embraces all.

Exclusivity is not a part of the measure of the Grace of God. Conversely, the Grace of God is universal.

All Existence Flows Through God's Grace

It is, rightfully, through the Grace of God that existence flows, that consciousness continues to expand. It is through the Grace of God that the cycle of life, or Wheel of Life (or incarnation, as so often referred to) is even possible. Consider you carefully, were it not so, then what would be the criterion? Where would be the measure of continuity, of worthiness, to perpetuate such existence and expression, were this not so?

The Grace of God is omnipotent.

It is not *held* in the heart or hand of one entity. It can be *demonstrated* through the heart and hand of one entity, to profound measure… as exemplified in the Master, as found in the teachings of the Buddha, as in the life and measure and expressions of guidance in Mohammed, in the tenets and truths and embrace of Moses and Abraham, and on and on might we continue but the meaning, we should think, is clear.

Each peoples, all who have their own uniqueness of focus and belief, are embraced by God's Grace. And within that literal expression of life potential, called grace, are all things possible… even errors… even that called misdeeds, mistakes, oversights, errors and sins of commission and omission. And yet, all throughout, one finds the brilliant light of God's Grace, shining. Only those who are adjudging upon their own balance scale or those offered by others, by mass-mind thought, by habit, by dictums of past judgment and such… these are those scales that limit.

Then the measure, in truth, is that which is found within yourself – ever, as a light, at times brilliant, and at other times perceived as dim – for it is the willingness to claim same that increases or diminishes its brilliance.

The Right to Decide

You must make decisions, in all of the realms who hear these words. And that is another of the wondrous great gifts of God, the very right to choose – the Law of Free Will.

Others can manacle your body, bind it with chain and all that sort. They can intern you physically. They can demean you and chastise you. They can call out to the masses, *Look you upon this one and compare to the standard which we hold as righteous.* But even so, throughout all, can you rise up of your own free will choice and claim God's Grace. At which point we might hear you state these words with authority and with compassion and love:

"Father, forgive them, for they know not what they do."

PARABLE: BLESSING

This is a small village in a time past, and it has in its company, in its inhabitants, several different divisions of what could be called the One Faith. Each of these divisions metes out, according to their interpretation of the Law. And while they, as a unit, as a village, are intact and sovereign unto the Law, within the village itself, they are divided. To those who would come from distant places and journey to and through this village, they would seem to be of one teaching, of one Law. It is as though they are cloaked in the measure of the Law as it is shared by all, and divided by its interpretation. According to happenstance, or chance (or perhaps one could say with a bit of humor, according to Providence) several travelers entered the village and, very weary from a long journey, sought shelter.

As they found one abode which accepted them after the offering of some coin, they were seated, partaking of their meal. And one asked of the head of the household, "What is the measure of your truth and your people's truths?"

And the man answered, "We are of the One God, and we are descendants of those who have gone before and who have evidenced the Truth of our One God."

The traveler, slowly consuming the food before him, turned to look at his two companions silently.

After a moment or two, the traveler again looked to the head of the household, who was seated across from them. "Where is this Truth, then, that you speak of?"

The head of the household was puzzled for a moment, and finally responded, "It is not a thing. It is not something that I can retrieve and show you. The Truth is within our lives."

The traveler again glances at his two companions and continues to take nourishment into his body. Finally, again, he speaks. "You have shared your food with us. Can you share your Truth with us?"

The head of household was startled and looked upon these three travelers. And in and about their countenance he saw that which was unfamiliar, unknown to him. And with mixed emotion and some confusion, he stated, "No, that would not be possible. You must be one of us in order to partake of our Truth."

The traveler again looked at his two companions, and there was an almost imperceptible nod. All three in unison arose from the table, thanked the head of household, and turned and left.

A short distance down the main way of this village, for it was of some size, again they knocked. And it was answered unto them. And the scene was repeated. They offered coin for nourishment. As they again sat before a simple meal placed before them, the same questions were asked.

And the head of this household looked upon them, when asked to share his Truth with them, and stated, "Well, I could share our Truth with you, but in order for you to truly be able to know it and for us to give it to you, you must stay with us and be one with us, for we live our Truth. It cannot be simply given."

Again, the center traveler turned to his two companions, and once again they arose, expressing quick gratitude and, without another word, departed.

A bit further down the way, they knocked upon a third door, and it was opened, and they were met with a smile.

And before they could ask, this is what they heard. "Welcome. You appear to have traveled a great distance. Come, let me give you shelter. Let me give you unto your needs."

The three bowed and entered and were seated. And the best of that within this abode was brought before these three travelers and given. Not a word was mentioned of coin.

"From whence do you come, dear friends?" questioned the head of household.

They explained that their journey was from a faraway land, little known by these peoples.

And the center traveler again spoke, asking the same questions, and when asked of his truth, the head of household spoke thusly: "This is my truth, dear friends... my truth is that I see you as my brothers from a distant land. I know not where, but it matters not. For our interpretation of the Law is that we are all one."

"Then this is your truth?" questions the center traveler.

"It is deep, it is broad, it is powerful," smiles the head of household, "and it is beyond my humble capacity to express to you in mere words, for I am not knowledgeable of many such. Therefore do I and my brethren strive to live our truth as we interpret the Law. And this is my expression of that truth... to welcome you, to offer you that which I have to give."

The center traveler turns to look at his two companions and, for the first time, they sit upright and their faces warm into smiles. And all three turn to look at the head of household, who is, indeed, smiling in return.

And the center traveler speaks. "You are that one for whom we have been searching. Your truth is as our own. And we have brought gifts for you."

The traveler on the left rises and reaches within his garments and pulls forth a small pouch. Placing it between his outstretched palms and bowing as he walks forward, he places it gently before the feet of the head of the household.

The head of household looks down in awe, for it is obviously a well-prepared pouch by some skilled artisan, and he cannot imagine what it might have as its contents. And so he looks from it, the pouch, back up to the giver, who is now backing away... hands together before his forehead, head bobbing slowly as he backs to stand by the doorway through which he entered.

The traveler to the right now rises and, giving the same gestures, comes before the head of household. And reaching within his robes, he pulls forth an exquisite box of some beautiful woods, decorated with gold and jewel, highly lacquered and polished, and with inscriptions of which the head of household has no knowledge. He places this to the opposite side of the head of household's feet, speaking not a word... hands folded, bobbing his head, as he backs to stand on the other side of the portal, the doorway, through which they entered.

All the while, the central traveler sits erect, his face serene and smiling, one hand placed over his heart throughout all of that we have just recounted. Now he rises, before the head of household can speak, having looked to his right side at the pouch, to his left at the beautiful box.

And now the central traveler walks about the table and to the head of household, standing ever so straight... the light of his love and warmth, his smile, all radiating as though he were illuminated by some unknown presence. Hands together, he stands before the now bedazzled head of household, who is struggling feebly, clumsily, to rise to his feet to stand before his honored guest.

The central traveler speaks thusly: "Your prayers and those of your peoples have been heard. There is a time before you of great import, a time wherein the Truth of Spirit can be a light... not only to those who hold it within, but unto those who would come unto it, just so as we three travelers, unknown to you, have come to you.

"We have come in answer to the prayers of your entire village, but only you and your peoples have truth in the form of the very Word of God. And so are we, then, honored to be in your presence. And these humble offerings which we have presented to you are to assist you and those who believe with you, in order that you shall, to the betterment of that work, be able to make the way passable.

"This, then, do I offer you in humbleness..." and he reaches up to un-secure his robe of travel. It appears dusty. It appears soiled by what obviously was a long, arduous journey. After removing it from himself, the central traveler turns it within.

And the head of household gasps, for it is covered with wondrous symbols, beautiful designs, the intersects of which are met by precious jewels.

The central traveler steps forward and gently, almost reverently, places it ornate side out, over the head of household's shoulders, then steps back.

The head of household cannot speak. He looks down, touching the garment.

And the central traveler also places his hands upwards together and begins to back towards the portal, as did his two companions before him. As they are all standing now before the doorway, the portal through which they entered, each places their hand over the heart of their body. "These are merely tools. You see them as great gifts and, indeed, in the Earth, they are the measure of humankind's value. What you do not see, dear brother, is that the greatest jewel of all is your expression of the Truth of God. We are messengers of that God. Take these tools and do good works with them."

And they are gone.

୫୦୯୪

The Harvest

Is it the measure of this humble peasant's expression of truth that brought to him these resplendent gifts? Is it the measure of his willingness to truly live his truth that brought about that which might be called by the Earth the *just reward*, the harvest of what he has sown? Or could it be said, in the eternal sense, that the greatest of all of these gifts... and they are bountiful as they were given to this simple man... was the affirmation to him and those of his grouping that their prayers are heard and answered.

Isn't it the greatest of all jewels, the greatest of all gifts, to know without question that your prayers are heard and answered, that your truth is the Truth of God?

You... answer that question for yourself.

And then see who it is that dines with you at your table on this ceremony of the Eleventh Hour.

Bring Forth the Golden Child

There are nine steps which have gone before.

And the tenth was the passage through the portal.

This, the eleventh, holds out the opportunity for you to claim the Rite of Passage... for you to express – to hear and know it to be good – the song of your own spirit... for you to bring forth the Golden Child from within you... nurtured, loved, forgiven, understood, given compassion, guided by truth and honor and righteousness... and seat that Child at the head of this table.

Bear the Atmosphere of Grace

Grace is not an idle gift. It is not suspended on some distant goalpost, awaiting those who would struggle to achieve it. It was the very first of all the blessings that were given to you upon your awakening... in the Earth, or whatsoever realm wherein you now dwell.

And the companion gift to it of Free Will empowers you to choose. For as is in that village, of the three different ways of interpreting the Law of God, two measure out according to an interpretation and it becomes very special, very beautiful, very empowering. But it is not lived in the Truth of Grace.

In the final household, it is easy to see, we should think... that grace is the atmosphere... that love is the shelter itself... and compassion and understanding are the essences which nourish all who enter into that good man's abode.

Be the Example

You are met with challenge. You are continually offered limitation and doubt and fear. These can imprison the most precious of all. True, the jewels, the coin, the beautiful robe, can be gained, can become possessions of one in any realm wherein such are present. But only through the purity of heart, only by way of claiming who and what you are in truth, can it be opened unto you and can it pass through you... that the light and love of God manifest in so many ways to those who come unto your presence.

But the most important of all, as this central traveler identified, is that of self. They did not gather all the members of that grouping who believed in this certain way, but went to one.

Now that one is the example. Let it be so within self. Let there be that one which is the example of the village of self... the aspects, the various memories and events, circumstances, and ways of thinking. Let these be exemplified and directed, guided, nurtured, and loved, through that one who knows and claims the right of choice. And through that empowerment, enables self to let the Grace flow into and through they.

We should begin in the first week by recognizing grace. We might do so in this way:

Lord God, help Thou me to see and know the presence
and expression of Thy Grace in all that I am about in
this day ahead.

Make your affirmation and conclude.

Upon the conclusion of the evenings of those first seven days, affirm in this way:

Thank You, Lord, for the expressions of Thy Grace
given to me in this day just past. As I enter into spiritual
sleep, guide me. Help me to better know and see these,

that on the morrow, as I awaken, even the greater shall
I be able to see and know and thus give to others.
Close with an affirmation or such... *Amen.*

In the second and third weeks, ask respectively:
Let me see the grace of others, no matter how slight.
And when I perceive it, let me nurture it and encourage
those who bear it to claim even more. Let me support
the grace of others.

And in the third:
Help me to see the grace of the world about me. Help
me to know goodness as it flows, even through the veils
of shadow or darkness. And let me call it such in my
own heart and mind, and let me speak of it to others.
Let me support it, nourish it, and welcome it within my
being. Amen.

In the fourth week, we humbly encourage you to do this:
All is supported and embraced by Thy Grace, Lord
God. Help thou me to contribute unto it, knowing that,
so as I do, the greater is given. And the greater then
shall it flow from me, and on and on. Let my prayers
and wishes for those beyond the Earth bear the grace of
forgiveness, love, compassion, long-suffering, and all
those tenets as I hold to be sacred within. Let me, O
Lord God, claim the righteousness as is Thy intent for
me.

Prepare for the Passage

One week's time, then – the fourth and final – hold this thought of Grace flowing through you and back to you. See it from the perspective of righteousness. For in our next meeting we would humbly ask you to baptize yourself with the Righteousness of the Christ Spirit within.

We are through here for the present, but our prayers and our Grace, given to us from God, is given to you, as is our right to do.

Fare thee well then for the present, dear friends.

GUEST LECTURE: The Angelic Host
Given October 26, 2000

ANGELIC HOST: We extend our greetings of love and joy to each and all of you.

We have come forward in answer to a call that is many-fold in its source and expression. One such as might be appropriately called, our brother – whom you know of as Michael – has beckoned to us. And there is a call equal in its brilliance and light which comes from the Sisters of Righteousness[15]. We have before us the vision of you. We have before us the knowledge of who you are eternally. We are presented with great offerings of what you have become in your current consciousness. And thus, it is with all of this before us that we bring to you the very light of God.

We have spoken recently through our brother in the Earth [in the Parable for the November open forum] and shared with you experiences of past. But now, what we would offer to you is a call. We call to you, that you should open to yourselves with the warmth, enthusiasm, and living essence, of your eternal nature – that you might see yourself as a weary traveler; and that the door of your own spirit is opened joyfully, warmly, unto that weary traveler; and that you would call, that the traveler should enter.

You are in varying expressions of consciousness that are a part of a journey, a journey many think of as having moved away from the presence, the loving embrace and consciousness, of God. But it is not so. And we are come unto this work to bring to you another gift – and that gift is the promise of your eternal nature.

How shall we give it? How shall it manifest? How shall you know of it? We give it to you now through these words and the form, the intent, the energy (as you call it) that flows with it. And we shall give it to you again as we enter with the Elders and Sisters[16] in a time just ahead.

But how shall you know it? There is but one way for you to truly know the gift, the gift that is eternal, and that is that you should live it.

---

[15] Sisters of Righteousness – refers to the Essene Holy Maidens and their teachers.

[16] Entering with the Elders and the Sisters – this refers to the entrée of the Second Wave of Light, which entered on March 18, 2001. We were told that this Wave (the Wave of Love and Compassion) would be brought in by Our Lady, Mary and Her Sisters, supported by the Elders on the wings of Love and Compassion.

You were asked to speak your answer to a call from the Master[17]. You were asked to confirm this. That was a great gift.

Some of you saw it not as a gift. Now we tell you: The gift is that you have given who you are, what you are, the promise of your spirit, to the realms of consciousness that are a part of the Earth and its measure which is adjacent to same. You have spoken out... even though some of you pondered this, yet you spoke out[18]. You confirmed to our brother and Susan your choice. Now the Law is fulfilled. Now The Way is opening.

Through what you saw as a simple act (albeit at times, for some, confusing) because you have spoken oft to our Lord in other ways. Did He need to hear your call: *Yea, Lord, I am with Thee. I accept*? No. Of course He could hear, and does, the message coming from your hearts and spirits.

But the expression of it... can you not see that that is the *living* of it?

When you speak what you hold in your heart and spirit, it is made manifest. No different than when He stated aloud... *"Arise and go. Thy faith has saved thee"* ...couldn't he have done this silently? Of course, and often did. But the speaking of it is the claiming of its power, the manifestation of its potential.

Speak what you believe, and then live it.

There is a secret place within you wherein the majesty of God's beauty manifested in you – only in that wonderful way that is specifically you – that yearns to be awakened. The portal to it is open; and that is the portal, the doorway, to which we referred just above.

Now, we are here to join with this work in a way that is now visible, and known. And we offer this, that all consciousness may know of our presence and that we stand at the side of our brother, Michael... and our brother, the Channel, as he has found his way once again, into the darkness[19], into the embrace of the presence of God. You who know of the darkness by way of your journey in the Earth

---

[17] The call – A "call" went out through this Channel from the Master, asking all to gather and open to receive a message from Him that would be given on October 11, 2000. His message is given in that reading: 20001011.

[18] Spoken out – those who answered that call were requested to do so by placing their name on a list, which many questioned as to its validity, its purpose.

[19] Into the Darkness – the Channel ventured into the darkness many times in the BORDERLAND *works*, which began midway through the giving of this course.

can well understand what has been the challenges. What you do not fully know at present is what has gone before. These we have before us and, just so as with all of you, we know these and they are good.

It is the mantle of Righteousness that is being offered to you. And that is within the secret place we spoke of.

The Call[20] comes forth, and it grows in its power and presence.

We are with this work unto its completion, evermore.

Shall you walk with us? If you speak, "Yea, I am with thee," then you are empowered. And we are with you.

Honor, Joy, Truth, Love, Compassion, Wisdom, Long-suffering, Patience, Humility... the Grace of God embraces all of these, just as it does and ever has embraced you.

The power of your spirit is the offering to you. That is the Master's work. That is the purpose for His Call to you. And that is the gift that we and others with us gave as the Golden Light [in that Call] to each of you.

Now, you are one with us. But you must step forward. *You* must empower yourself.

He comes.

---

[20] The Call – in this reference, the Call that which will be issued by the Master, the Christ, in those times ahead prophesied.

GUEST LECTURE: Theresa
Given October 26, 2000

THERESA: I am called Theresa. I am greatly honored, beyond words, to be permitted to speak to you all again. And at first, when I was so invited, my reaction was, "I have recently spoken before the Master to so many beautiful souls in the Earth and beyond.[21] What more could I give?" But these beautiful (as they are called) Elders have encouraged me, that perhaps from my recent experiences and such, that this might be of service to you... maybe even an inspiration.

For those of you who are not intimately familiar with the works I know of so well now (and they are called the *Borderland Project* in the Earth) I was among the lost. I was dwelling in what is called the illusion of separateness from God. Believe it or not, only a few Earth months ago I was alone for all practical purposes, and the most bare, minimal of my needs were supplied to me by those who dwell in Darkness and seek to dominate through those varying aspects of same.

When it occurred that I saw a challenge between what you call, categorically, the Forces of Light and the Forces of Darkness, I thought (as we were told) that it would be an opportunity for me, and the others with me, to see the Darkness strengthened as it conquered one of the Light. You can imagine, after having dwelled in the embrace of Darkness and the illusion of so many aspects of it, the utter shock of seeing one of (what we considered to be) incredible power literally neutralized by this one of Light. It was an opportunity to have hope again.

Many of us fell to our knees in confusion, and a collage of emotive content followed. Some ran from that place, believing that the Light was now going to destroy all Darkness. For they had been told this... that Light, you see, destroys.

Some of us gathered together. And we found that, as we did, we were able to make our way along the filamental path of light, and to actually emerge from the darkness to a place of comparative refuge, called the Borderland. From there, the remainder of the events are recounted, so I shan't reiterate them here.

---

[21] Recently Spoken – Theresa became known to those involved in the Borderland works. Those following that work shared her life-transforming experience, so transformative, that the Master invited her to speak in the reading referred to earlier in this course as "The Call" given on October 11, 2000. Having only recently, at that time, broken free of feeling herself to have no worthiness whatsoever, she was amazed to be called yet again to offer her thoughts.

But this is what I most of all wish to share with you…

I was lost. I had no hope. Each day was met in darkness. Each new event was an energizing of limitation. I knew not the joy of being able to share without fear, of being able to give without fear of retribution. I couldn't even express a phrase of kindness or embrace to another. I was lost in the darkness of my own despair.

And now I have stood before the Master (as many of you know, when you came and heard the recounting in *His Call*). I am free. The Light is with me. And I am with it.

Though he would have me not speak it here, the one who brought this light and made the way passable for me and the others, the Channel, is loved beyond any capacity that could be comprehended by mere word.

What are *you*, then, if not the same? Isn't it true that we are all one? And because this one (he who brought us this light) is being spoken of here honorably and lovingly… what about you? What about you in that distant land who continue to hope, who continue to look and search, who look for the means to prove to yourself that you are a Son or Daughter of God?

All you have to do is believe it.

This one who brought us the light told us again and again that it is yours, now… not tomorrow, not next year or another lifetime. It does not need to be earned. It isn't the kind of thing that you need to apply a rote or dogma to, or adhere to rigid doctrines or procedures. It is yours now. That's what he told us. And here I am as proof of that. I am going to serve with him and his mate and those of you who are with him in that work. I have asked our Lord if I am worthy, and the Master, the Christ Jesus, said to me, *"You have always been worthy. It is I who called you, through my brother, to come and stand at my side. And your spirit called you, and said,* 'Here is a work that will bring some light to the darkness, that will bring a light of hopefulness and expectancy to those who are lost.'" The Master said to me further, *"Go. Walk with them. Stand at the side of my brother, as he seeks to bring my light to those who are lost."*

So isn't it fitting, dear friends, that as I am passing by to join him and his mate in the continuation of their works for those I have left behind in what you may call the Underworld, that I might pause here to share this joy with you?

Every one of us is special.

Every one of us is beautiful.

Some are called to the forefront and are spoken of by name or by their work, and this is purposeful and a part of the path.

But we know *you*... every one – we embrace your beauty, your uniqueness; your contributions of prayer and loving intent are warmly gathered by all of us here as a harvest of God's Light.

Now, I shall take my leave of you for this time, to go and stand with Susan and the Channel and the Great One with them.

Won't you stand with us, too? So many... so very many... have lost their way. You can help them.

Thank you for honoring me.

And thank you, Master... and all of you... for the gift of Life.

GUEST LECTURE: Joseph

Given October 26, 2000

JOSEPH: May the blessings of the One God surround and embrace you all. I am honored to come to be with you in these works which are preparatory to the return of our Lord, the Master, the Christ.

In those times past, I was guided often through dream and vision. In the process of taking those guidances into daily life and evaluating them, testing them, weighing them, there was always the challenge meted out to me by the forces which were surrounding me, my very life in the Earth. It was of no small consequence to me that I should have been chosen to be a part of those works which were, as you all know, to bring forth a Light of Hope to the Earth.

And now – in your current time – the Light is coming. It is being offered to the Earth. As it was then, so is it now... first offered to those who would open themselves and make Him welcome within.

When I mentioned in those times past to some closest to me of the visions and dreams I had been given, I was met with doubt and confusion, scorn, even ridicule. Some, who were dear to me, walked away. And yet, again and again, as I sought and asked, it was given, *Joseph, be of good cheer. Be strong – know that I am with thee.*

And so my Lady, in her sweetness and love and compassion, was chosen to be the vessel through which the Lamb of God might enter. So was God's Promise fulfilled before me in the moment of His entry, in that simple stable, on a bed of straw.

And so, what I would share with you now, in your current time, those of you in the Earth and those who are in realms adjacent to it:

If He would come then... upon a bed of simple straw, in a manger, a stable, with many of God's creatures looking on to enter into the care of Our Lady... and I, an old man of the Earth, filled with question and doubt, yet strong in the belief in God... if He could come under those circumstances to such means of entry, don't you think He would come to you?

Don't you think if He would ask or call you, that you could answer mightily? I know that you can, and I believe that you shall.

I look about you, all of you, and I see many whom I have

known in those times returned to the Earth and drawn to realms adjacent to it, who are answering His call once again. And I see the one from cousin Elizabeth and Zachariah. And I see the others of the sisters. And I see the brethren, brothers and sisters, whose names are not so well-known or recounted, but whose works and love were equal in every measure to all the rest, including I, Joseph.

As the measure of the Earth metes out to each of you such challenges as I met when sharing the message with my closest friends, forgive them and release them.

Do not cling to the need of the continuity of them if they cannot see, if they cannot hear; but bless them and release them, and make your temple stronger because it is builded upon that which is pure and righteous.

And so, dear friends, brothers and sisters, we are all Children of God. But among us, comes that Light again. And we can help It to shine. We can help It to be known… to be seen and claimed by those who are His. I know that my Lady is with you in this, and that her sweetness is ever the offering given to you.

Perhaps I shall not speak again in this way, for there are others greater than I whose works are so much of purpose in your current time. So I would leave you with these closing thoughts…

My heart and my spirit are with you, with my Lady, and our Lord. It shall be my prayer that you will open yourself and let your light shine.

Thank you. God bless you.
Hello… to you all in the Earth, and these other realms.

STUDY GUIDE

Weekly Exercises for Grace

Week 1
Morning Prayer:
Lord God, help Thou me to see and know the presence and expression of Thy Grace in all that I am about in this day ahead.
Make your affirmation and conclude.

Evening Prayer:
Thank you, Lord, for the expressions of Thy grace given to me in this day just past. As I enter into spiritual sleep, guide me. Help me to better know and see these, that on the morrow, as I awaken, even the greater shall I be able to see and know and, thus, give to others.

Week 2
Morning Prayer:
Let me see the grace of others, no matter how slight. And when I perceive it, let me nurture it and encourage those who bear it to claim even more. Let me support the grace of others.

Evening:
Offer your own prayer and affirmation.

Week 3
Morning Prayer:
Help me to see the grace of the world about me. Help me to know goodness as it flows, even through the veils of shadow or darkness. And let me call it such in my own heart and mind, and let me speak of it to others. Let me support it, nourish it, and welcome it within my being.

Evening:
Offer your own prayer and affirmation.

Week 4
Morning Prayer:
All is supported and embraced by Thy grace, Lord God. Help thou me to contribute unto it, knowing that, so as I do, the greater is given. And the greater then shall it flow from me, and on and on. Let my prayers and wishes for those beyond the Earth bear the grace of forgiveness, love, compassion, long-suffering, and all those tenets as I hold to be sacred within. Let me, O Lord God, claim the righteousness as is Thy intent for me.

Hold this thought of grace flowing through you and back to you. See it from the perspective of righteousness.

Prepare in your consciousness and intent for next month's closing ceremony, in which you will baptize yourself with the righteousness of the Christ spirit within.

NOTES:

_____

_____

_____

_____

_____

_____

_____

_____

_____

_____

_____

_____

_____

_____

_____

_____

_____

_____

_____

_____

_____

_____

_____

_____

_____

_____

_____

_____

Further Exploring Grace

NOTE: The thoughts listed here are merely suggestions to get you started in further exploration of this subject. Use any portion of them, or not, as your personal guidance leads you.

POINTS TO PONDER:

Lama Sing said, "We have come in answer to the prayers."
Do you remember what your prayer was? Do you feel, do you know, that your prayer has been answered?

"The greatest jewel of all is your expression of the Truth of God."
"Isn't it the greatest of all gifts to know without question that your prayers are heard and answered… that your truth is the Truth of God?"

What is the expression of your Truth?

In the story, it was said by the three travelers, "These humble offerings which we have presented to you are to assist you and those who believe with you, in order that you shall, to the betterment of that work, be able to make the way passable. This, then, do I offer you in humbleness." What were the gifts offered, in your opinion? How would they apply to you in the present time?

How would you define in the sense of this Course, the "eleventh hour?"
"This is that eleventh hour call. Know this to be the moment of truth - the eleventh hour of your spirit's song."
"It is the call to worthiness."
Why are we being urged to claim our worthiness in this, the "eleventh hour?" How does one achieve worthiness? What does this have to do with Grace?

To what or whom does Lama Sing refer when it is said that what is being given applies to "those, here, from other realms" or "to those listening who are from other realms?"
An example of this is in the statement "This is the eleventh hour. For it is that time of determination of so many aspects that are borne within self as the product of the journey through life in the Earth. And for those of you here who are from realms beyond the Earth, all of this and so much more is offered and applies to you, as well."

And "We have heretofore offered many things, humbly and with loving grace, that you might be, in your current consciousness … whether in the Earth or beyond … re-awakened to the power and simplicity of those things as have been given."

Why do you suppose the Lama Sing grouping has "let us in on" the fact that these readings are being offered to others beyond the consciousness of the Earth?

What are the vestiges of you self still remaining to side, that are seeking to be invited in to your embrace? "As you move unto that called the Christhood, call upon those which are the aspects of self still standing to the side, observing, looking, questioning, asking ... yes, and perhaps even doubting and fearing."

How would you define:
- righteousness
- grace
- wisdom
- worthiness
- truth
- honor
- claiming

How do you see Grace and the Law of Free Will as going together? As being the two that hold the place of honor as the first in God's list of gifts to us.

We are being invited to understand what it means to "struggle through the passage-way of darkness, which seems to limit and yet, all the while, embraces." What DOES this mean, and what is its significance as important to be given in one of the final messages of this Course?

This, the eleventh, holds out the opportunity for you to claim the Rite of Passage ... for you to express, to hear and know it to be good, the song of your own spirit ... for you to bring forth the golden Child from within you, nurtured, loved, forgiven, under-stood, given compassion, guided by truth and honor and righteousness . . . and seat that Child at the head of the table.

NOTES: _____

_____

_____

_____

_____

_____

_____

_____

_____

_____

_____

_____

_____

JOURNAL

Step 12:

Righteousness

Given November 29, 2000

A CLOSING PRAYER FROM AL MINER

Lord God, as we come before You today, we ask humbly and joyfully that You would guide us to that information which You know to be the very highest and best. We wish to thank the Lama Sing grouping, the Elders, the Sisters, the beautiful teachers who have come forward, Michael for his protection and guidance, and all those many beautiful beings in the Earth and beyond who are a part of this work, some of which we may not even know by name.

In this final work for this series, we ask that the Master, the Christ, be with us as never before... that each heart and mind which hears this work receives His presence and His blessing... and those who would follow would know that time is only an illusion, and that we claim you and extend our love and our blessings to you, wherever you are in whatever time you might be in.

We claim in this work, Lord God, our oneness with You. And we ask that You awaken our spirits, our minds, our hearts and emotions, and our physical bodies. We ask that You unify us in all respects into a state of oneness. Help us, Father-Mother-God, to claim the righteousness that is promised to us.

Susan and I offer our profound love and blessings to each of you for joining us in oneness in this work. And perhaps as is fitting here... you, Master... we extend our eternal love and joy in oneness with you; thank you for being the example, for setting the pattern, for showing us the Way. Lord God, help us, every one, to fulfill the Master's prophecy... that we might do all those things as He has done, and even greater. We pray of You, Lord God... in our Brother, the Christ's Name... awaken us, strengthen us, guide us, help us to claim, help us know always – without question, doubt, or fear – the power of your presence eternally within us. Help us claim our righteousness. We offer this to those who have asked of You, Father. And to those who have not or know not to ask, our love and our prayer are constantly offered to you. We call out to you. Join us in oneness. Leave behind the separateness and the illusion. Come and rejoice with us.

Father, Mother, we claim You. In this work, guide us... guide those who will share it with u, now and in future. With profound joy, humbleness, and love overflowing from our hearts, Susan and I and all those who are a part of this work now say thank You. Amen.

OPEN FORUM ON RIGHTEOUSNESS

LAMA SING: Yes, we have the Channel then and, as well, those intents and purposes as are a part of these works. As we come together in this intention, let us join into oneness, offering this prayer of joyful affirmation unto God.

> *In the trinity of Thy expression, Lord God, is the potential for each one to find their way. So do we call out to Thee in this moment... that You would awaken within all, the expressions of potential which are their uniqueness. And from this discovery within, that each would experience the joy and wonder as Thou hast given to them in the first moment of creation. Let them find this wellspring of inner light and bring it forth, that they shall know it, claim it, and live it.*

> *Here, as we are gathered, we submit our joy, our oneness, to all who would accept same. And we do so in Your name, Lord God, knowing that Thou art the spirit and the life, the pattern and the force of righteousness which can prevail against all challenge.*

> *We thank thee, Master, for your presence in these, and works which are now past. And we thank you for being the example, for embracing each one who has asked of thee, for gifting each of us with thy loving compassion, with the grace, with the love, with the wisdom and truth, which are the mantle of Christhood.*

> *Unto all those who are gathered in the Earth and other realms seeking from this to find the Way... here are we to bring the gifts of the Christ within and without unto your consciousness... For those of you who may know of these works but have chosen to dwell in limitation or darkness, we are ever at the ready. Should you choose, we are here.*

> *We thank all of those who have come forward... and exceptionally so this, our Channel, and his mate, for permitting the birth of these works into the Earth in this time of their need. We thank each soul in these and realms beyond who has presented an offering of light.*

These we have gathered, lovingly accepted, and have placed in the continuum of Consciousness for any who would harvest same.

So, Father-Mother-God, we come now before Thee, in the presence of Thy light and spirit, asking only that Thou would guide, that that which is given herein shall be as is most needed, most joyful, to those who shall partake of same.

We thank Thee, Lord God for the wonder and joy of service, for the blessing of miracles answered by way of prayer, for the hearts which are opening and knowing themselves, for those who have taken forgiveness and claimed it and who now are offering it outwardly. These and so much the greater we give to you as our gratitude and love.

So let these works be written in hearts and minds eternally, as seeds from whence the greater can grow and bear harvest. So do we thank Thee, Lord God... and all of you, dear friends. Amen.

THE CROWN OF CONSCIOUSNESS

As we are come together in this work, we encourage you to remember that there is no work which is final nor absolute; that each work, as we would give it here, humbly, is offered in the understanding that it comes to you with our prayer of support and encouragement, never with a mantle of responsibility or that which will cause less than the greatest potential for joy that is within you. We are, as ever, your brethren (brothers and sisters, if you will) only a step or two away.

As you contemplate that which has been given, we might lovingly encourage you to ofttimes review same, for within those works which have gone before this are the potentials which can strengthen and free you, which can empower and ennoble you... ultimately, that you shall, through the power and wonder of your free will, claim the Grace of God and be free.

In this work, as has been given, we are focusing upon that which is called *Righteousness*. And while we might here offer many diverse commentaries which would exemplify the meaning, nature, and potential of righteousness, we say to you in humbleness, all that which has gone before does just this... as you would see the first nine steps likened unto a golden pathway, leading you to the crown of consciousness; and from this, then, the vantage point to see all else. Not as a division between finiteness and infiniteness, but in the sense and comprehension of oneness, which bodes eternal, in terms of its understanding.

Calling Forth the Channel

We have, as ever, in all those works which have gone before (some three decades of Earth measure) embraced this, our Channel, in the consciousness of truth. And as we have so done, he has reciprocated this to us and returned, as well, the tenet of honor... ofttimes, to the diminishment or negation of claiming his own. It is, perhaps, these attributes (as they are called in the Earth) of selflessness that have endeared him in the hearts and minds of so many of you.

Now, here is a work which has come to its completion. As a good gardener in the service of God has tended his crop, as the good shepherd has tended their flock, now the harvest is at the ready... the flock is ready to multiply.

So our first work here is to call forth now our own Channel, that the righteousness of service is no longer relegated to that which lies beyond, but is claimed in the personage of self. And in the so doing, exemplify that which has been given in past in this life and share it, enriched by the presence of each of your loving hearts and minds.

Calling You

So is it, then, your spirits which hear our request humbly to our Channel, and know, simultaneously, that those who are with you in the personal sense wish us to now state to you: You are similarly called.

You are called to claim your righteousness.

You are called to build this upon the pillars of truth and honor, to embrace these with love and compassion, and to crown this, as the eternal foundation, with the glory of God's Grace.

It is no small matter, no small work, which has gone before. Neither is it so that you are less than wondrous in your potential. You, collectively, are the Children of God. And you, individually, are a Child of God. When the Master spoke as the man called Jesus, He was and is speaking to you: *"All these things and the greater shall ye do."*

THE HARVEST

Here is a time, as given, which is rich with the potential for harvest. It is, as well, that time foretold, wherein those who bear His mark – not a mark of disfigurement, but a mark of Light – shall come to the fore and proclaim Him, embrace Him, and be one with Him.

But how to do this?

What are the means by which I, as one so named, can do all that is possible for me to do?

Review

Review those steps, as given.

And in the flame of Truth… See, Know, Claim.

Infill yourself with the fruits of Forgiveness, for it shall free you.

Use Gratitude to affirm, empower, through the claiming and acknowledgement of what is.

See the self expressed in varying forms and expressions, and yet, know Self to be One.

In the Channel's opening prayer from his heart was the request for oneness, for unification of Self, not separateness. Let the body be known as the vehicle of spirit, the living temple in which the heart of the Christ can be found.

Choose

Shall you be companions or followers? Shall you be student or teacher? Shall you be healer or one in need? Shall you open and make The Way passable through you for the Master's prophecy to be made manifest?

So are each of you called, as our Channel and Susan are called… setting aside that which could question or qualify, which could shelter or even obscure the beauty of the gifts which are within.

That which is aright is righteousness. That which is not, is in that stage or those stages of discovery. You, then, can be the light, that they might see, know, and claim their own discovery.

We humbly encourage you to oft look at that as has been given in these works, and the great teacher – of Life itself – which is ever an expression of God's Spirit striving to nurture His/Her Children.

Let thoughts of separateness be used only to compare and discover the incredible beauty of the uniqueness of the individuality. And bring that as the gem of your own being, and place it upon the altar, that all can see it, that all can know it, and that its contribution unto the greater whole can take its rightful place. Those of you who are in the Earth, hearing these words, might see that altar as life itself.

Or you might look within yourselves and perhaps know, to some varying degree, the journey that you have followed in past to reach this point; and from that, gain the understanding of the diversity of expressions which are the potential for the Children of God.

And while there may be that moment here or there which seems to have gone astray, think of these as the rungs of a ladder upon which you are empowered to ascend, if you would but place them into such an understanding and perspective. How great a transgression can you adjudge to be sufficient so as to separate you from God? How great an error might you find and adjudge, and thereafter claim, that can place you apart from the Master? And what division could be sought after, known and claimed, that can, in the reality of your current expression, separate you from those who are, in truth, one with you?

Never Compromise Your Path

Each has a path they have chosen to follow, and that path may be evaluated by self to be distant. Never should one compromise their path, their ideal, their truth, their honor, that they would, as a byproduct of so doing, abandon their own path, to follow one which is lesser than their truth.

This is an aspect of righteousness: that one within knows, Yes, there have been these experiences here and there which I would rather not hold before God as an achievement of righteousness. And still, I can look upon these and forgive them and myself, as I might just so forgive a child who has just broken an object of personal love and beauty, in the material sense in the Earth.

Exercise the Law of Grace

Whether willful or passive, or any measure between those poles, error is the experiencing of that which is, through which one can purify themselves... or burden themselves.

Clinging to the past in terms of responsibility can be as the millstone about one's neck; claiming the past as the rung upon the ladder of ascension can be accepting the gift or blessing that those experiences – however painful, however deviant from that which thou knoweth now – as the path of Righteousness.

No matter what, God's law of Grace transcends all.

The righteous not only claim this Grace, but they make essence of it. They materialize Grace into the foundational stones, the step-stones, the rungs on that ladder. And they rise up upon them. They know them not in the manner of finiteness; but know them, claim them intimately, for the gift and energies that are offered through same.

THE LOGOS

So we began these works, asking humbly of you to begin a work in forgiveness. Some of you resonated with this powerfully, immediately; others of you still have this as an offering. And in time, wherein it is appropriate, you will see it, know it, and claim it, as some have before you. So is it appropriate that the crown of this work also honors the power of forgiveness – for the beginning and ending are one.

Oneness with the All

The circle, the Logos, comes unto its beginning, always.

So as you might find in the cycles of your own lives, the circular path which (when one can see, can know, can claim... as we gave those as topics) understands that it is not a closed circle, but an open one – ever receptive, ever growing, ever ascending, through the gift of experience, amplified through understanding.

So as we return to forgiveness, it is no longer at the level from whence it was originally given, but a level above that – the circle, then, being the upward spiral of ascension into righteousness and oneness with the All.

There Is No Separateness

There are those of you who have tested, challenged, and sought the purity of who and what you are. Some of you have done so of recent times, in small gatherings, and others will follow this; and you might well be examples, lights. That they, too, shall find the shelter of love, compassion, and understanding, in which their uniqueness can be uncovered, released from the limitations and illusions which had heretofore bound them into obscurity.

You, then, are in a group of such dedicated souls... whether you are alone in the Earth (by the example of the Earth)... or whether you are together with one who shares intimately, as a mate... with those who share intimately, as true friends, colleagues, fellow travelers upon the path... or whether you have ascended such that you can go beyond, and claim oneness with all those who are in the light seeking, claiming, in their own unique ways as individuals and groups following that lamp of example which is unto their belief true: there is no separateness; there is only oneness.

GOD

If you could imagine for a moment with us a beautiful sphere of light comprised of a collage of unimaginable brilliance, of indescribable spectrums of color, of sound, of energies which, to the present time in the Earth, have no means of description; if you could imagine this sphere pulsing, moving, vibrating; if the very contemplation of it brings a surge of joy, of expectancy, of harmony, of compassion, of love; if the very contemplation of it makes you think of the word *GOD* then you are where we wish you to be.

Individualized Expressions

In this contemplation of this majestic sphere... timelessly, eternally, moving, growing, breathing in and out... offering creation and the powers inherent in same to those who would have it... drawing in the needs, the requests, the prayers, the desires of heart, mind, and body...and breathing out the answer... if you would consider that sphere in the very next moment to – gently not vigorously, to lovingly not with force – disperse itself... inestimable numbers of particles of that sphere moving away from the center of it, never diminishing the sphere itself, but seemingly expanding it... these tiny spheres are identical to the Source Sphere: the Logos of Light birthing itself into a multitude of individualized expressions.

These inestimable numbers of spheres could be called Children of the Greater.

And they are, of course, each of you.

They are as their Source.

They are going forth to know themselves... to begin a journey which must ultimately return to the Source of their being. But when they do so, they bring back to the Source many great gifts and blessings. They bring back the gift of understanding gained through individualized experiencing. There is the knowing of the expression of finiteness, thereafter to be placed, appropriately so, in conjunction with the infiniteness of their being.

EMOTION – THE SUBSTANCE OF WHICH MIND BUILDS

Emotion is an energy in the Earth.

It has been given so oft so many diverse ways that mind is the builder; and that it builds, when in harmony with its own spirit, according to the perfect pattern. But it is the substance called emotion which is that of which mind builds.

The Momentum of Desire, The Worker of the Mind and Spirit

Emotion is the momentum of desire. Emotion is the worker dispatched by the will of mind, by the pattern and light of spirit.

Look at your emotions often. Examine your emotions. Are there vestiges of same which are limited because of self-imposed judgments or even the comparative judgments imposed by the mass-mind thought of Earth?

The Power of Your Work

Emotion is the power that goes before you in the works that you do. When your works are devoid of emotion, they are like a conduit with naught flowing through same – the conduit can be present, but within it, flowing through it, there is little or naught. See the power of your emotion. Connect this with the Grace of God, which tells you continually, gently, always: All is aright and true.

Let your emotion be the vehicle upon which your prayers go forth. For after all, love is an emotion.

Compassion is a statement of being, amplified and empowered through emotion. You can empathize, sympathize, realize the factors which are a part of another's journey, and thus, compassion is possible. But it is difficult to have compassion, if you cannot forgive yourself first.

FREE WILL

The wellspring of your potential, the energies which can flow from you, which doeth the work in the finite expression and beyond, must be freed.

Force Vitae

Righteousness is a state of consciousness – it is a state of living, of being, of doing, of knowing. Righteousness rests upon the structure previously described: truth, honor, love, compassion, and capped or centered around grace.

But what is the envelopment of this beautiful structure, as we have defined it? Which gives meaning to all of it? Wherein? Of what? Where is the nature or source of the force vitae, the force of life vital? It is free will.

You choose to meditate… or not.

You choose to pray… or not.

You choose to believe in the words and paths of others… or not.

You choose to find an ideal, and purposes and goals which you believe, in that time, shall lead you to and empower you to accomplish your ideal… or not.

We mentioned above that the Master was prophesizing to you, but it is your free will which shall give life to that prophecy… or not.

The Offering Before You

We are one with you, and you are one with we. And yet, the veil of separateness is that called death. The journey begins with birth and ends with the passage through the portal called death.

And yet, all the while, some aspect of you has known and does know that there is no death. There is only the transformation from one form to another.

So was it, then, that you came from the Tree of Spirit as its fruits, born into finiteness called Earth, into physical body, in order to express and interact according to that which is to be honored in that expression called Earth. And when you depart, you shall leave the vestiges of that expression (the vehicle, if you will) behind. And that is righteous and appropriate. For thou art eternal, and that is but an expression of your eternal nature.

Now, the cycle comes to its point of ascension. And the question comes forth for some: *If I am eternal spirit, if I am a particle of that Great Sphere, which has been birthed from it, of it, going forth to experience, then can it be that I am ever less than that? Is it possible for me to set aside my oneness with what is called, collectively, God?*

Free will. You can choose to believe in the finite or the infinite, or both.

So that is the cycle of ascension. That is the offering before you.

Your Intention and Ascension

The body is one with its own spirit. And your works, your destination, your intention, has ever been to come to the point of realization that this is truth; and from the realization and claiming of that as truth… to honor it.

How? Through the seeing, knowing, and claiming, as given in the works before… to see the small *s* self and the capital *S* Self in the truth of your eternal wisdom.

And so as you do, to ascend on this cycle now upon you in the Earth and growing, as the Earth weeks, months, and years ahead shall come to you bearing their gifts.

You have never been less than a Child of God… the mini-sphere birthed from the Great Sphere, with all of its inherent qualities and nature with the addition of one very precious aspect… called uniqueness.

This uniqueness now has become an expression for you of your current life. As you have sought to express and understand your uniqueness in this – yet one more physical body, one more lifetime, one more journey – here you are with us and the others: contemplating the possibility of claiming the greatest of all: considering actually, truly, literally, freeing yourself.

RIGHTEOUSNESS

Righteousness is a state of being which is ever aware of its oneness with the All.

Placing All in Perspective

It does not labor over individual opportunities or challenges, and linger, dwelling, contemplating, immersing itself into same. Righteousness is continually in motion, flowing forth, growing, discovering, understanding, and embracing. Not stumbling over the needs and wants of the flesh, but placing in true perspective and focus that that same flesh or temple of spirit is not separate nor limited, but is ever the expression of the Child of God who is seeking.

As you come upon the needs of others, or perceive those who are in states of varying degrees of dis-ease, you can, as righteousness, be seen as a vehicle... as a momentum which is never static, never limited, but always alive and flowing... as that which can give to their needs, whether individuals, groups, or such. And knowing in that moment of giving, that all, and greater than is the need of that one receiving your gifts, has been given. That you are the companion to Him whom we have for so long honored here, and for so long has been the focal point of the honor of so many of you, not the least of which, our Channel and his mate.

Companion to the Christ

Do you revere the Christ? Do you look upon the Master as the Ascended One? Perhaps even considering, to some varying degree, as a position or stature unattainable by self?

We lovingly encourage you to set that aside now.

He calls to you, *"Come. Walk with me. Be my brother; be my sister. Be my brethren, my companions. Co-create with me. Let us, together, be the path, be the light, and answer the needs."*

And is it not so that, as the Son of God comes to exemplify, to demonstrate, to show the Way in whatsoever expression is your comfort and shelter and belief, there is no difference? But in this, the Son of God is the same with God. For we know that God awaits our return as companions, as brethren, equal... one.

The Children of God Coming to Be God

We are the Children of God in the process of discovering that we are one with God... that we, collectively, shall come to be, through our oneness, God.

The very statement of such a potential may disarm many. But it is impossible for something to be of a source and not be the source. Unique? Yes. Individualized? Yes. But if you take water from water, it is still water. It molds itself to its container. It becomes, according to the intent of that one who takes from it, according to their desire and need. And yet, it is ever one with its source, which is water. And even in the Earth, it is defined that water always returns to its source; that, that is the continual journey, the evolutionary cycle, its ideal.

Exercising Righteousness

So is it then here that, as you seek to claim righteousness, that we might suggest the following.

In the first week of a lunar cycle, consider in morning and evening: *Who am I?*
And this might be the prayer:
Lord God, here am I, (and state your name)… *awaken me.*
Nothing more.

In the second week, think on this: *Why am I?*
Your prayer might be:
Lord God, guide Thou me to know myself in all expressions, and unify me.
In the *Why am I* you will find many differing perspectives by way of which individuals will search. *Why am I...* Do that. It is expanding and good for you.

In the third week, ask only, in morning and evening, *What is my work?*
Your prayer might well be:
Lord God, show me the way. Awaken me.
For one's work is their way, and there is the greater ever that one is capable of, that one can claim. Your work is the expression of your intent, the potential of your creativity.

In the fourth week, consider only this: *Oneness.*
Look for that that thou knoweth or see. Follow it to its point of creation… backwards, upwards, howsoever it must be. Go beyond this to consider all of the expressions of your life, past, present, and as potentials in future. And reflect upon them from the position of oneness. You are not striving to literally be one with all things; you are striving to understand and know that all things spring forth from the same Source… that that beautiful sphere of light which sent forth molecules of itself is the Source of all existence.

You are striving in that Earth week to understand; to see, not to subscribe; to know, not to be one with a certain expression in the Earth, because its path and intent, its ideal, may be literally divergent from thy own; but to know its source, to understand that it is one of those particles in motion, journeying out to discover and understand. Sometimes unsuccessfully by the measure of analyses in the Earth, but always being offered the gift of discovery, the potential for growth.

Whether that be the worst among thee or the best, these are particles of the one God in motion. If you know this oneness, then you can release yourself from the potential limitation or confinement of subscribing to that as separate.

This would be the prayer we would consider:

Lord God, help Thou me to see, to know, to claim, and to become Righteousness.

Find the Connection in Oneness

The Master could look upon dis-ease and know it to be one – one with the source, a potential which (by the measure of those who possessed such dis-ease) as that imbalance between the polarities of all that which has been given in these works before. For dis-ease to exist, there must be some counterpoint to one of the truths we have offered in the previous eleven works.

The first nine are the steps which are relevant interactively to finite expression (that is self-apparent, we should think, humbly).

These, the final three, offer the potential to congeal the understanding into oneness. And that oneness is titled *Righteousness*.

So the Master looked upon such dis-ease and did not see it to be alien; did not see it as some powerful, individualized, negative force having taken residency in or about that one who was infirmed. But in the twinkling of an eye, as you call it, could find its connection in oneness and, thereafter, it was simple, straightforward, for that entity to be healed.

For, see the dis-ease flowing from the potential, the oneness of God, just so as the ease; see the light and the darkness as unable to exist, either one, without the presence of the other.

It is in the venue of claiming, choosing, the application of free will, that one comes forth to manifest whatsoever they are. So, we have suggested that as one of your works. Knowing who you are, where you are, what your work is, what your willingness to go forth and claim and be unique, be individual... all of these things will empower you to be able to claim righteousness

But remember, here is a weary traveler, dis-eased, having come before the Master and asking, "Lord, Lord, if ye would but say the word, I am healed."

And the Master, looking upon the entity, instantly sees the connection between all that is before Him with the oneness of God. And he can answer, *"According to your belief, so is it given to thee. Arise. Go. Thou art healed."* And only but a moment's glance, thereafter, given by the Master… and He continues His journey.

And the one who has come and asked and has been given, must thereafter claim, nurture, and give life to the gift given them. See?

Look to the Pillars of Righteousness in All

So know yourself. *Who am I? What am I? Where am I? What is my work? Where is my oneness?*

But do not be led astray. Do not believe that you must now, in order to demonstrate your oneness, embrace all that is about you. Neither should you become as them, in order to evidence to them your oneness.

For look at the pillars of righteousness: truth (your truth… remember that teaching?) Honor is paramount, in order for one to truly claim righteousness. Love, and compassion… first, fill to overflowing within, and then mete it out to those who are met in daily life.

There is that when oneness is truly known which may call to you, *Come. Be one with this one, or that teaching, or this way of life.* Have a care not to subscribe too heavily to such, remembering that mind is the builder, and emotion the material from whence mind can build. All whom you meet have applied this. Have had, perhaps, many sojourns in the Earth and elsewhere, and have constructed, *Who am I? What am I? What is my work?*

Honor self in the truth of that which you know. Then, certainly, cooperate and honor others. But only so as the ideal is in oneness should you cleave unto that, never to the relinquishment of your unique gift of individuality. If that is called for or asked of you, then it is, perhaps, not the best path for you. Conversely, if your uniqueness is revered, is held up and is honored by those whose ideal you are considering joining, then that is the first test to know that this is right.

Righteousness honors all of the tenets of God, not just one or two, not just this part or that. But righteousness embraces all that is. It is the joyful journey unto return into oneness with God.

LOOK TO THE DAWNING

We have been of great joy here to have been a part of these works with you. And as we bring this work to conclusion, know that we continue to be with you, and know and claim and empower yourselves, first as individuals, and then as groups. And perhaps coming together as many groups, honoring one another, honoring the source of your being. But never losing sight of the importance of your individual honor, and the honor of others, as well.

A Place of Residency

You know when you claim righteousness that you are complete.

You know when you have claimed righteousness that no thing is impossible.

But perhaps most of all, when you have claimed righteousness, you make residency possible for true love and true compassion to live on eternally within you.

Rejoice

We will continue to contribute as it is sought of us here, in ways which will be intended to support those works as have been given... and importantly, to support those individuals and groups who strive to apply and live same.

And so, as we come to conclusion, recognize in that same moment, dear friends, that the dawning is before you. As you conclude, it is like giving closure to night, to the darkness, and turning to welcome and receive the dawning.

And in this dawning, He comes.
Rejoice.

Fare thee well then for the present, dear friends.

GUEST LECTURE: Judith
Given November 29, 2000

JUDITH: I, Judith am sent to you by the Master, the Christ, to sweep you up in His embrace of love… to rejoice with you that you have reached this point of discovery.

In the light of our eternal Father-Mother-God, there is the embrace of hopefulness. There is the wonder of the potential for unlimited creation.

As the spirit of the Christ is stirred and perhaps, I should pray, awakened within you now as this particular work comes to its fruition, reach out your hand and heart. I am here. I, Judith, am at the side of the Master, the Christ. And together, we reach out to you, with many more doing the same.

We are all one. And it is the path of loving self – and the empowering of that path through the application of the gifts given by the Lama Sing grouping, the Elders and others, and through this called our Channel, and his mate – so do we reach out to you now.

Hear these words, and, as ye can, believe them…

You are eternal. Your current journey is an adventure into finiteness. It is not a separation from your eternal self. It is as the thrusting forth of a finger of Consciousness into the awareness and interactive creation of others… knowing.

Know, too, then, that our love and our prayers are always with you.

I thank you for the gifts you have given in the form of your prayers and your efforts on behalf of others, and most of all, for your efforts on behalf of yourselves. For as you discover and free yourself, you are giving one of the greatest gifts that you can to those about you.

Good journey… joy… and many blessings.
Fare well for now, dear friends.

GUEST LECTURE: The Elders

Given November 29, 2000

ELDERS: We are honored to come forward in this meeting to offer you these humble comments. We are called the Elders.

We have experienced much of what you call finite expressions. We have dwelled within and through them. Many, of our grouping, have served others in the Earth and other realms of long tenure, in the capacity of that which you would call guides, teachers, counsel, to those who were journeying in said finiteness. Through those collective experiences, we have moved into the understanding of the nature of God's Law.

As we came together, first as individuals and small groupings, we did so because we had a common quest. As we shared that quest, we realized that we could not, each one, conform to a standard belief or definition of what was right. For we attempted to do this and, in so doing, we experienced many diverse events… lifetimes, if you will. And as we came together, summating that collage of our group's experiences, we saw the beauty arise from same as the phoenix from the ashes. That it was, after all, our individual uniqueness that must be seen, claimed, and lived in order to make the greater whole into oneness. It was by the very nature of striving to be what was expected, of striving to conform to what might be called one right way, that we saw the fallacy of this, that forcing unique individual beauties to live and thrive within the confines of such limitation of definition simply did not bear good fruit.

And so, in a point of time and space (as you would call it) the movement of our consciousness suddenly became one. In that oneness and the momentous joy of our discovery of it, we, of course sustaining yet vestiges of finiteness, sought to test this. We went forth with expectation… challenging, so to say, our new discovery, because we wanted to know *Is this true? Can we truly honor this, in the knowledge that it is truth?*

In the process of so doing, we became, as you might expect, entangled with the vestiges and aspects of our own desire to evidence to ourselves, to challenge, and thus to exemplify that truth. And we were, for a time (quote) lost (end quote). Not lost, as separate from God, but lost in the focus of our chosen work. We became the object of our quest. And through our prayers, through our ideal as we kept it pure within, our call was answered… and we are here.

We are called the Elders because we are looked upon as those who have passed through the challenges that so many of you who hear these words or read them are still embarked upon. And indeed, we have so accomplished our journey. But were it not for the journey and the challenges, and the opportunity to explore the breadth and depth of all that we could be, we tell you... our journey would have been considerably longer. And perhaps that which we are now, as we are honored to speak to you, might not yet have been realized.

Certain who are present here, even as we speak, were a great light unto us. And we have, thereafter, pledged with great love, gratitude, humbleness, and joy to be a part of such works evermore.

And so we bring to you this message... that you would know the Way is passable. That it is possible for each of you – no matter how so you believe, no matter what you see yourself to be, with only the casual consideration of what your work is – you, right now, could claim righteousness.

To do so is only to believe, to have faith, and to honor that belief and faith, that it can be given life... to love it, that it is sustained and nourished... to hold it compassionately within you, that whatsoe'er the challenge and limitation which comes forth unto it, your compassion surrounds it, embraces it, and perpetuates it.

Righteousness is the life.

And God's Law is that continually awaiting any who would recognize and claim same to be foundational in the ascension into righteousness.

There are, amongst that called God's Universal Law, those aspects, as tools, which can help you with each and every one of the steps which have been given. And we are pledged to remain with this work and our Channel, to serve in whatsoe'er ways will contribute unto you and your quest to claim same.

God's Laws are perfect... in so many ways misunderstood, by even those who have studied them with dedication and deliberateness. And that is because God's Laws simply are. They are the manna of existence upon which the intentions of the Children of God can be born and realized.

God's Laws are like the loving parent who gently guides a child through the experiences of their growth in childhood. This is heart. And that is called the polarities of tactile sensation. This is light, and this is dark, the complements of the expression and presence of

God. One does not know itself without the other. Thus, they are as brother and sister. Their journey must bring them together, or they shall never know who they are.

So did we share that small snippet, if you will, of our background, that you can see from our journeys that we have used these same truths, these same teachings... and we are now one with God.

And yet, who and what we are individually is so much the greater, because we are together.

We have the power of God, because we claim it. We live and rejoice and celebrate every moment of existence. And we await you. We look forward to when you, too, will choose to be one with us. Until that time, here are we, with you... serving this, our Channel, and his mate, and each of you, in whatsoe'er works you, individually or collectively, shall choose.

God's Law is one with you. Do not deny it, but know it, and live within it, in truth, honor, love, and compassion... becoming the grace of God... and ascending into the righteousness, that has *always* been yours.

We depart, leaving you our prayers and blessings.

GUEST LECTURE:
[No Name Was Given]
Given November 29, 2000

Selah. Selah.

Glory to you, brothers and sisters.

Here is my hand. Wilt thou not grasp same? Together, let us journey, rejoicing and celebrating our Oneness.

As a work cometh unto you, claim it, as though it were a jewel given of our Father-Mother-God. In the claiming of that jewel of opportunity, let us rejoice. For here, the gifts can be given. And as these flow through us and we see the claiming and awakening of another, our number shall grow. And the path becomes, thereafter, even greater.

Before you, many changes await. Those cycles of change are nigh at hand.

Meet them from the completeness of your own being, and I shall be with thee. And as you do this and know we are one, let this shine upon others, that they, too, shall wish to come and partake of it.

Believing unto yourselves and knowing the Way to be passable is a wondrous work unto itself. It is that work which shall, without question, bear the fruits of a wondrous harvest to come.

The teachers of righteousness are among you – as am I. Would you call them forth? Will you see in one another that which is holy? And will you rejoice with them, for them, and for yourself – as do I – upon the claiming of same?

Be of good cheer... for the glory of God awaits us.

STUDY GUIDE

Weekly Exercises for Righteousness

Week 1:

In the morning and evening:
Ask… "Who am I?"

Morning and Evening Prayer:
Lord God, here am I, (and state your name)… Awaken me.

Week 2:

In the morning and evening:
Ask… "Why am I?"

Morning and Evening Prayer:
Lord God, guide Thou me to know myself in all expressions, and unify me.

Week 3:

In the morning and evening:
Ask… "What is my work?"

Morning and Evening Prayer:
Lord God, show me the way. Awaken me.

Week 4:

In the morning and evening:
Consider only this… "Oneness."

Morning and Evening Prayer:
Lord God, help Thou me to see, to know, to claim, and to become Righteousness.

NOTES: _____

_____

_____

_____

_____

_____

_____

_____

Further Exploring Righteousness

NOTE: The thoughts listed here are merely suggestions intended get you started in further exploration of this subject. Use any portion of them as your personal guidance leads you.

POINTS TO PONDER:

What does it mean to you: "You are called to claim your Righteousness."?

What thoughts of separateness" might Lama Sing be referring to and how are we being encouraged to transform those thoughts?

How would you yourself put into words the reasons this Course in Oneness returned to Forgiveness?

Lama Sing refers repeatedly to Edgar Cayce's words, "Mind is the builder." And Lama Sing almost always adds the addendum, "Emotion is the substance from and with which mind builds." What is the encouragement for us in this concept?

Consider again these words:
Righteousness is a state of consciousness. It is a state of living, of being, of doing, of knowing. Righteousness rests upon the structure previously described - Truth, Honor, Love, Compassion - and capped or centered around Grace.
But what is the envelopment of this beautiful structure, as we have defined it? Which gives meaning to all of it? Wherein? Of what? Where is the nature or source of the force vitae... the force of life?
It is Free Will.
You choose to meditate... or not.
You choose to pray... or not.
You choose to believe in the words and paths of others ... or not.
You choose to find an ideal, and purposes, and goals which you believe in that time shall lead you to and empower you to accomplish your ideal ... or not.
We mentioned that the Master was prophesizing to you, but it is your Free Will which shall give life to that prophecy... or not.

Consider these words given to Al in a Work Reading, by the Master, looking directly into Al's eyes, with love and joyful expectation: "Did you free your spirit yet?" How would YOU go about freeing your spirit, so that you could be a companion to the Christ?

How would you describe "the dawning"?

JOURNAL

_____

_____

_____

_____

_____

_____

_____

_____

_____

_____

_____

_____

_____

_____

_____

_____

_____

_____

_____

_____

_____

_____

_____

_____

_____

_____

_____

_____

_____

_____

_____

_____

_____

_____

_____

_____

_____

_____

_____

_____

_____

_____

_____

_____

_____

_____

Rite

Of

Passage

Given December 31, 2000

RITE OF PASSAGE

LAMA SING: Yes, we have the Channel then and, as well, that request, as given just above, now before us. As we commence with these works, let us join together in this joyful prayer of oneness.

We call out to Thee, O Father-Mother-God, asking that Thou would look upon us. In Thy spirit all things can be known, all works can be accomplished. So is it, then, our request that You would awaken within and about these works that which is Thy Spirit eternal. So let that Light which is ever of Thee permeate the entirety of all who shall know of these works and this prayer. We come unto Thee in gratitude and joy. We extend ourselves in the spirit of oneness. And upon the wings of our intent do we send ourselves to be one with all those who have come unto this work in Thy name.

We thank each of you who have ever been a part of these works... now in the Earth, in the past, and those who shall follow. Thou art blessed in the presence of our intention for you, and it is ever our will that sends forth that blessing unto all those who may hear this call. There are those forces eternal which are awakening. There are those forces finite which are cleaving unto that of the call within. So is it then written that as it is sought after, it shall be given. As one knocks, it shall be opened. So has it been, according to your will. And now, so is it given.

We thank Thee, Master, for Your presence 'round and about these works ever, and for the light of Thy example which shineth through all that would seek to obscure same. And we thank You for those gifts of Your healing grace, Your love, Your compassion, and wisdom. We know these now to be within us, as well. So then do we summon them forth in that very spirit as we have asked and claim the presence of, from God.

Unto all of you who are weary or who have challenges brought before you, we are with you. Those of you who hear these words from the recesses of your own illu-sion, we have extended our hand to you, and our prayer is ever at the ready so as thou art willing.

So then do we, as well, conclude this prayer with our expression of gratitude to each of you, as well. For you cannot know the wonder and joy of the presence of your willing hearts and minds, nor can you recognize fully the beauty of the growth of your own light. With each passing Earth day, so is it contributing unto illuminat-ing the Way.

And lastly... Look you upon our brother, for these works could not be were his heart not open to receive same.

So, Lord God, do we thank Thee for those gifts Thou hast given to we... above all else, those of joyful service and oneness with our brothers and sisters in all realms. We thank Thee, Lord God, and this, our Channel and his mate in the Earth. Amen.

As you might gather yourself into oneness, you would do so by searching. Perhaps using some of that as has been given previously to recognize those aspects of self which are serving here and there as portions of the greater Self. So might you, then, gather these into oneness and prepare.

So might you, then, as well, take these aspects of self into the heart and mind, and look upon them. Know them. Then unify self in spirit, mind, and body. Doing this, perhaps, as thou knoweth to be the very best for you... perhaps through that methodology of preparation as has become a blessing to you.

But if you have not these, or if none such comes to the forefront of your thought, we now offer this in humbleness, open-handedly, for you to choose or nay, so as your spirit guides:

Preparing for the Ceremony

Items

Prepare a small container, and a single candle.

The container should be of such nature that you might place your fingertips together within it. In the container you would, of course, place water.

Self

You should prepare yourself, if you are following this, in a manner that promotes the greatest of all comfort and ease:
- Firstly, for your physical body
- Secondly, for your mental and emotional self
- And thirdly, for your spiritual consciousness.

The intention therein to be such so as to promote a state of joyful ease; that you are positioning yourself in the Stream of Life to be in such a state as to become one with it; and of course, that Stream of Life is that Spirit of God which we asked for above. And so as you do prepare, you can open yourself to become one with it.

Remove that from your body as would take your focus or attention, and place it aside.

At the least, you should have bathed your hands and perhaps your face, that there is the sense of purification so, as you do this... that a portion of your consciousness would recognize that you have begun the process of purification, making for the greater, more receptive, more open.

There should not be the footwear upon the body.

Neither should there be that excess which is metallic or of a substance which can resonate, other than that which is within.

(Noting here that this should not become burdensome, but considered only as guidance, suggestions.)

The posture of the body should be such so as to be comfortable for a period of ten to twenty Earth minutes.

Once this has been seen to, and the other necessities of the body and the physical environ are attended to, place yourself in that position so as ye have chosen to be the best of all.

OPENING THE CEREMONY

Disconnecting

Now take that moment or two, close your eyes, and recognize that as you do, there is the elimination... the disconnecting with the visual and thus with stimulations which can arouse the flow of thought.

Removing the Thoughts of Finiteness

So doing, with the eyes closed, raise your hands so as to place your fingertips to the temples, and let your thoughts be one with your fingertips. In other words, your consciousness should flow to this area, applying gentle pressure so as you do.

Then there might be these words spoken by self:

I am eternal. The thoughts of this moment, this day, this lifetime, are a part of the continuum of who I have been, who I am, and what I might become. As I remove my fingertips from my temples, for this time to come I also remove these thoughts from my consciousness, thereby opening self as I do.

PREPARING TO RECEIVE

Awakening Self to Oneness, Eternal Truth, and Righteousness

Slowly remove your fingertips, but do not lower your hands. Instead, bring them together in front of your face. Do not clasp the fingers, but keep them open, so to say... not spread awide, but hands together at the palms, and the fingers just a bit apart. Hold this position for a moment.

Now these thoughts and words might we speak:

Here am I, Lord God, in a state of completeness. I seek oneness with Thee. Let the tenets of Truth flow to me, awakening that which is my Righteousness within.

As you do this, open the hands a bit wider, as though you are receiving from above. Do so for just a few moments.

And now gently bring your fingers together, that they are touching one another, and each hand touching the other, in the traditional symbol of prayer:

I claim these, Lord God, now and ever.

Hold this position for a few more moments.

RECEIVING AND CLAIMING

Awakening These Gifts Eternally

Now, turn your hands, that the palms are facing your face. Take the fingertips and place them upon the forehead (perhaps together, perhaps a bit apart... you choose, as thou art guided), Hold the fingertips against the forehead gently.

As you do, let this be the thought or prayer:

These are the gifts eternal which I now claim, according to the Master's own words. In Thy spirit's presence, Lord God, do I awaken these within me and claim them evermore.

Keep the fingertips to the forehead for a few more moments.

Imparting the Spirit of God

Now, bring the hands together again in the traditional form of prayer, slowly lowering them until you can place both palms above the heart or approximate center of your being. Hold these here, now reclining, resting. And here might be the thoughts:

Within and without is the Spirit of God. So as I have acknowledged and claimed same, do I impart this to my own being. My life is the life of God eternal. Those teachings and truths as are eternal are mine within. I recognize them. I feel and know them. And I claim them.

Pause a few more moments.

And now, simply allow your hands to come to rest wheresoever thou has chosen to place them for the remainder.

Illuminating the Golden Child Within

Now, open your eyes, and illuminate the candle with these words:

This flame symbolizes Thy spirit's light, Lord God. This candle symbolizes me. From the light of Thy spirit to mine own being do I illuminate who and what I am... Your Child.

Now, lean back and simply gaze at the candle. Think of its flame as being you. See in the flame the potential to eliminate drosses, to purify... to bring light and warmth to the heart, to the thoughts, to life itself. See in this single flame the potential to illuminate many others, never with a loss to self. See in this flame the potential to do all manner of work, and to do it in joyfulness. See in this flame the spirit of expectancy...the joyful hope, for that which can be.

Illuminating the Flame of the Four Pillars Within

Close your eyes for a moment, and open them again, focusing upon the flame. Perhaps several times you might do this.

And as you do, remember the flame within.

As you do this, remember, too, that thou art claiming it and awakening that same flame of truth and honor, of love and compassion, within you.

Claiming Grace – The Guiding Light Within

Open your eyes one more time and look at the flame.

And think of it -- its power and its delicacy, its beauty, warmth, and light. And think of the potential that this offers to you as you might take this, symbolically and literally, within your own being as an eternal guide, as that which you can turn to in a moment of challenge or a time of need. That in the form of your prayers to one who is in need or in darkness, who has lost their way, or whose ease is no longer present – a simple flame to illuminate that of others' hope and purpose, to give them rise to recognize that they are the masters of their own destiny.

And as you hold that flame in your sight and thought, remember God's grace as the crown upon which all else can find its path, its way unto freedom, that path which can lead one to claim righteousness within.

Hold that thought, symbolically and literally, in that place within you which is now open.

And think this thought, and hold it a moment:

I am that Spirit Eternal which is the unique gift of God to all whom I meet. I am the wellspring of God's gifts and abundance to those who would come unto it. For as I am here in the Earth, in this body, experiencing this lifetime, it is always in the spirit of oneness with God. I am always in the presence of His grace.

Feel the growing essence, the sense of stimulation, the glow, the warmth, the energy that rises within you. Call it forth.

You have forgiven yourself and all others for actions, which are merely step-stones on the path of self-discovery. You have seen through the eyes of wisdom. You have held in the heart the compassion and love which is the Christ. You have looked upon those things in the Earth, and you have seen them – not as finite expressions whose nature is limited, whose function is superfluous; but you have looked upon them and seen them to be the creations of opportunity, to be the parameters, the expressions, of an opportunity made manifest for the Children of God to discover their own nature.

BAPTIZING SELF IN THE CHRIST SPIRIT

Let the love, which is the Christ, and the compassion which is ever His spirit, flow all throughout you. There is no part of your being that is apart from the Spirit of God. There is no part of your being which does not know the Spirit Eternal, called Christ. All throughout you does It flow. Its light, its energy and sweetness are all about. Feel it. Let the laughter of His love resonate within you, and the compassion of His understanding and wisdom transcend any last vestiges of limitation.

Making His Mark on Spirit, Mind, and Heart

Open your eyes, and reach out with your fingertips and immerse them gently into the water you have prepared and bring them forth, placing them against your own forehead.

And this might be the prayer:

Lord God, in Thy sight and in the presence of the Christ spirit, so do I baptize myself in the eternal Spirit of Christ.

Make that symbol or mark, as ye will, upon your forehead.

And bring the hands back to the center of your being and place it here, as well, that not only in spirit and mind, but also in heart and body, do you claim and baptize your Self in the Christ Spirit.

Receiving the Celebration

Having so done, now rest your hands together as ye would… somewhat as you might *receive* in them. And feel the glow of acceptance and acknowledgement. And hear those who are beyond finiteness rejoice and celebrate about you.

Preparing to Receive the Christ

Now, rest a moment and consider all this.
Let it flow all throughout.

Take a deliberate breath in. Hold it, and exhale. As you do, consider that you are releasing, finally, all those things which would limit.

Do this again, and as you draw in a breath, know that you are drawing in that which is your rightful heritage.

Receiving the Christ

Now let your breathing and body become relaxed and normal.

As you rest… see, know, feel, that He comes before thee.

Know that, now, it is His hand which dips fingertips into the water; and it is His hand which touches, now, your forehead.

Know that it is His word which recognizes you as brother or sister.

Receiving the Christ Blessing to Gift to Others

His hand moves now to the center of your being and rests here. And hear these thoughts and words:

"My heart and your heart are one. My love and your love, together, are the gifts we offer to those who are in need."

OPENING TO THE PORTAL

<u>Claiming the Full Potential of Self</u>

And now, as He stands before you, claim yourself.

For it is this, as is our humble offering in the suggestions above, that can be used to pass through that portal... beyond which lies the full potential of who and what you are.

═══════════════════

Whether you do this alone or with others is a matter of choice and joy; but we are with you, whether you are several-fold or singular in this ceremony.

Whenever there is the desire to have a closer walk with He and we, do this or similar, either literally or in mind and heart.

And we are ever with you.

EXPLORING MASTERY

Exploring Mastery

NOTE: The thoughts listed here are merely suggestions to get you started in further exploration of this subject. Use any portion of them, or not, as your personal guidance leads you.

Lama Sing has said "This course contains the keys which can set you free"?
In this context, what key or keys to setting yourself free did you find in:

Forgiveness

Gratitude

Hopefulness

Truth

Self

Faith

Seeing

Knowing

Claiming

The Four Sacred Tenets (the pillars of Righteousness)

Truth

Honor

Love

Compassion

Grace

Righteousness

Relate the parables in each of the Open Forums to the steps in Mastery. In other words, relate...

Forgiveness to Releasing –

Gratitude to Thanksgiving –

Hopefulness to Expecting –

Truth to Empowering –

Self to Honoring –

Faith to Trusting –

Seeing to Perceiving –

Claiming to Exemplifying –

Truth, Honor, Love and Compassion to Soaring –

Grace to Blessing –

This is a course in Mastery...

    Mastery of what?

This is a path to Awakening...

    Awakening to what?

On the final pages, there is room for you to journal your thoughts, such as your thoughts on this course... on awakening... on oneness... on mastery...

JOURNAL: Closing Thoughts

_____

_____

_____

_____

_____

_____

_____

_____

_____

_____

_____

_____

_____

_____

_____

_____

_____

_____

_____

About Lama Sing

"The source, which has become known as Lama Sing is, indeed, a teacher to the Channel. The Channel has functioned with this source in previous life experiences not limited to the Earth or physical planes. The source, known as Lama Sing, is a part of the Channel's group soul purpose, which then functions under a different accord or tenet, celestially speaking.

"We identify ourselves only as servants of God, dedicated to you, our brothers and sisters in the Earth. ...Do not associate the title Lama Sing as an individual name. Though the name has been an individual soul's name in past, it should not be thought of just as an individual in its present use or connotation, but rather, as a group or purpose, rather than a name. It would be as though one were speaking to a consciousness, comprised of collective aspects."

About These Works

"Know that it is our prayer throughout eternity that these works shall heighten that consciousness in each who shall hear it, and only to the need and the usefulness of thy soul's will do we ask that it be given. Each shall hear differently, for each is the unique creation of God—each one hears within himself or herself, and shall understand a different word, a different comprehension. So, dwell not upon this word or that, but cleave unto the spirit, which is given in each."

"The purposes of functioning through this Channel are to give to mankind only that as would urge them to find God within themselves. There is no wish among those present here that these words shall ring throughout eternity or be inscribed in great books or great halls. It would rather be our most humble prayer that the thoughts which are given with these words should have some meaning in the hearts and minds of those who hear them; and that the thoughts and attitudes shall live on, not these words or these works or the name surrounding same."

About This Channel

"Channel is that term given generally to those who enable themselves to be, as much as possible, open and passable in terms of information that can pass through them from the Universal Consciousness, or other such which are not associated in the direct sense with their finite consciousness of the current incarnation. ...It is the purpose of this Channel to be a lamp unto your footsteps, to be your servant, and to be that which gives unto you when you are needy and which shares with you when you are joyous. But we here, and the Channel, are no greater than the least of thee."

– Lama Sing

About Al Miner

A chance hypnosis session in 1973 began Al's tenure as the channel for Lama Sing. Since then, nearly 10,000 readings have been given in a trance state answering technical and personal questions on such topics as science, health and disease, history, geophysical, spiritual, philosophical, metaphysical, past and future times, and much more. The validity of the information has been substantiated and documented by research institutions and individuals, and those receiving personal readings continue to refer others to Al's work based on the accuracy and integrity of the information in their readings. In 1984, St. Johns University awarded Al an honorary doctoral degree in parapsychology.

Al conducts a variety of field research projects as well as occasional workshops and lectures, and while he occasionally accepts requests for personal readings, he is mostly devoting his time to works intended to be good for all. Much of his current research is dedicated to the concept that the best of all guidance is that which comes from within.

Al lives with his family in the mountains of Western North Carolina.